Advance Praise for

CALM THE CHAOS

"Parents, this is the book we've all been waiting for. Dayna Abraham's compassion for parents who are at the end of their rope and kids who don't quite fit the mold is unprecedented. Where conventional parenting tactics trap families in a cycle of disconnection and mistrust, *Calm the Chaos* sets families free from power struggles—and the heartaches that go along with them. Using small, digestible steps and enlightening illustrations, Abraham equips parents to uncover the root cause of challenging behaviors so they can respond in ways that foster growth in their child and peace in their family."

—**Rachel Macy Stafford**, *New York Times* bestselling author
of *Hands Free Mama*, *Only Love Today*, and *Soul Shift*

"This book is bound to help parents of challenging children feel seen and supported. It also offers hope and a path forward."

—**Joanna Faber and Julie King**, coauthors of
How to Talk When Kids Won't Listen

"This book is *incredible*. *Calm the Chaos* gives parents, teachers, and anyone working with kids evidence-based, practical strategies for addressing every hot-button behavior issue. Dayna Abraham has masterfully woven together her experiences as an educator and a mother to create a one-of-a-kind resource that is simple to use in real time. Best of all, it's filled with real hope for helping everyone thrive."

—**Michele Borba, EdD**, author of *Thrivers* and *UnSelfie*

"*Calm the Chaos* offers a practical road map for exhausted, frustrated parents who are navigating challenging behaviors. With compassion and clarity, Dayna Abraham has devised a five-phase program to help adults and kids of all ages work together to leave behind outdated behavioral advice and instead focus on regulation and restoring connection. This book is an essential reset button that gives every member of the family hope and a path to safety and success."

—**Tina Payne Bryson, LCSW, PhD**, *New York Times* bestselling coauthor of *The Whole-Brain Child* and *No-Drama Discipline* and author of *The Bottom Line for Baby*

"Just when a parent feels at their wits' end, *Calm the Chaos* comes along like a true friend. This long-needed book provides a straightforward and non-judgmental way for understanding even the most challenging of children's behaviors and how to approach them in an accessible and supportive manner. Having experienced major child challenges herself, Abraham understands well what it's like for parents in these very-hard-to-handle situations with their children. The book provides an empowering, clear, and compassionate path for helping your child, helping yourself as a parent, and moving forward in the most positive way. I'm glad this book has arrived!"

—**Tovah P. Klein, PhD**, director of the Barnard College Center for Toddler Development and author of *How Toddlers Thrive*

"In *Calm the Chaos*, Dayna Abraham has thoughtfully considered just about every tricky scenario parents might be navigating with their differently wired kids. The relatable examples, doable actions, game-changing reframes, and sweet visual doodles bring her road map to life in a way that feels accessible even for the most overwhelmed parent."

—**Debbie Reber**, founder and CEO of Tilt Parenting and author of *Differently Wired*

"If you've got a chaos causer (or two) in your home, get this book! With warm wisdom, Dayna Abraham leads you to restore calm and help your children love who they are, accept others, see how they can fit into the world, and develop values. Her method employs tiny steps to determine the challenge du jour, take care of yourself, connect with your child, understand the underlying reason for the chaos-producing behavior, and empower everyone to build a joyful family team. You can do it, Dayna says. You got this!"

—**Carol Stock Kranowitz, MA**, author of *The Out-of-Sync Child: Recognizing and Coping with Sensory Processing Differences*

CALM THE CHAOS

A Fail-Proof Road Map for Parenting
Even the Most Challenging Kids

DAYNA ABRAHAM

SIMON ELEMENT

NEW YORK LONDON TORONTO SYDNEY NEW DELHI

SIMON
ELEMENT

An Imprint of Simon & Schuster, Inc.
1230 Avenue of the Americas
New York, NY 10020

First Simon Element trade paperback edition August 2023

SIMON ELEMENT is a trademark of Simon & Schuster, Inc.

For information about special discounts for bulk purchases, please contact Simon & Schuster Special Sales at 1-866-506-1949 or business@simonandschuster.com.

The Simon & Schuster Speakers Bureau can bring authors to your live event. For more information or to book an event, contact the Simon & Schuster Speakers Bureau at 1-866-248-3049 or visit our website at www.simonspeakers.com.

Interior design by Ruth Lee-Mui
Illustrations by Dayna Abraham

Manufactured in the United States of America

3   5   7   9   10   8   6   4   2

Library of Congress Control Number: 2023937796

ISBN 978-1-6680-1428-8
ISBN 978-1-6680-1429-5 (ebook)

To my kids:
Thank you for teaching me to be a better human every single day.
I love you exactly as you are.

To Jason:
Thanks for being my steady rock in the worst of storms.

To my community:
Thank you for trusting me as your guide along this journey.

Love you all to the moon and back.

CONTENTS

INTRODUCTION

The school was calling, yet again.

"Come fast. Your son is out of control, and we've tried everything."

Despite being nine months pregnant and forty-five minutes from school, I drove as fast as I could. I replayed every word the teachers, doctors, and even my family had told me:

"If you just set firmer limits."

"If you just used stronger consequences."

"If you just changed everything about your parenting."

Or at least it felt like that's what they were telling me.

None of this was new. My son was asked to leave preschool. In elementary school, I was repeatedly asked to pick my son up early. By second grade, he was suspended more days than he was in school. In other words, this was the same thing, different days.

The principal, teachers, office staff, and even the police gathered around me as I entered the school. In the midst of piercing stares, I spotted my son hunkered under a table in a glassed-in room, screaming at anyone who approached. The authorities had turned my son into a caged lion for the whole school to observe. As I entered the office, my sweet, loving, and humorous child roared and gnashed his teeth, ready to pounce.

"How did this happen?" I asked through my tears.

"It just came out of nowhere," the principal said. "We don't know what happened."

She ushered me past the window where my son was beating on the glass. "Mrs. Abraham, please come into my office."

"You have two options." She pointed to the frowning fellow who had joined us.

"One, let this officer take him away.

"Or two, take your son and don't bring him back until you figure out what's wrong with him."

An entire staff of trained professionals, bewildered by my son's behavior, throwing their hands in the air, made one thing painfully clear: *something had to change.*

I believe these teachers were doing their best. They were throwing everything they knew at the situation; however, it wasn't good enough. I was getting calls daily. My son was coming home with bruises and saying things that scared me.

"Why do I have to be this way?"

"I'm such a bad kid."

And the worst of them all: "I wish I was dead."

It scared the crap out of me. I couldn't keep the worst-case scenario endings from spiraling out of control in my head if we continued treating his meltdowns with the same one-size-fits-all disciplinary approach used for decades.

I'd seen it before with my brother, who was expelled from school after school, tossed from treatment center to therapists and a camp for troubled kids. He blamed everyone for his struggles. "They just don't get it" turned into violence, abuse, arrests, identity theft, and multiple jail sentences. I couldn't let my son end up in jail and disconnected from everyone who ever loved him.

I also knew the risk of what could happen if my son took his anger and pain out on himself. Growing up, I battled thoughts of being broken, not fitting in, and not being good enough. Luckily, my attempts to remove myself from the planet left only scars, but my friend Sarah wasn't so fortunate. She'd spent years trying to fit in and conform. Sarah blamed herself for being so much "trouble." During her senior year of high school, Sarah ended her life.

Hunched over and hiding my head in shame in the principal's office that day, I saw the future flash before me once again. I was determined to change my son's trajectory.

We had to help my son.

We couldn't just pass it off as "unpredictable" behavior that couldn't be prevented. We couldn't just label him as "challenging" and believe we could discipline it out of him.

He deserved better.

I didn't have a clue how I was going to help my son, but I knew I was the only one who was determined to take on the challenge.

LET'S TALK ABOUT "THAT KID"

For a dozen years, I taught in inner-city schools with class sizes up to forty-eight (yes, *forty-eight*) children at a time. My passion was for students who didn't quite fit the mold. They came with a paper trail behind them, and were considered too loud, too emotional, too distracted, and, for most teachers, too much trouble.

In my classroom, there were more than one every year. The teachers before me had warned me, and the children's parents even dropped them off with their heads hung low.

The part that hit me in the gut: *that kid knew it.* They not only felt the disappointment and frustration. They owned it.

I was obsessed with finding out what others didn't know—the part that people didn't see or tell me about that child. I was determined to learn how to connect with and understand these kids.

That day after the principal sent me home with my son to "figure out what was wrong with him," I was on the phone with my best friend, tears running down my cheeks, heart heavy. Suddenly, I realized what was going on.

I muttered, "I *have* that kid."

THE REAL CHALLENGE

I wondered if anyone would ever get to know my child. *Would they ever truly see the kid I loved and saw at home, when all the stressors were gone?*

After realizing my son was that kid and no one else could (or wanted to) hear or see what he was trying to communicate through his tantrums, outbursts, and meltdowns, I did the unthinkable. I quit my job, pulled my son from school, and dove in headfirst.

I had two goals:

1. I wanted my son to stop blaming himself for not fitting in, and
2. I didn't want him to blame the world for not understanding him.

My son didn't need more diagnoses, more therapy, more strategies, or even more discipline.

He needed *one* person who could see him for who he was behind the outbursts, who believed he was worth fighting for, who knew he wasn't a lost cause.

I was that person.

And because you're reading this book, I know that *you* are that one person for your child.

Whether you've just started your journey or have been trekking down this path through endless storms, I want you to know you're in the right place.

Find a quiet spot (my favorite is my purple chair in the corner of my living room), grab a hot cup of coffee or tea (it's okay if you need to microwave it a few or a lot of times), and settle in.

YOU'VE GOT THIS

The first thing you need to know is that you are exactly the parent your child needs, exactly as you are with your imperfections, unshowered bed head, cold coffee, and messy kitchen.

You can do this, no matter how little you believe that right now. With all my heart, I know this to be true.

How do I know?

For more than a decade, I've helped thousands of at-the-end-of-their-rope parents go from barely surviving each day, drowning in the torrential downpour, and dealing with a child with massive tantrums, outbursts, and meltdowns, to having a child who feels seen, heard, and even understood, and who isn't shunned because of their unruly behavior.

I've witnessed hopeless parents succeed in creating families that see each other for who they are, problem solve together, enjoy spending time together, empower and advocate for each other, and have hope for the future.

But more than that, I've been in the trenches and survived. I can't count the number of holes in the walls, broken dishes, toys thrown at my head, cracked doors, and torn pictures from this period in my life. It was ugly. I went days without showering, and my other kids rarely saw me without a frown or a scowl on my face. I was constantly battling with my husband over how to handle my son's dangerous and aggressive behavior.

We tried what felt like absolutely everything, from things we believed in and aligned with my core beliefs and values as an educator to things that

I was completely against but willing to try. I was grasping at straws, desperate for anything to work. You name it, I tried it: medication, time-outs, rewards, consequences, and even therapy.

I can hardly believe the contrast between that war zone and the writing studio I'm sitting in now as I write this. I hear birds chirping and kids playing, and our family just finished a lovely lunch together around our kitchen table. All three of my kids hugged me this morning. I've been able to cuddle with my daughter, interview a fabulous expert, meet with a team member, and write this book, all without a single argument or battle.

There is hope. And a lot of it.

There has never been a better time for a new way to parent, especially for our most challenging kids. The Calm the Chaos framework changed everything for my family and thousands of others too. The good news is you're probably already doing a lot of this. I'm going to walk you through the step-by-step road map I created to inch my way out of the darkness to a life I had never thought possible, where our family advocates for and empowers each other.

Calm the Chaos offers you not only the most up-to-date brain-based parenting concepts but also actionable strategies and a step-by-step guide that you can implement in the midst of even the most challenging behaviors, regardless of what type of child you have at home.

HOW TO USE THIS BOOK

Calm the Chaos is designed so that you can read it whenever you have a minute or five, with bite-sized chunks meant to be consumed at your own pace. I know that right now imagining any more time than that to read a book seems difficult. By the end of this book, however, you'll have more time than you know what to do with. That's what I aim to do over and over again: help you believe that what has felt impossible is indeed very possible.

This journey is presented in five stages you will need to go through to get from surviving to thriving. I call this the five-stage family road map.

These stages are:

- Stage One: Surviving the Storm
- Stage Two: Your Energy Reserves
- Stage Three: The Calm at the Center of the Storm
- Stage Four: No More Storm Chasing
- Stage Five: Building a Storm-Proof Infrastructure

Since I know most overwhelmed parents work best when things are broken into small pieces, each stage includes six chapters where you can easily leave the book and pick up where you left off. Each chapter title in each section begins with the same element:

- Your Challenge
- You
- Connect
- Understand
- Empower
- Putting It All Together

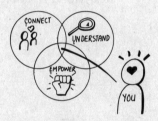

In each chapter you will find:

- **The Challenge and Path Ahead:** This is where you will gain your footing and get clarity on what is needed for the journey ahead. I'll explain the challenges you may face and the most important shifts required.
- **Actionable Sections:** Each plan is divided into four distinct pieces that correspond with the Calm the Chaos framework, which I'll introduce throughout this book. The ideas will be brought to life by examples, science, and stories. Then you'll find an action step to help you keep moving forward.
- **Putting It All Together:** Finally, the last chapter of each stage includes a plan (there are five in total). These plans will help you overcome painful challenges while allowing you to fall in love with your child again.

All the new ideas and tools will be put into one complete action plan that you can use with your family to stop feeling overwhelmed, respond in the heat of the moment, and even get your family on board.

ICONS AND DOODLES

There are some common icons you will see throughout the book to help you process information:

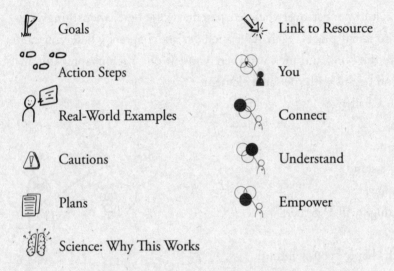

Goals

Link to Resource

Action Steps

You

Real-World Examples

Connect

Cautions

Understand

Plans

Empower

Science: Why This Works

WORKSHEETS AND RESOURCES

There are a lot of visuals and lists in this book, along with plans to create with your family. To make this easier to use and implement, I've created a free resource pack you can download.

Simply visit www.calmthechaosbook.com/toolkit to download your printable cheat sheets, lists, and blank plans (along with some other goodies you will find to help you on your journey).

FROM SURVIVING THE STORM TO THRIVING EVERY DAY

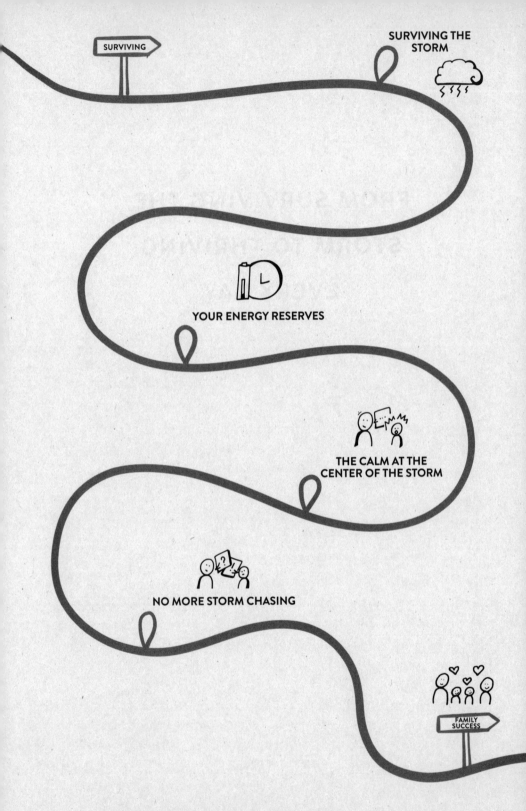

SURVIVING

SURVIVING THE STORM

YOUR ENERGY RESERVES

THE CALM AT THE CENTER OF THE STORM

NO MORE STORM CHASING

FAMILY SUCCESS

TIME FOR A NEW PLAN

You've got enough on your to-do list. The last thing you need is one more "guru" giving you their magic one-size-fits-all parenting advice. But on the flip side, you don't have to try to figure out this whole parenting-a-challenging-kid thing on your own. You shouldn't need to get a PhD in parenting just to parent your own child. Instead, you need an out-of-the-box approach to parenting that considers your unique child, your background and upbringing, your values and beliefs, and your whole family, combined with best practices for raising a challenging child.

You need a framework that simplifies parenting in even the most challenging situations and that can be used no matter what stage of the parenting journey you're currently wading through.

The Calm the Chaos framework will organize and simplify everything you've already learned and help you create action plans with your family

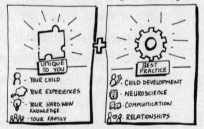

that actually work. This framework is the culmination of over twenty years of my own work in the classroom, parenting my own challenging kiddo, and working with thousands of other families around the world. It draws from time-tested research and rock-solid science about the brain, neurodiversity, education, communication, and relationships.

THE CALM THE CHAOS WAY

I'm here to make a bold claim: *More than structure, discipline, or even consistency, your child needs to be seen, heard, understood, and empowered.*

Whether you're barely surviving or your family is working together smoothly, you need a way to keep moving forward even on your hardest days.

To understand just how revolutionary the Calm the Chaos system is, consider the following paradigm shifts:

1. Rather than seeing challenging kids as problems to fix or, in dire cases, get rid of (by way of expulsion and isolation), what if we could uncover what makes them tick?

2. Instead of parenting with a discipline-from-on-high approach, what if we treated children as fully-fledged members of a team, rather than people who must obey, or else?

3. What would be possible if we made even the most challenging children feel seen, heard, and accepted, and allowed them to express their opinions and preferences while fully being themselves, instead of trying to mold them into who we think they should be?

4. Instead of always searching for solutions to "get kids to behave," what if we worked together to create safety, understanding, and relationships that allowed children to take risks, make mistakes, and advocate for themselves?

The Calm the Chaos way is a family team approach in which kids' and adults' needs are considered and you put your heads together to find an out-of-the-box solution that works for everyone involved.

THE CALM THE CHAOS SYSTEM

Calm the Chaos will walk you through the two-part system needed to go from surviving to thriving as a family.

1. **Five-Stage Family Road Map:** This will serve as a guide through your family's relationship-rebuilding journey and will give you the blueprint needed to storm proof your family.

2. **Calm the Chaos Framework:** Every plan you create includes four essential ingredients known as You-CUE. As you go through each stage, the framework builds on itself, but never more than you can handle, given the amount of chaos in your current situation.

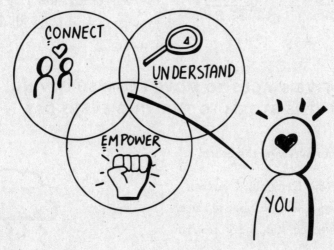

THE FIVE-STAGE FAMILY ROAD MAP

Although there is no one-size-fits-all solution for all families, there are clear stages that all families go through as they navigate the journey of raising a challenging kid. My goal is to explain the distinct stages so that you can easily determine where you and your family are. Each stage has a role you must play, a mission, and a plan to follow to create a family that works together.

WHAT'S IN A PLAN?

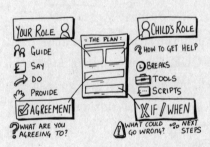

You'll be building a repertoire of plans to solve different struggles in your family. The more plans you make and agree on ahead of a crisis, the smoother your days will be.

I've even created a road map to make sure you go down a trail with the right equipment.

FIVE STAGES TO MOVE FROM SURVIVING THE STORM TO THRIVING EVERY DAY

Stage One: Surviving the Storm

Your Role: Determined Survivor
Challenge: Get Everyone to Safety
Plan Needed: Ride the Storm Plan

Goal of this stage:

The number one goal in this stage is safety, which can include physical, emotional, and mental safety. This could include anything from large emergencies that are life altering (such as a death in the family, dangerous outbursts, or drug and alcohol use) to smaller struggles that wreak havoc on your family (such as a new school or diagnosis). In this stage, you will develop a Ride the Storm plan so you can get through the challenges with minimal damage or disconnection.

Action Steps:

1. The first step is to create your own safety and calm your nervous system so you can remain calm in any storm and keep from adding your own chaos to an already volatile situation.
2. Next, you'll make simple shifts in your body language and movements, so you become your child's safe place.
3. You'll develop an important perspective shift about your child's behavior to create a foundation of trust and empathy as you move out of crisis mode.
4. Finally, you'll develop a habit of gratitude and noticing that will allow you to keep moving forward even on your darkest days.

Stage Two: Your Energy Reserves

Your Role: Brave Parent
Challenge: Having Energy to Face Another Battle
Plan Needed: The Five-Minute Energy Plan

Goal of this stage:

Let's face it—without any time or energy, you can feel overwhelmed, leading you right back to stage one, Surviving the Storm, which might be worse than when you first started. So often, parents want to skip this stage and jump right to the "let's fix it" stage, but I assure you, this stage is vital if you're going to have any long-term change.

While you might feel like jumping into solving behaviors and working out what to do about all the chaos, this is actually when you need to focus on your needs. Your number one goal here is to get out of feeling overwhelmed and have a path forward that feels sustainable and possible.

During this stage you will create a Five-Minute Energy plan that allows you to regularly shift your mood from disempowered to empowered.

Action Steps:

1. You'll start to prioritize the things that are most important to you so you can finally kick the whole "balance" myth to the curb. This means putting yourself back on your to-do list and finding time for yourself (even if only five minutes to begin).

2. Next, you'll find small ways to boost connection and build your support system.

3. You'll identify what boosts your energy, while removing things that drain you each day.

4. Finally, you'll build tiny habits for taking care of your own health (mental, spiritual, and physical) so you can weather any storm to come.

Stage Three: The Calm at the Center of the Storm

Your Role: Chaos Wrangler
Challenge: Defuse the Chaos without Adding
    Fuel to the Fire
Plan Needed: In-the-Moment Plan

Goal of this stage:

Your number one objective in this stage is to defuse the situation quickly without creating more chaos. You and your children are building trust and deepening your connection while creating a safe environment for big emotions, outbursts, and mistakes, not teaching and skill-building (this will come later). This stage is where parents spend the most time, rebuilding, rediscovering, and rewiring from the inside out. Trust and bonding are the foundations of any future skill-building or change.

Action Steps:

1. The first step in this stage is to challenge your deep-seated thoughts and beliefs about your child and their behavior, swapping the disempowering thoughts for more empowering ones.

2. Next, you'll work to defuse the situation before it spirals into more chaos and mayhem by creating connection and empathy in the heat of the moment.

3. You'll do some detective work and start to become an expert in your own child by digging under the surface to find the root cause of their outbursts so you can understand your unique child and their challenges.

4. Finally, you'll craft an In-the-Moment plan for exactly what to say and do in the moment to defuse the outbursts and get through the battle unscathed.

Stage Four: No More Storm Chasing

Your Role: Problem-Solving Partner
Challenge: Stop the Whac-A-Mole Parenting Approach
Plan Needed: Ahead-of-the-Moment Plan

Goal of this stage:

This stage is a turning point for so many families and is where long-lasting change starts. Days start to feel easier and lighter. However, in the beginning you may feel as if you're constantly jumping from one challenge to the next and running in circles. In this stage, your top goal is to become your child's guide and mentor. You'll get ahead of the battles, outbursts, and meltdowns before they ever begin.

Action Steps:

1. Your first step is to prioritize and focus on the primary chaos causer wreaking havoc on your family.

2. Your connection will grow deeper with intentional connection out of the moment, building your child's repository of belonging and trust.

3. You'll spiral out and recognize signs of the storms brewing so you aren't caught off guard (heck, you'll even be able to stop the outbursts before the point of no return).

4. Finally, you'll problem solve and communicate with your child in a new and revolutionary way that allows you to create plans that work for both of you. Not only will you have an Ahead-of-the-Moment plan to remain calm or solve problems but your child will begin to build the skills needed to advocate for their own needs and get them met without the use of screaming, back talk, distraction, or aggression.

Stage Five: Building a Storm-Proof Infrastructure

Your Role: Team Builder
Challenge: Minimize Future Chaos
Plan Needed: Family Success Plan

Goal of the stage:

This stage is the ultimate destination of your journey: an empowered family, one that works together, enjoys spending time together, has fun together, and supports each other. Now that you've strengthened your one-on-one relationship with your child, the rest of the family needs repair and reconnection. This stage prepares you and your family for lifelong change (rather than a quick fix). By the end of this stage, family discussions will be a daily habit and a way of life. When a problem arises, you'll notice your children calling a huddle to brainstorm solutions that work for each member of the family.

Action Steps:

1. The first step is to swap your child's struggles (the very thing that makes them challenging) for their superpowers.
2. Next, you'll work to create a family ecosystem that's connected and centered on working together as a team.
3. You'll create a profile for each family member so they understand and accept each other on a deep level.
4. Finally, you'll create a Family Success plan so everyone is in agreement and your family can run smoothly. You'll redefine rules, routines, and even personal boundaries based on common family values so everyone is on the same page.

ACTION STEP: QUIZ

Your number one action step right now is to assess where you are in your journey.

1. Is each member of your family safe (physically, emotionally, and psychologically) and the adults seen as the calm, safe place?   Yes ☐ No ☐

     If yes, move on to question two. If no, you're in Stage One: Surviving the Storm.

2. Are you able to take time for yourself each day to take care of your own needs and desires?   Yes ☐ No ☐

     If yes, move on to question three. If no, you're in Stage Two: Your Energy Reserves.

3. Do you know what to say and do to calm your child's outbursts in the heat of the moment without making things worse?   Yes ☐ No ☐

If yes, move on to question four. If no, you're in Stage Three: The Calm in the Center of the Storm.

4. Can you recognize, understand, and prevent challenging behaviors before they happen? Are you able to avoid challenges before they begin?   Yes ☐ No ☐

If yes, move on to question five. If no, you're in Stage Four: No More Storm Chasing.

5. Does your family have routines, systems, and plans in place that allow each family member's needs to be met?   Yes ☐ No ☐

If yes, congratulations! You've created an empowered family. (This book will be a great way to enhance connection, boost problem-solving skills, and handle any small challenges that creep up in your family.)

If no, you're in Stage Five: Building a Storm-Proof Infrastructure.

You can also visit www.calmthechaosbook.com/roadmap for a more in-depth quiz. This assessment will not only tell you which stage you're in right now but also indicate your immediate next steps. Think of it as your CliffsNotes to the book, giving you exactly what to focus on for your specific family.

THE CALM THE CHAOS FRAMEWORK

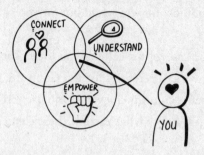

One of my favorite connection activities with my kids is to watch *Nailed It!* You know the show? They bring amateur bakers on and ask them to create master-level cakes that look like real-life items (imagine cakes that look like cars, elephants, zombies, and everything in between). What ensues is a comical hot mess.

This is equivalent to what happens when we try to follow elaborate parenting methods without first learning the fundamentals.

Every cake has four basic ingredients: eggs, sugar, butter, and flour. Sure, you can have different kinds of sweeteners, bases, liquids, and fats, but for any basic cake you need these four things. Like a cake, the Calm the Chaos framework has four essential elements: you, connection, understanding, and empowerment.

The Four Elements of the Calm the Chaos Framework (You-CUE for Short)

1. **You:** a person who is determined to see the situation for what it is, flaws and all; focused on one simple thing at a time; and a grounded, safe place in the storm.

2. **Connection:** true acceptance of the child you have, not the child you wish you had.

3. **Understanding:** a deep knowledge of your child including their likes, dislikes, struggles, superpowers, skills, and neurology.

4. **Empowerment:** out-of-the-box solutions that build problem-solving, self-regulation, and life skills along the way, not just for your child but for you as well.

Warning: As is the case with a cake, if you forget the flour or the sugar, it's just not going to work. Therefore, for the Calm the Chaos framework, you need all the elements combined, even if you use just a sprinkle of each.

It's also important to know what each of these elements are.

YOU

The Calm the Chaos framework starts with you, because you are the linchpin holding it all together.

Contrary to popular belief, this isn't meditation and bubble baths (which feel completely out of reach when you are barely surviving). Instead, it's more about your state of being: your mindset, ability to see your children and their behaviors differently, and capacity to shift your thoughts and beliefs to transform your outcomes. It includes your ability to ground yourself in the moment, remain calm, and be present for your kids, even when things are really nasty and ugly.

One of the most important aspects of the "you" element is the ability to give yourself permission to just focus on one thing at a time. As parents of challenging children, we are often pulled in five thousand different directions, feeling like we need to solve everything at once to make any progress. However, right here and now, I want to give you permission to focus on just one thing at a time (don't worry, I'll show you how to do this in Stage Three).

CONNECT

Connection is a core principle of most modern parenting methodologies, but it can be misunderstood, leading to more disconnection than connection. The desire for deeper connection may have led you to try spending more one-on-one time with your kids, getting down on their level, and/ or asking them about their day. However, simply adding more time and attention doesn't necessarily lead to better relationships. As the pandemic showed us, we can spend all day together but still feel disconnected.

Building a strong connection with your children isn't about the quantity of time you spend together but the quality of the time. This means being present and fully engaged during the time you have together. It also means approaching your interactions with a positive and compassionate attitude rather than nagging, criticizing, or blaming. Connection is about accepting your child fully for who they are, validating and supporting their feelings and beliefs, and creating a safe and supportive place for them to make mistakes and be themselves.

UNDERSTAND

If you've ever asked yourself *Why in the world did my kid do that?* this element is for you. It's true that each child is unique, and what works for one might not work for another. That's why it's so important to truly understand your child, their specific needs, skills, triggers, and preferences; in other words, what makes them tick. Unfortunately, assumptions and labels often get in the way of this understanding. Many behaviors are dismissed as bad or naughty before anyone looks for a root cause. On the flip side, some parents are so focused on understanding their children that they seek outside opinions and lose confidence in their own ability to parent. They exhaust themselves searching for answers and trying to "fix" their children.

The understand element equips you with tools to unravel your child's behavior and helps you and your children communicate needs, wants, and emotions in a way that everyone can understand. By embracing your expertise and teaching your child to be an expert in themselves, you can build a more empathetic and in-tune relationship with your child.

EMPOWER

If you've ever thought *I can't let my kid get away with this*, then you will love the empower element of the Calm the Chaos framework. It takes the old way tactics of "do as I say" commands and flips them on their head. Instead of forced compliance or surface-level "buy-in," parents can work with their child so both the parent and the child are empowered with a path forward.

Contrary to popular belief, empowerment doesn't come from giving your child choices, rewards, firm boundaries, or imposing consequences. It's about working together with your child to make plans, truly listening to their opinions, and valuing each family member's input. Not only does this allow your child's voice to be heard without the need for aggressive fits, outright refusal, or shutting down, it teaches them how to problem solve and find their own solutions.

Here's the cool part: the empower element is about teaching your child to advocate fiercely for themselves in a way that others can understand. By working together with your child, you can create plans that work for your unique situation through experimentation, iteration, review, and tweaking along the way. The rest of this book is designed to empower both you and your child with plans that work for each challenge and stage you face as you go from surviving to thriving, with each one building on the last.

⚠ CAUTION

At a glance, many of these strategies might look familiar (because they're based on best practices and the science from the last fifty years). While seeing familiar tenets might be comforting, for many it can feel hopeless. "I've tried all this. Nothing works for my kid." Which leads right back to feeling overwhelmed and exhausted. So I want to caution you: *Do not try to do everything on the last few pages at once.* It's impossible to implement all of these strategies at the same time. Instead, it's how you combine the elements that makes all the difference.

Through the rest of this book, I will walk you step by step through these concepts so you can apply these four elements in any situation to quickly calm any challenging behavior and give your kids the skills to handle their emotions and solve problems on their own. This is how you will create a home with no bickering, teasing, or yelling, and a family that can actually play board games together without the board being flung across the room. We will start with the most basic plans, and then build to more elaborate plans as we progress. For now, take a deep breath and remind yourself to take it one baby step at a time.

Action Step: Assess Your Base

Your action step for this section is simple. Use the assessment below to find your primary parenting style. The category with the most *yes* answers will indicate your primary style. As you move through the stages and create plans with your family, you can build on this strength and notice small areas where you could boost the other areas.

You

- Are you able to remain calm during tantrums, meltdowns, or outbursts without yelling?   Yes ☐ No ☐

- Do you take time to recognize when things go right (e.g., gratitude journal, small celebrations, and/or shouts of joy)?   Yes ☐ No ☐

- Do you know how to change your thoughts when you're feeling worried, overwhelmed, or frustrated?   Yes ☐ No ☐

- Do you have a daily practice to prioritize your day and keep yourself from feeling overwhelmed?   Yes ☐ No ☐

- Do you take at least five minutes a day, every day, to focus on your own needs?   Yes ☐ No ☐

- Do you give yourself permission to not do everything on your to-do list?   Yes ❐ No ❐

- Are you able to focus on one challenge or struggle at a time without jumping from one thing to the next?   Yes ❐ No ❐

- Do you know what recharges your batteries and actively make time daily to do it?   Yes ❐ No ❐

Connect

- When your child is upset or having an outburst, do you check your own body language and voice before engaging?   Yes ❐ No ❐

- Do you have a support system with other adults in your life, either virtually or in person?   Yes ❐ No ❐

- When you need your child's attention, do you move closer to them instead of talking to them from the other room?   Yes ❐ No ❐

- Do you have planned connection time with each child in your family?   Yes ❐ No ❐

- Can you list ten positives about each child in your family?   Yes ❐ No ❐

- Do you make time with other important adults in your child's life for them to connect?   Yes ❐ No ❐

- Are the majority of the interactions between family members positive and fun?   Yes ❐ No ❐

- Does your family have ways they describe themselves as a united group?   Yes ❐ No ❐

Understand

- Are you able to recognize and calm your own triggers that lead to burnout, anger, and losing your temper?   Yes ☐ No ☐

- Do you know how your child responds when they're stressed, worried, excited, or afraid?   Yes ☐ No ☐

- Do you know how to calm down your child in the moment when they're having a meltdown, outburst, or frustrating behavior?   Yes ☐ No ☐

- Can you identify the reasons behind your child's challenging behaviors?   Yes ☐ No ☐

- Are you able to list likes, dislikes, struggles, strengths, sensory preferences, and skill deficiencies for each family member?   Yes ☐ No ☐

- Are you able to recognize the buildup and predict a tantrum, meltdown, or outburst before it happens?   Yes ☐ No ☐

- When an argument or challenge occurs in your family, are you able to get details from everyone involved to fully understand what happened?   Yes ☐ No ☐

- Can each family member recognize and accommodate the needs of other family members?   Yes ☐ No ☐

Empower

- Are you able to notice small wins and progress even when things are still hard?   Yes ☐ No ☐

- Do you have a plan for what to say and do that works when your child is struggling?   Yes ☐ No ☐

- Does your child have a plan for how to handle frustration, feeling overwhelmed, or not getting their way that doesn't include screaming or refusal? Yes ☐ No ☐

- Is your child able to voice their concerns and frustrations without getting in trouble for talking back? Yes ☐ No ☐

- Does your family have a set of values that each member took part in creating? Yes ☐ No ☐

- When there's a problem or concern, do all family members come together to problem solve and listen? Yes ☐ No ☐

- Do you have routines in place (morning, evening, electronics, schoolwork, etc.) that meet the specific needs of each member of the family? Yes ☐ No ☐

- Does everyone in the family know and agree with the agreements, routines, plans, and personal boundaries ahead of time? Yes ☐ No ☐

- Do you include your children in the creation of family values and plans, routines, and agreements? Yes ☐ No ☐

Add the yes responses from each category. Your highest score correlates to your primary parenting style. If you scored highest in:

You: you are a **grounded parent**.

Connect: you are an **affirming parent**.

Understand: you are an **in-tune parent**.

Empower: you are an **empowered parent**.

Note: No matter what scores you got, it's okay. Over the course of this book, you will learn to fill the gaps using the You-CUE framework so you can calm challenging behaviors while creating a family that empowers each other, advocates for each other, and enjoys each other's company.

If you'd like to learn more about your primary parenting style and get tips on how to use this style as you go through the rest of the book, you can go to www.calmthechaosbook.com/parentingstyle.

BEFORE YOU BEGIN

If you're wondering how you'll ever be able to get your family around a table to come to any kind of decision without fights and arguments breaking out, you aren't alone.

Maybe you have a partner with a different parenting style than yours, or children who are accustomed to you acting a certain way and don't relish change. Getting them on board with decision-making and problem-solving may help bring you and them closer, but trying to get there without a lot of hubbub feels impossible.

So, before we dive into the stages of the road map, here are my top three tips for getting other family members on board with ideas and plans.

1. RELEASE YOUR FEARS

Often the thing that holds us back from getting buy-in is our own fear. We bring a certain energy to the table that radiates a lack of belief in ourselves and our ability to effect change. Tell me you haven't thought some of the following, which is why you picked up this book:

- I'm heartbroken for my child.
- I hate that this is my life.
- I'm just so damn exhausted.
- I feel like such a fraud.
- I'm just so overwhelmed.

- What if it never gets better?
- I'm so effin' done and ready to give up.
- I'm just so scared for when my child goes into the real world.

THE RELEASE FEAR

These thoughts are quite common. In fact, scientists call this "rumination," and studies show that more than 70 percent of our thoughts are negative thoughts. We're hardwired to think the negative, worried thoughts that will ensure survival. But the thing is, if left unattended, these thoughts can steal your happiness and joy.

Clear that nothing-will-ever-change mindset away and you'll start to see some interesting things. One way to do that is to get clear on your own beliefs and worries, and then find proof of the opposite. We'll be doing that as we move along.

2. MEET THE TEAM MEMBERS WHERE THEY ARE

When we can take a step back from what we want and consider what our children or spouse might need and want, we can approach any situation with a different perspective. By listening to your team's concerns and meeting them where they are, you're far more likely to get them on board over time. This step takes patience on your part, but I assure you the outcome is so much more pleasant than trying to cram your ideas into a situation where it just won't fit. Ask yourself the following questions to get at issues you might easily gloss over:

- What are your kids' concerns and hang-ups?
- What background is your partner bringing to 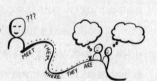 the conversation?
- What worries or fears do others have?
- How do they want to solve this problem?

3. IDENTIFY WHAT'S IN IT FOR THEM

Anytime I come up with a plan or an activity, I put the other person's needs and wants first. I pause and evaluate why this person should care about what I'm bringing to them. In other words:

- What's in it for them?
- Why would they want to change?
- What benefit does it bring to them?
- How does this help them?
- What does this make possible for them?
- What's at stake for them if this doesn't change?

Patience is key. This is a long-term process, not a short-term fix. Because of this, you will have days when all your best efforts are met with total resistance and disdain. You will attempt to rally the team, and all hell will break loose. Expect it, then plan for it.

PERMISSION TO FREAK OUT

It never fails. In the aftermath of a storm, the chaos in my own mind always seems to be worse than the physical damage around me. I start to spiral into overwhelming and catastrophizing thoughts. I'm betting that the same holds true for you.

The first tool I want to share with you is useful for each stage of your journey, not just when you're starting out. I'm bringing it right up front because until you have new ways to handle the stress and chaos in your family, you need a way to process and move forward when life feels way too difficult. Because your well-being and ability to remain calm in any storm is essential to this equation, we need to set you up for success.

The "freak-out" system is a proven process that has been used thousands of times by our students to help them move from emotional shutdown and spiraling thoughts to a place of peace and logic within just a few minutes.

At the end of the day, there comes a time when we must move from catastrophic thoughts to more active problem-solving. But before we can do that, we have to offload the chaos.

The Freak-Out Timer

"Can I just vent a minute?" How many of us have said this once or twice or a million times? However, I'm guessing when everything came out, you didn't feel any better or have any new ideas for how to move forward. (You sure didn't get any relief by word vomiting on social media!) That's because science has proven that venting and complaining only leaves you feeling worse than when you began. In fact, it can be incredibly detrimental to your overall mental health.

The freak-out timer is designed to help you acknowledge your feelings, express your thoughts, and then move into active problem-solving quicker and easier. This process will help you move from a downward spiral of ruminating and negative thoughts to active problem-solving so you don't have to spend days, even weeks, using up the little energy you have left stuck in feeling overwhelmed.

The key here is not to whisk away all your troubles, or pretend life is butterflies and rainbows. It's important to acknowledge your feelings and thoughts and not suppress them.

But how?

How do you allow your feelings while moving from feeling fearful and overwhelmed to productively creating plans and reconnecting? How do you find a next step when everything feels so huge? Where do you even start?

You freak the eff out with the freak-out timer.

My good friend Kaylene, an autistic adult raising six neurodivergent children and founder of AutisticMama.com, created and used a process as a child when she would get hit with debilitating anxiety. She then shared it with me during one of my toughest years as a parent, when my son was getting hospitalized and police were being called on him on a regular basis. Together, we adapted the process and shared it with other parents around the world.

The freak-out timer is broken into three steps:

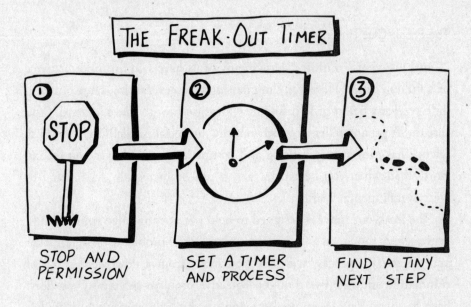

THE FREAK·OUT TIMER

① STOP

② (timer)

③

STOP AND PERMISSION

SET A TIMER AND PROCESS

FIND A TINY NEXT STEP

1. Stop and give yourself permission.
2. Set a timer and process.
3. Find a tiny next step.

Step One: Stop and Give Yourself Permission

This first step is essential, as the tendency when faced with a crisis is to jump into action and start trying to fix or solve.

Think back to the last time you started to slip into spiraling thoughts and behaviors. What did your body or mind do that led to the desire to shut down, complain, or vent?

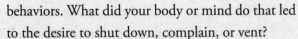

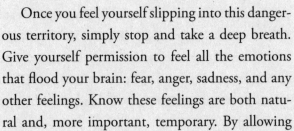

HOT FLASHES
RACING THOUGHTS
HOLD BREATH
CRYING
TIGHT CHEST
TENSE SHOULDERS
HEART POUNDING
SWEATY PALMS
UPSET STOMACH

SIGNS TO STOP AND NOTICE

Once you feel yourself slipping into this dangerous territory, simply stop and take a deep breath. Give yourself permission to feel all the emotions that flood your brain: fear, anger, sadness, and any other feelings. Know these feelings are both natural and, more important, temporary. By allowing yourself to embrace these emotions, you will in turn diminish their power, intensity, and control over you.

Remember: This isn't about pretending that bad days don't happen and negative thoughts don't exist. Instead, it's about confronting these feelings head-on, so they don't take over your life.

Step Two: Set a Timer and Process

Step two is to process, be curious, and begin to move your thoughts and attention from doom and gloom to the facts you see in front of you. You will want to set a timer for a random amount of time (we recommend between five and fifteen minutes). It's imperative that you set a timer because this will give your brain a limit to how long you can spiral as you process.

How you process isn't important; simply allow yourself to work through your deepest, darkest fears and worries. Be careful not to label your reactions as good or bad.

After you do this step a few times you will start to notice patterns about what helps you. Simply play the role of an observer:

- Do you notice repetitive inner dialogue?
- Do you shut down?
- Do you become aggressive or snappy?
- Do you critique and/or blame others?

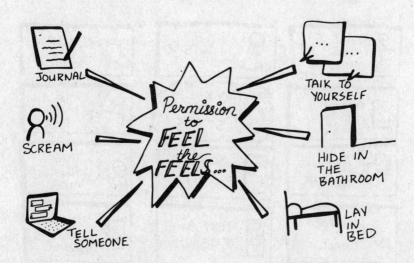

JOURNAL

TALK TO YOURSELF

SCREAM

HIDE IN THE BATHROOM

Permission to FEEL *the* FEELS...

TELL SOMEONE

LAY IN BED

Remember, there is no wrong or right way to process. It has been scientifically proven that you can't be curious and "freaking out" at the same time. Therefore, setting a timer and asking how bad it is on a scale of one to ten immediately allows your mind to stop, get out of crisis mode, and begin to be curious about the next steps (even if you don't feel ready for them yet).

Step Three: Find a Tiny Next Step

A few years ago, when I lost my mom unexpectedly, my son was struggling in school and life felt suffocating. I felt completely stuck. A mentor told me, "Dayna, you don't have to know how you're going to get to your destination. You simply need to know where you're headed with the very next step in front of you. Once you take this step, you'll find your next step, and the next and the next. But right now, you don't need to worry about all the steps ahead, only the very next one."

When your timer goes off, that is what I want you to do: find your tiny next step, the one that is so simple it's impossible to fail.

Examples of Tiny Next Steps

BETTER TOGETHER

The goal of the freak-out timer is to be able to do this on your own, to be able to notice the negative emotions rising and the downward spiral of negative thoughts, and then take these three steps. However, after working through this process with thousands of parents, I know this can be hard to do by yourself. That is why in our Calm the Chaos community, we use the timer along with a freak-out partner.

The benefit of having a partner support you through this process is that they set the time, hold space and energy for you while you process with zero judgment or advice, and then help you find a next step when it feels impossible.

Note: Before expecting someone to take this role for you, introduce them to this chapter and do a practice run. The process shifts slightly when you have a partner to walk through it with you. It looks like this:

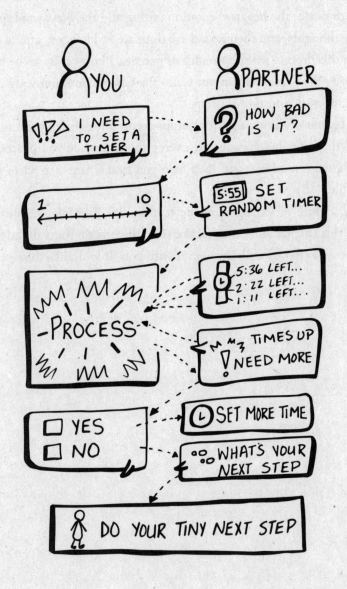

STORY OF HOPE

"I can't do this. I give up. I can't parent him anymore."

All Zoey wanted when she grew up was to get married, have kids, and be the best mom in the world. And yet, sobbing on the other end of the line, she sounded completely defeated and ready to give up hope.

As a parent, Zoey had done everything by the book. She'd been consistent, set firm boundaries, been loving and calm, and given her child all the connection she could muster. Yet it still wasn't enough. Her five-year-old son was in crisis mode. In just one week, the school had recorded fifty-three occurrences of aggression, which spilled into the home. She knew she needed something to change. With despair in her voice, Zoey confessed, "I just have to give it over to the professionals. I can't do this anymore."

Now, as she cried on the phone, I couldn't help but sigh. I had seen what the professionals suggested with kids like ours: heavy medication, ignoring the behavior until they learned, or, worse, physical punishment. I had tried it all to no avail.

"Do you trust me?" I asked her.

Together we took a deep breath and went to work with one thing in mind: simplicity. Her approach had to be so simple that Zoey could use it during the next episode. She could also start rebuilding her trust in her own parenting skills and repair the lost connection between her and her son. Because that was her biggest source of grief, the feeling that she was dealing with an alien, not her own flesh and blood.

We began crafting a plan using the four basic elements of the Calm the Chaos framework.

STEP ONE: YOU

"What can you do to get yourself to calm?" I asked Zoey. "How will you get yourself out of the reactive emotional state and stay present in the moment?"

Zoey thought about it and said, "I can picture him as a baby. When I brought him home from the hospital, he was dependent on me. When he cried, I responded. When he got fussy, I helped him. All he could do was cry to tell me he needed something. So I will picture him as a baby." She vowed to grab some baby photos and put them around the house so she could easily remember being in the moment. "I'm also going to remind myself that nothing he says can be taken personally, so I can stay calm and continue to see that he needs me."

STEP TWO: CONNECT

"All right," I said. "Now that you have a plan to stay calm, how will you connect with him and show him that you're there for him? How can you find a way to help him see he doesn't have to go through this big, scary outburst on his own and that you love him unconditionally? Can you think of anything that has worked in the past?"

Zoey was no longer crying. "Well, I don't want to get hit, but I know he needs to know I'm there. So I'll get closer." She hesitated for a moment. "But not too close. I'll just move near him and sit down on the floor, far enough away that if he kicks, he can't reach me, but close enough that if he wants hugs, I can move closer. I'll just simply say, 'I'm here if you want a hug.'"

STEP THREE: UNDERSTAND

I walked Zoey through the next step. "Now, what is one tiny way you can show your son that you understand his frustration and you want to help him?"

"I sure as heck can't solve it in the moment," Zoey laughed. "So I will simply listen and keep words to a minimum. I'll say, 'I hear you. We can solve that in just a bit.' That way he knows I'm not ignoring his real concerns." Zoey thought some more. "After the outburst passes, we can problem solve together and I can dig into what caused the frustration in the first place. But my goal in the moment will be to simply listen, validate, and empathize."

STEP FOUR: EMPOWER

I was impressed by how resourceful Zoey was. "Finally," I asked, "how will you both move forward and empower him with tools for future success?"

It took a few moments before Zoey responded. "After the dust has settled, we'll make a new plan for what he can do when he feels frustrated, upset, or scared. We'll practice going to a safe place and I'll have him help me come up with ways he can let me know he's upset without having to use words." She knew from our work together that her son couldn't access his logic in distress, so creating a way for him to feel heard in the moment would be key.

To summarize, Zoey's plan was:

You: Picture my son as a baby who needs me.

Connect: Move closer and get down on the floor.

Understand: Listen and keep words to a minimum.

Empower: Problem solve afterward and create a custom plan with
my son.

Neither Zoey nor I expected this planned approach to chaotic behavior to be a magic bullet, but at this point, she was willing to try anything.

It wasn't long before the new plan was put to the test. Inevitably, Zoey's son got angry at his little sister, and fists started flying. Zoey took a deep breath and went into action. *Picture him as a baby, move closer, stay quiet and listen, problem solve later.* And it worked. Not only was Zoey able to remain calm, the outburst lasted only minutes instead of hours.

When her son started yelling at his dad the next day, she tried it again. And again, it worked. Each time she used the plan, she remained calm, and her son calmed down faster and easier. This resulted in Zoey and her son being able to build trust in each other during these tough moments. This went on for a week and a half.

Things were looking promising until one day Zoey was touched-out, noised-out, and exhausted when the yelling started.

That's when Zoey simply couldn't remain calm. She screamed one of those screams that leaves your throat sore the next day. She was sure all the progress they'd made would unravel. But instead, her son simply said, "Mom, don't forget, breathe and picture me as a baby. I'm here when you're ready. Do you need a hug? We can solve this when we both are calm."

What kind of witchcraft was this? Zoey's son was using the plan we'd created to calm *her* down.

Not long after, a fight broke out on a play structure. Too many kids and a small structure was a recipe for a lot of angry five-year-olds. Normally, Zoey's son would have been the ringleader of the anger brigade, but when she arrived to try to help, she saw that her son was taking charge of problem-solving. "I notice we all want to play, but there isn't enough room for all of us. What if we made a plan that works for all of us? What are your concerns? How would you like to solve this problem?" Within minutes, the kids had worked out their frustration, created a plan that worked for everyone, and were back to being pirates on a voyage for hidden treasures. And all of this was possible because Zoey stuck to one simple plan (based on the Calm the Chaos framework) to remain calm in the moment. I share this story with you now to show you that progress and change are possible.

STAGE ONE:

SURVIVING THE STORM

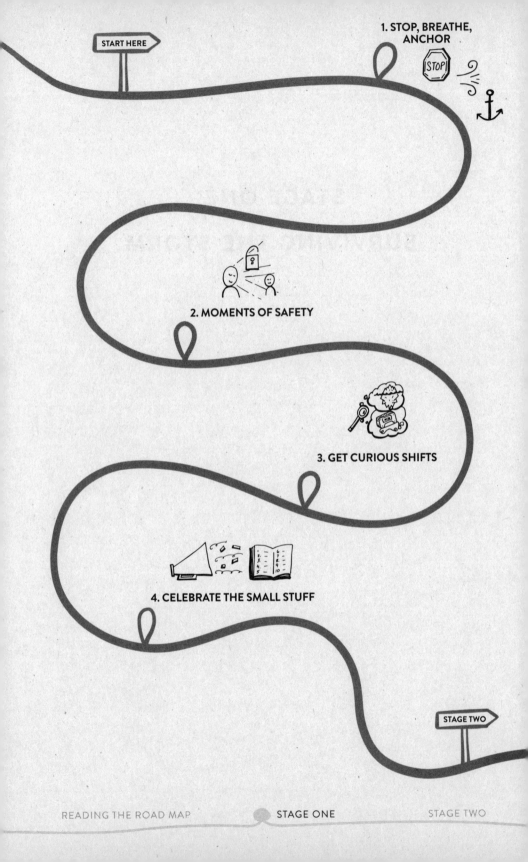

START HERE

1. STOP, BREATHE, ANCHOR

2. MOMENTS OF SAFETY

3. GET CURIOUS SHIFTS

4. CELEBRATE THE SMALL STUFF

STAGE TWO

YOUR CHALLENGE: GET EVERYONE TO SAFETY

"I can't live like this anymore." Standing there in our kitchen, my husband said the words I had feared hearing for years. My oldest son had just had yet another massive meltdown. This time our three-year-old daughter got stuck in the crossfire. Despite his love for me and our family, I knew my husband was contemplating divorce just to free himself of the constant chaos. He scooped up our daughter, loaded the car, and headed to his parents' house. I wasn't sure if he was coming back, but deep down, I was pretty sure our marriage was over.

I'd spent the last five years reading everything I could to help me understand my son, weathering gale-force winds and destructive stormy meltdowns, and even trying therapy after therapy to get ahead of the damage. I'd—okay, we'd—tried everything: cognitive behavioral therapy, counseling, applied behavior analysis (ABA), occupational therapy (OT), speech, social work; you name it, we tried it. Yet I still found myself in constant survival mode.

This was *not* the life I had signed up for or the family I'd imagined. It was clear it wasn't going to get better anytime soon unless I did something different. And right there, on my thirty-seventh birthday, I decided I wanted not just to survive but to thrive. I didn't have the how quite yet, but I was ready.

⚠ PREPARE FOR THE WORST

I know at this stage you might want me to tell you what to say to your child, how to stop the chaos from happening in the first place, or what you can do right now to have a blissful family evening together. But I just can't do that. You see, I know that you can't whip out a power move if you're in the middle of a storm of any kind, especially a category three storm. You just can't. There's only one thing that will help you when all hell breaks loose: getting everyone to safety, including yourself. That's your one and only focus.

Most of us tired parents would like to believe that breaking out one simple strategy will stop the storms dead or quell the chaos once and for all, but that's not how this stuff works. That's just magical thinking. Not only will your challenging kid continue to challenge you but life's little curveballs will continue to drain your reserves, making you less resourceful.

Growing up in Tornado Alley, I learned early on that storms are inevitable and no amount of ignoring or pretending makes them any less likely to happen. Every Wednesday at noon the sirens would blare, and kids across the state would practice going into the halls of their schools, kneeling facing the walls, and placing their hands over their heads. It was our emergency preparedness training for when the real tornado touched down. Then at home, we'd run through the entire scenario again and again until everyone knew their part. When the sky would turn yellow and the sirens would sound, everyone knew exactly what to do and where to go. Our safe place was under the stairs where two adults, three tired and cranky kids, and three large dogs would cram with our radio and flashlights until the coast was clear (sometimes this would last hours).

This stage is all about preparing for the inevitable, much like tornado drills: coming up with a plan so you don't have to think about what to do in the heat of the moment. The Ride the Storm plan we're going to develop together will keep you and your family safe in the worst scenarios (even ones you can't possibly fathom at this point).

But first we need a reality check.

YOU CAN'T AVOID THE STORMS

No one wants to admit their family is in survival mode, especially if you've worked your ass off to get past your worst days. Parents are constantly telling me, "I don't want to go back to the storms. I want to be past them." And when they utter these words, I want to reach out and squeeze them, whisper in their ears, "But, friend, storms are inevitable."

Storms are a fact of life. It's unrealistic to expect sunshine and rainbows every single day, and as clichéd as it might sound, you can't have rainbows without rain. Storms are part of the cycle; they aren't failures or signs that you've taken a wrong turn. Instead, acknowledging and prepping for what's ahead gives us strength. We can prepare ourselves while building resiliency, skills, and confidence to weather anything that comes our way.

THREE TYPES OF STORMS

When beginning stage one, it's inevitable to feel as though your entire world is about to crumble into tiny pieces. Unfortunately, this keeps you fearful and perpetually on edge. Approaching every interaction as if it's a sign of the end of times is exhausting and will eventually lead to burnout. Not to mention, this way of life makes it difficult for your family to know when the real emergency appears. Therefore, it's important to recognize the different types of storms. This differentiation will allow you to not only prep for the hurricane but weather the smaller storms and breathe.

Category One: Cloudy with a Chance of Showers

Small and uncomfortable stressors that can pile on top of each other and feel overwhelming. Interruptions, sibling bickering, changes in routines, or talking back are just a few examples of small storms.

Category Two: Thunderstorms

Larger stress- and worry-inducing challenges that can take more than a day to solve. These storms could include anything from refusing to go to school to lying or cheating, picky eating, trouble at school, or even a sick parent.

Category Three: Hurricanes

Giant life-altering challenges that have the potential to derail you for weeks, months, or longer. These typically affect everyone in the family and can be dangerous. Level-three storms might include physical aggression, suspensions or expulsions, divisive divorce or custody battles, drug or alcohol use, or self-harm.

📑 THE PATH FORWARD:
YOUR RIDE THE STORM PLAN

When you're in the shelter hunkered down waiting out the storm, you know you need a plan for survival. You want to know precisely what to do and how to do it, but everything feels so difficult and challenging. Yes, you know your job is to let go of the things that just don't matter right now, but you need so much more.

In the following chapters, I will break down the Ride the Storm plan one part at a time. Finally, in the last chapter, we'll put it all together.

YOU: HEY, BRAIN, YOU OKAY UP THERE?

I'm sure you've heard the phrase "be the calm in the storm." As parents, our job is to calm the chaos instead of adding to it. However, ignoring our own stress response only sets us up for perceived failure and self-blame, sending us into a nasty shame cycle that feels as if there's zero hope for improvement. I think we can all admit we don't need any more reasons to doubt our parenting skills.

What do I mean by stress response? In an attempt to keep you safe at all costs, your brain will trigger an automatic stress response (fight, flight, freeze, fawn). This results in you:

- yelling (fight),
- hiding in your room behind a barricade (flight),
- shutting down with your feet glued to the floor (freeze), or
- giving in to keep the peace (fawn).

(This is an oversimplification of the neuroscience; more on this later.) When you're in survival mode, remaining calm in the middle of an outburst or fight with your child is next to impossible.

What can you do instead? You need a technique that will deactivate this natural stress response and allow you to access your logic and thinking in the middle of the storms. That is exactly what Stop, Breathe, Anchor is designed to do.

STOP, BREATHE, ANCHOR

When you're in the middle of a storm, this technique will help ground and calm your nervous system, leaving you able to respond with love and empathy versus turning into a monster in the middle of your living room. This technique takes zero time in the moment and can be done even while your child is throwing toys at your head, lunging at their sibling, or refusing to do anything you've asked. You can do this anywhere and anytime, even if you feel like you have no time at all.

Stop, Breathe, Anchor consists of three small steps:

1. **Stop:** Pausing before reacting or responding.
2. **Breathe:** Disarming your nervous system with deep breaths.
3. **Anchor:** A strong memory, affirmation, or thought that removes emotion and grounds you.

I'm going to walk you through precisely how to do this, but first I want to talk about your brain, whose primary job is to keep you safe.

WORKING WITH WHAT YOU'VE GOT

For the last twenty years, parents have been told that they must be calm and consistent if they are to raise resilient children. And while this advice is a vast improvement from "do as I command at any cost," it fails to address the individual parent and the emotional resources we each bring to the table. We must consider the effects of our own trauma, personalities, needs, and unique nervous systems.

For far too long we parents have been expected to remain calm at all costs even if our own mental health is shaky; we must remain consistent with our responses, even when we lack the wherewithal to do that. When we falter in the slightest, we tend to spiral into self-hate: *I'm not good enough. I'm a terrible parent. I'm a failure.* To add insult to injury, as children, many of us were never taught mindfulness or self-awareness techniques to remain calm. We are forced to rely on willpower, counting to three, or stuffing our feelings so deep down we forget they exist.

Unfortunately, this doesn't work, because when our kids don't listen, or they go into meltdown mode, we're suddenly flooded with all sorts of emotions and feelings that cause our brain to perceive danger. The brain is designed to protect us, so your child might as well be a big grizzly bear rearing to attack you, because that's how it interprets their behavior.

As for remaining consistent, without faltering in the least, give up on that idea because it ignores your child's own need for safety and a lack of skills to combat their natural response system, not just yours. For example, if you tell your child, "It's not okay to hit," but your child doesn't know how else to express those emotions, then they're going to keep hitting. In these moments, your child is dealing with their very own fight-or-flight response. And let's be honest, most of us have never learned how to handle this automatic stress response, yet we're asking our kids to do so. Get good at managing your own response, then start teaching them how.

Step One: Stop

In the moment of chaos, our instinct is to run in and fix the problem. I want to caution you that if you aren't calm (and your child isn't calm), this will end badly. Your brain needs a second to know that it is, in fact, not in danger. This pause is essential for breaking you out of the automatic reactive state and calming your nervous system. This pause is responsible for rewiring your brain, so this becomes intuitively second nature.

This step is exactly what it sounds like. Simply stop. As an added benefit, your child will receive your nonverbal cues (pausing instead of reacting) before they ever process your words. By stopping, you become a grounding force for them as well.

Stop talking.

Stop moving.

Stop pointing your finger.

Stop all interactions with your child.

If possible, plant your feet on the ground and imagine roots extending into the earth, holding you steady.

Step Two: Breathe

Yep. I just told you to do something you believe you do naturally: breathe. But think about it, what do you typically do when you jump off into a tailspin of anger? For most people, their instinct is to hold their breath and jump into action. When we hold our breath, our brain gets the signal that something is seriously amiss. Breathing is life, and if you're not breathing your brain believes something must be wrong. "Hey, why'd she stop breathing? She must need our help. Send in the big dogs. Fight or flight?"

JUST breathe

The easiest way to call off the fight-or-flight response is to breathe into the situation and get oxygen to our brain. But how?

Start by shifting from short, shallow breaths in your chest to breathing deep into your belly and out of your mouth until you begin to feel your heart rate slow. I am not asking you to do a fifteen-minute yoga routine here; that would be ludicrous. Instead, simply take three to ten seconds to breathe in and out. Your stress response will thank you later (and so will your mama guilt).

One of my absolute favorite ways to breathe in the heat of the moment is the hand-to-heart breath.

Place your right hand on your heart. Next, place your left hand on top of your hand. Now, simply take in a big deep breath through your nose and into your belly. Then breathe out through your mouth. Repeat this three to five times until you sense your heartbeat starting to slow.

The reason this method is so powerful is because the hand to heart gives your heart a hug and tells your brain, "Hey, we are safe."

The best part is this breath can be done anywhere. You can do it while your kids are kicking in front of you, while your spouse is yelling at you, or when you get another call from school. It takes no extra time or energy and is a tool you can carry with you anywhere you go.

Step Three: Anchor

The final piece of this grounding technique is your anchor. This tells your brain, "Hey, friend, it's okay. We got this. No need to react."

If you've ever latched on to a cute mantra or meditation only for it to fail in the moment, the reason is likely twofold:

1. You didn't believe it enough to calm your nervous system.
2. You didn't practice out of the moment, so it wasn't a habit when you needed it most.

My work with parents around the world with various backgrounds and triggers has made it clear that anchors are incredibly personal to the individual. That said, I've discovered several types of anchors to add to your toolbox that you can use right now. Find one that resonates and feels simple enough to try.

Types of Anchors:

1. **Memory Anchors**

    These are any positive memories that flood your brain with serotonin (the happy chemical). For some parents, the birth of their child was traumatic, therefore more recent memories might be more soothing. The key is to remember one moment where you and your child were connected and happy.

    Examples:
    - The first time your child hugged you or said I love you
    - A special day with the family
    - A time your child helped a sibling
    - Reading or cuddling at nighttime
    - A recent win or achievement
    - Something funny your child said or did

2. **Sensory Anchors**

Evoke different senses to bring you a sense of calm, regardless of what's going on around you. Of all the senses, your olfactory sense (sense of smell) is the fastest path to your brain, which is why including a calming scent works wonders to calm the nervous system.

Examples:

- Soft piece of fabric
- Familiar fidget
- Stone or crystal
- Necklace or beads
- Favorite tune or sound
- Your favorite scent

3. **Affirmation Anchors**

For many parents, having a small word, phrase, or mantra to repeat in the heat of the moment (often in their head on repeat) is the easiest way to ground themselves when they feel themselves slipping into an old way of parenting. Again, this isn't about finding all the mantras and hoping you'll remember them in the moment. Instead, start by finding one mantra that speaks to you and reminds you that you're safe when the shit is hitting the fan. If this doesn't work after attempting it a few times, then you can swap for a new anchor.

Some of our students' favorite affirmations:

- All behavior is communication.
- They need me here now.
- I am safe.
- They aren't doing this to me.
- This isn't about me.
- There is no bear.

Practice, Practice, and Practice Some More

I want you to know that it's completely normal to try a few of these anchors and still lose your ever-lovin' mind. It takes time to create the habit and to rewire your natural response. Give yourself permission to be imperfect, and don't worry if it doesn't work 100 percent of the time. This is no way a sign that you're a failure or this won't work for you.

STOP, BREATHE, ANCHOR IN ACTION

Clare: Triggered by Violent Attacks

Clare, who had been physically abused by her brother growing up, could muster all her calm to keep from blowing up during the first physical attack from her daughter of the day. However, by attack number three, she would lose any ounce of patience she had left and scream back at her daughter. She desperately needed a way to separate her reaction to her daughter from the traumatic memories of her own childhood, no matter what her daughter threw at her. Her first anchor was "Just wait it out. Breathe. Don't respond." She moved on to:

1. "She's not my brother. I am safe. Breathe."
2. "I'm okay. I can get through this. Breathe."

The more she told herself she was safe and remained calm, the shorter and fewer the attacks became.

ACTION STEP: CHOOSE YOUR ANCHOR

Your next step is to choose one to five anchors that might work for you the next time your child is yelling, arguing, or spiraling into the danger zone. Feel free to use the anchors in this chapter (no reason to invent something new if you don't have to). Choose the one that resonates the most that you want to test first.

Next, write this anchor on a Post-it note and place it where you'll see it regularly (the kitchen sink, the bathroom mirror, the car dashboard, etc.).

Finally, decide when and where you will practice your anchor before the storm, so the next time the storm hits, you can jump into action with Stop, Breathe, Anchor.

Note: Taking this first step is a huge accomplishment. While it may not feel like it now, this is the one step that unlocks the rest of the journey. To encourage you to pause and take this step, I've created a special video just for you. It will give you the momentum and the boost you need to keep going on this journey, even on the hard days.

You can visit www.calmthechaosbook.com/anchor to get your special message and a printable sheet of simple anchors you can use to remain calm in the heat of the moment.

CONNECT: ARE WE SAFE YET?

Let's face it—in the middle of the storm there isn't a lot of time for lots of connection, hugging it out, or playing a game. You're trying to survive the storm and just praying everyone comes out unscathed.

In a crisis, humans must first feel safe and secure before taking any other actions, thinking logically, or regulating their emotions. So how can we as parents use kinder words, change our tone, take pauses, turn toward each other, and soften our bodies to create safety *as connection* in the moment?

This is where the next step in the Ride the Storm plan was born. We call this moments of safety.

MOMENTS OF SAFETY

Moments of safety are the signals you send to your child both during and after storms. By providing your child with small bits of connection, even during the roughest moments, you can show your child you're on their side, you're there for them no matter what happens, and that they will be accepted even in their worst moments. With practice, you can become your child's safe haven in the storm.

The truth is, when our nervous system is overwhelmed, overstimulated, or senses danger, it's nearly impossible to access reason, logic, or self-regulation. In addition, blood circulation to the inner ear is restricted, making it difficult to differentiate voices from background noise; our other senses heighten causing touch, restraint, or physical input to send us into a further spiral; and our bodies automatically respond to the signals being sent by the others meaning we might kick, hit, or push to avoid this sensation. Any of these can be exaggerated if there is prolonged history of exposure to danger (perceived or tangible). That's why, in the middle of an outburst, tantrum, or meltdown, your child may act as though they're trying to escape from a wild bear attack.

You, a bear? Hardly. Right?

Yet, think of the last storm you weathered with your child. If someone was in the room with you with a video camera, what would they have seen?

- Were your shoulders raised?
- Were your teeth gritted and were you speaking through them?
- Were your eyebrows furrowed and were you glaring at your child with "the look"?
- Were you standing tall over your child on the floor pointing a finger at them to "stop right now"?
- Were you moving quickly around the room and making sudden movements?
- Was your voice raised a few extra octaves as you repeatedly told your child for the millionth time to "get it together"?

Note: If guilt is starting to rear its ugly head, I want to stop you right now. Remember, you're human. Not only is your nervous system reacting to the danger but you've probably had little practice in responding in a way that helps both you and your child feel safe. Now that you're aware, you can do things differently and begin to create moments of safety for you and your child.

But how?

CHECK YO' SELF

So often as parents we tend to interact on autopilot. We answer or nod without looking up from our work or making dinner. We say things simply because they're ingrained in us, such as "Because I said so," "You heard me the first time," or "Why would you do that?"

When we're in the middle of the storm, our autopilot response can often send signals of danger to our children instead of the calming safety signals we would like.

Often I've had parents tell me, "I'm not a yeller. I stay calm and my child still gets upset." Unfortunately, nine times out of ten, nonverbal cues get flung into the mix. Think about it: Have you ever walked into a room where an argument has been happening, and even though no one is speaking you can cut the tension with a knife? The same is true when you interact with your children. They can feel your frustration, disappointment, and anger, even if you're not saying anything to them.

Challenging children often have heightened emotions. They can feel other people's emotions so acutely that they're sometimes unable to differentiate their own feelings from those of another. I believe this is a superpower of challenging children, but on the flip side, it can cause miscommunication. Even if you don't say anything at all, your children can feel your exhaustion from a long day, stress over work, or frustration over an argument with your spouse. Unfortunately, children don't yet have the cognitive development to decipher what energy is directed at them and what is coming from another source. Therefore, doing a body scan and checking yourself for cues (of both safety and danger) being sent to your child is vital.

Body Scan

You can do a body scan to check yourself both during and after a heated moment. In fact, I encourage you to do this exercise a few times when you aren't trying to ride out a three-hour meltdown, so it's easier to notice your signals and tweak them for maximum impact during the next storm.

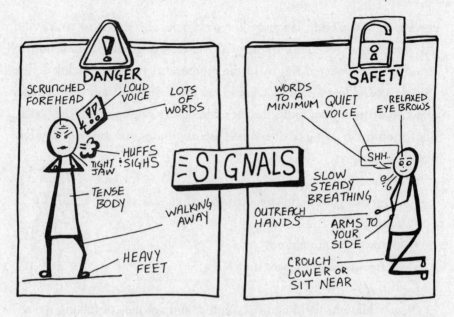

Close your eyes and imagine the last tantrum, meltdown, or outburst that occurred with your child. My guess is your first visual was of your child, their actions, and their responses. Yet, you have no control over anyone's actions but your own. I want you to shift your focus to your own body. Starting from the top of your head, imagine an infrared scanner moving slowly down to your toes and back up to the top. Is your body sending signals of danger or of safety?

When I started doing this exercise, I realized that my groggy, tired morning voice sounded to my child like I was angry at him. Because he was so sensitive to other people's anger and was instantly triggered when he believed someone was angry at him, he would spiral into a full-blown meltdown just at the sound of my "time to wake up."

Keep Words to a Minimum

During a storm, it can be tempting to talk it out, problem solve, or even help your child process their emotions. Resist the urge to create moments of safety with your words (verbal language) in the heat of the moment. Instead, keep words to a minimum, use a softened voice, and actively check your own body language for ways you can signal to your child that you're there for them. In Stage Three, we will go deeper into how to create calm, connected scripts in the moment so you can quickly defuse a situation and know exactly what to say the next time your child refuses to get ready for school, pulls the cat's tail, or starts jumping on the couch. But for now, I'm going to offer a few useful phrases that may signal safety instead of danger:

- I'm here.
- I hear that you are (mirror what your child is saying).
- You are safe.
- I know it's hard right now.
- I see you're having a hard time.

Now, while our word choice, volume, and amount of talking matter, the focus right now is on our body language and the signals we are sending during the storm.

Swapping Danger for Moments of Safety

Now that you've done a body scan and are more aware of the signals your body is sending your child in the middle of a tantrum, meltdown, or outburst, you can swap the signals of danger for body language that tells your child in the moment of chaos that they're safe, loved, and secure. If you remember from the last section, the first step in the Ride the Storm plan is to stop, breathe, and anchor yourself so you're ready for whatever comes your way during the worst moments. Not only does this anchor help you find your calm, it allows you to access the body scan tool to create moments of safety.

After you've taken a moment to anchor yourself, do a quick body scan (one to three seconds long) from head to toe. Where you notice signals of danger, simply swap them for signals of safety.

Examples:

- Put down phone or activity
- Lower your body
- Soften your voice
- Keep words to a minimum
- Loosen your jaw
- Unfold your arms
- Slow down your movements
- Gently touch if possible
- Steady your breathing

Practice, Practice, Practice

As with each tool I introduce, practicing these out of the moment is essential to feeling confident in the moment. First responders practice the same routines and movements for hundreds of hours so that when faced with danger, their bodies intuitively know how to respond in the moment. The same is true for surviving the storm. Practicing the body scan and the softening of your body out of the moment will help you so you don't revert to old habits when you're met with a stressful situation. This is not one-size-fits-all but rather a guide to follow so you can make it work for you and your children.

THE MAGIC FIVE-TO-ONE RATIO

Dr. John Gottman, in his research on what makes happy, connected couples, found that for every one negative interaction, you need five positive interactions to establish a high level of affection and trust. This is the magic five-to-one ratio. The same is true with parent-child relationships.

Throughout the rest of this book, I will dive deeper into the concept of connection—what it looks like at the different stages of your journey, and how you can make it a sustainable and doable practice, even if you're completely overwhelmed by the chaos. For now, I want to focus on what this looks like in the middle of a storm. How do you connect when shoes are being thrown at your head, your six-year-old is spitting in your face, or your teenager is cursing you out for the third time today? You create moments of safety.

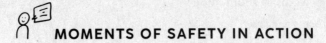

MOMENTS OF SAFETY IN ACTION

Tamara and Hannah: Volatile Mother/Daughter Arguments

As a single, homeschooling mother, one-on-one time was all Tamara's daughter knew. That didn't matter. Their relationship was completely volatile. Anytime Tamara asked Hannah to do anything, whether it was cleaning up, doing her schoolwork, or taking a shower, they would end up in a screaming match. However, when Tamara learned about moments of safety, things started to change almost immediately. Tamara simply walked over to her daughter, sat beside her, rubbed her back, and calmly said she noticed Hannah was having a hard time. Hannah says, "I could feel the difference in my mom immediately. I knew she wanted to help me, and I wasn't afraid of what would happen next."

ACTION STEP: CHECK YO' SELF

Your simple next step is to think of simple ways you can create small moments of safety during your next storm. After you do a body scan, what will you shift to physically be the calm in the middle of the storm?

Will you soften your voice, lower your body, or let go of your clenched jaw? What is one small phrase you can use to create safety and connection in the moment without adding to you or your child feeling overwhelmed?

UNDERSTAND: ALL BEHAVIOR
IS COMMUNICATION

Unfortunately, the middle of a storm is the worst moment to attempt any logical discussions or problem-solving. You get that by now. So how do we as parents understand the *why* behind our children's behavior in the middle of chaos, when we are about to lose our ever-lovin' mind and our kids have glued themselves to the floor, refusing to budge?

We need a technique that doesn't require any dialogue, allows us to remove emotion, and gives us enough empathy and understanding to deal with the storm.

As I've mentioned before, the goal of surviving the storm is to get everyone to safety. This means there isn't enough time to do a deep dive into understanding your child's behaviors in the moment. Instead, we need to shift our thinking from "he's being such a brat" to "wow, he's really struggling." Because the truth is, all behaviors are communication. Meaning your child is trying to tell you something with their behaviors. They have no other way to tell you with their body or words when their stress responses are triggered.

So how do you find the deeper need driving your child's behavior?

ICEBERG THEORY

I want you to picture an iceberg, this big island of ice in the middle of the ocean. Did you know that what you see of an iceberg is only one-seventh of the full thing? That means 85 percent more of the iceberg is under the ocean than above.

Your child's behaviors are much like this iceberg. What you see is only a sliver of what's really happening beneath the surface.

For example, you see a child who:

- clings to your legs and doesn't like to be alone for one minute
- screams and cries over the seemingly tiniest problems
- bounces off the wall when new guests arrive at your house
- refuses to do anything you ask, and tantrums at the mention of "no"
- hits, throws, punches, and kicks anytime they get upset

It's easy to look at these behaviors, throw your hands in the air, and say, "What's wrong with my kid?" However, it's important to remember when your child hits, screams "I hate you," refuses to clean up, or has a meltdown, something more is going on below the surface.

If you look deeper, you'll find there is a reason they do what they do.

- The child who hides behind your legs might be unable to verbalize their big worries and fears.
- The child who cries and kicks over the smallest things might be struggling with skills to calm themselves down.
- The child who jumps on the furniture and plays too rough with others might lack the ability to recognize when they're overexcited or nervous.

Remember, all behavior is communication. Everything your child does is a clue to what they're thinking and feeling. They're pointing you to what they need.

Below is one of our behavior charts that's been shared online more than one million times. It's a great way to do a quick misbehavior swap and see that there are so many possibilities under the surface, and why in the moment you can't possibly identify the specific one. (Please don't try; you'll drive yourself batty.)

COMMON MISBEHAVIORS	POSSIBLE BENEATH-THE-SURFACE CAUSES
Overemotional or Highly Sensitive • Cries over smallest problems • Gets sad when you leave • Doesn't like being alone • Can't watch super sad movies • Whines often	**Strong Need for Safety and Belonging** • Lacks emotional regulation • Feels unsafe in new places • Needs connection • Big feelings and empathy • Lacks verbal skills
Aggressive or Explosive • Yells and screams often • Throws or destroys property • Curses or shouts mean words • Kicks, hits, or bites • Threatens or runs after others	**"Fight" Stress Response** • Lacks problem-solving skills • Needs sensory input • Pushing others away feels safer • Lacks emotional regulation • Lacks communication skills
Defiant or Strong Willed • Can't handle when plans change • Wants things their way • Struggles with criticism • Ignores requests • Repeatedly breaks rules	**Strong Desire for Autonomy** • Needs repetition for safety • Lacks problem-solving skills • Strong need for connection • "Freeze" stress response • Needs are still unmet
Wild or Hyperactive • Makes inappropriate jokes • Jumps on furniture • Constantly on the move • Hyper around new people • Plays rough with others	**Unmet Sensory Needs** • Seeks connection and belonging • Lacks body awareness • Seeks movement • Automatic "flee" response • Lacks self-regulation
Lazy or Scattered • Easily distracted • Unmotivated • Doesn't help around the house • Shuts down easily • Unorganized and messy	**Lacks Organizational Skills** • Curious about the world • Has no desire for task • Fearful of doing it wrong again • Lacks safety when overwhelmed • Lacks organizational skills

Note: The beneath-the-surface causes are all speculation at this point. Don't get sucked into the maze of trying to align your child's behaviors or causes one to one or trying to categorize your child. These are simply common struggles and causes I've worked with over the last twenty years and is not a definitive list in any way, shape, or form.

In Stage Three, I will share how you can truly understand what your child's behaviors are telling you, and even how to figure out their most common stress response. For now, the focus is on realizing that there is indeed a need behind every behavior. Notice this isn't about a diagnosis or a particular

label. Instead this is about understanding your unique child. While a diagnosis can be extremely helpful in understanding our children and informing decisions, a diagnosis isn't a "reason" behind the behavior.

The biggest takeaway from this shift is to move from "my child is (insert label)" to "my child needs me." In the moment, this can be added to your anchors so you can remain calm and empathetic. Discovering what is under the surface will come later, so let your mind ease if you're already starting to get pulled down that rabbit hole. I urge you, don't go there just yet.

IT'S NOT ABOUT YOU

Now, I don't know about you, but I'm a sing-in-the-shower type girl, and one song always reminds me not to take my child's behaviors personally. It's by Carly Simon, whose hit song in the seventies had this line: "You probably think this song is about you, don't you, don't you?"

Here's the point: Your child's meltdowns, defiance, aggression, and other behaviors aren't about you. They're about them. They're about their own reactions, struggles, needs, and automatic stress responses.

If you've ever thought:

- My kids are always giving me such a hard time
- My kids are mean or rude to me
- My kids don't respect me
- My kids don't care about me

You aren't alone.

But I promise, your child's behavior is not something they're doing to you.

Remember, all behavior is communication. (Sounds like a mantra, I know. Go ahead and use it.) Your child is struggling, has a need that isn't

being met, and doesn't know how to express it or work through it, yet. So in the middle of your next storm, remove the blame and let go of the idea that the behavior is about you. It's simply not. Keep the focus on your child by staying curious and telling yourself, "This isn't about me."

Instead of thinking *Why is my child giving me such a hard time?* change your question to *Why is my child having such a hard time?* This can immediately release the stress and pressure that you feel in the moment and allow you to remain open, curious, and empathetic in the middle of the worst storms.

Some behaviors, phrases, and jabs might be directed directly at you. You might have a child say, "You're the worst mom ever." Even though they're directing their frustration at you, the real challenge and need is still under the surface.

Think about it: Have you ever blown up at someone who truly didn't deserve to be on the receiving end of your wrath? Maybe something like the following has happened in your home. You've been with the kids all day, cleaned up messes, rewashed the dishes fifty times, folded and refolded laundry, carted kids to multiple places, made fifteen meals to appease each member of the family, and then finally, at the end of the night, your kid goes haywire because you're out of banana oatmeal and you completely lose your mind. You snap, start yelling, say unkind things, send everyone to their rooms, and then immediately feel guilty? My guess is your blowup wasn't about the banana oatmeal at all. Instead, you were depleted, touched-out, noised-out, overwhelmed, and ready to end the day.

The same is true for your child's behaviors.

Note: The idea that all behavior is communication takes time to understand and put into practice. Give yourself grace and space to slowly shift from automatic responses and thoughts. In addition, if your child is non-speaking or has apraxia or tics, the behaviors are typically signs of a misfire. While they might not be communicating exactly what your child wants them to, they're still signals that your child needs you, not that they're being manipulative or disrespectful.

 ## THE POWER AND ATTENTION TRAP

The biggest trap I see parents and professionals fall into is when they believe that all behavior is a sign that the child is seeking one of two things: **power** or **attention.**

You know you've fallen into the power or attention trap if:
- You've ever given your child choices with very clear boundaries—like whether they can get the blue cup or the red cup, or whether they can clean their room or do the dishes first—but they must do both.
- You praise the good and ignore the bad.
- You've ever found yourself refusing to back down, because you know if you give in, they will learn that their power ploy works.

The usual remedy for a child presumed to be seeking power is to simply give them two choices in order to avoid defiance. If attention is the problem, you're counseled to be careful, because if your child doesn't get enough positive attention, then they will seek out attention in negative ways.

There are three problems with this limited way of thinking.

1. **Resentment**

    Looking at your child through an attention-seeking lens can lead to you resenting your children. If you see all their behavior as attention seeking yet you give them all the attention in the world, you'll be resentful that they still want more from you. You might even feel like your kids are entitled or disrespectful brats who just want more and more and more, and you can never give them enough.

2. **Power Struggles**

Seeing behavior as a bid for power leads to constant power struggles because you just see your children as power hungry and feel a constant pull to set firm limits so your kids don't walk all over you. The fact is, it takes two to have a power struggle. When you're constantly on the lookout for who's winning, a power struggle will follow, just as crying follows screaming.

3. **Eliminates Other Possibilities**

The biggest problem with this power and attention trap is that it ignores the other possibilities. Your unique child could need connection, feel overwhelmed, lack the confidence to do the task asked, be overstimulated from the surroundings, and on and on.

ALL BEHAVIOR IS COMMUNICATION IN ACTION

Rocio: Generational Guilt

Rocio was raised in a family that believed children shouldn't ever talk back or speak out of turn. You listen, you do what is asked, and that's the end of the story. So when Rocio had a young daughter described by others as "strong willed," she assumed her daughter hated her. After all, her daughter never listened, spoke up and out of turn all the time, and didn't do what Rocio asked. If Rocio took it personally, it set her off into her own raging spirals. After learning that the behavior wasn't about her, Rocio was able to remain calm in the middle of the storm. Suddenly, she didn't take her daughter's lack of listening as an attack; instead she got curious as to what could be hiding under the surface.

ACTION STEP: GET CURIOUS

Your tiny next step is to get curious. As you think about the last tantrum, meltdown, or outburst you found yourself in the middle of, what assumptions did you make about the behavior you saw? How did these behaviors make you feel? Did you take them personally?

Now that you've been introduced to the iceberg theory and the idea that it's not about you, what simple shift can you remember during the next storm to stay curious and empathetic?

Here are a few of my students' favorite "get curious" shifts:

- All behavior is communication
- My child is not giving me a hard time, my child is having a hard time
- This is not about me
- My child needs me

EMPOWER: CELEBRATE THE SMALL STUFF

When you first begin this work, it can feel near impossible to get through the day, let alone focus on any small growth and wins. You may feel as though you're barely treading water, so your win is simply that you made it to the end of the day with your family alive. And while this win could be encouraging a few days out of the year, when this is all you can latch on to every day, it can feel depressing. Nonetheless, challenging yourself to find something small to focus on helps break up the drudgery of your daily life. Sure, you want the big wins, but trust me when I say little wins turn into a safety net that you can fall back on when storms strike again. Because let's face it, life will continue to throw lightning bolts your way.

By focusing on only large wins, completed goals, and complete transformation, you hinder your progress. Find proof that you are in fact growing, changing, and working toward moving out of the constant storms, and you will be far more likely to build a family that works together and gets along.

SIX WAYS TO CELEBRATE THE SMALL STUFF

Fact Check
Look for proof that your catastrophizing thoughts aren't true.

- Your child played with their sibling. (They don't *always* fight.)
- You had five minutes to yourself. (You don't have *zero* time to yourself.)
- Your child got upset but didn't resort to aggression. (They aren't *always* angry.)
- Your kids followed an agreed-upon plan even though it was a challenge. (It's not true that they *never* listen.)

Progress, Not Perfection
Look for proof that you're making small steps toward a goal.

- You didn't yell when your child refused to get ready.
- You read a chapter of a book you've been meaning to read.
- You stayed curious and present when your child was upset.
- Your child did their homework even if it was hard.

Decreased Chaos
Look for proof that struggles are getting better even if they aren't gone yet.

- Your toddler sets something down gently instead of throwing it.
- Bedtime took two hours instead of three.
- You faced fifteen occurrences of aggression instead of thirty.
- Your child had fewer meltdowns (five instead of fifteen a week).

Increased Connection
Look for proof of connection when it feels all connection is lost.

- You laughed for the first time in a long time.
- You noticed something amazing about your child that you hadn't seen before.
- Your child asked for your help.
- One child helped another sibling.

Gratitude
Proof that there are things in your life that are positive and worth being thankful for.

- You enjoyed a quiet moment with a cup of coffee in your favorite chair.
- You got good news from a friend.
- You got some much-needed rest.
- You scheduled an appointment with a specialist.

Strength and Resilience
Proof you can get through hard things.

- You or your child were able to pivot and shift with changes.
- You accepted help from someone else.
- You had a difficult conversation.
- You advocated for your child when others disagreed.

THE ULTIMATE TEST

I will never forget the moment our Calm the Chaos students had to put this practice of finding small wins to the ultimate test. At the time—during the onset of the whole Covid lockdown—we didn't know what we were about to encounter. We just knew that the world felt uneasy, unpredictable, and full of chaos.

Our community is used to chaos: kids getting kicked out of school, parents having to leave a job to take care of a challenging kid, arguments breaking out over small things, siblings fighting, meltdowns over electronics and schoolwork—you name it, they get it. But the lockdown felt different. It felt like the world was starting to turn upside down. As a reset, I challenged our community to post #onewinaday, no matter how small. I wasn't sure if this would help the energy and mood of the group, but I figured if it worked for me and for others over the years, it was time to put this to the test. Could focusing on one win a day really help us collectively get through this tough time?

More than ever, our community needed to focus on small growth, what was working, and small wins. As schools shut down, parents focused on *progress, not perfection.* As the Covid death toll started to rise, the community focused on *gratitude* for the health of their family. As families were stuck inside with nowhere to go but their own home, our families focused on the small proof of *increased connection.* As days turned to weeks, weeks into months, months into years of uncertainty, change, and chaos, our students focused on their *resilience and strength* to get through hard days. And when the worries and fears would spiral, when another shutdown was announced, when kids had to return to school, and when all else seemed to fail, our parents focused on *fact-checking* their fears to find proof to contradict their catastrophizing thoughts.

When our community shifted from focusing on all the things that were going wrong in the world and in their families to empowering themselves with proof that they were, in fact, going to be okay, what happened feels almost magical. While the rest of the world was struggling to get through the pandemic, our community was thriving. Obviously, there were days where it felt like too much to handle, but every single student who participated in #onewinaday saw a shift in their mood, their ability to remain calm, and their ability to show up for their family. Many of these students even said 2020 was their best year as a family, and it all started by shifting their focus from everything that was going wrong to the small proof of what was working.

As I write this book, more than ten thousand wins of all sizes have been documented. Some students are reaching their thousandth day of focusing on #onewinaday. What started as celebrations for things that were too small and not worth noticing slowly grew into much bigger wins and rippled across entire families.

Don't be discouraged if your wins feel too small or not enough right now. The key is to find one small thread of hope, even on your dark days; eventually you will have enough of these threads to weave your own safety net to fall back on when another storm arrives.

BONUS: DON'T KEEP THE CELEBRATION TO YOURSELF

Focusing on these small wins and growth, especially if you build a habit of collecting at least one small win a day, can be incredibly powerful. If you want to supercharge this exercise and habit, you can include your children or your entire family. Not only will this increase connection during the break between storms but it can also help your children start to shift their thinking away from always or never, all or nothing, or negative self-talk. In Stage Four, I will share more about how to collect wins with your whole family, but for now know that you don't have to keep this powerful tool to yourself until you get there. We have students who write one win a day as a family on a sticky note and keep a wall of wins. Some have small notes they add to a jar and then read them when the jar is full of wins. Others simply say the wins verbally during dinner each night as a way to connect over the progress and growth happening in the whole family.

TRICK YOUR BRAIN

You might often find yourself wondering why this has to be so hard. Why do our kids have to have such terrible behavior? Why can't our kids act "normal"?

While these thoughts are completely normal, stop. This only serves to turn your brain into a negative accomplice, whose sole job is to search for supporting evidence that you're in danger, all to protect you. Because if you can spot the cause of pain, you're more likely to avoid it. In fact, negativity bias, which is what this is called, has an evolutionary function: The more attuned to danger we are, the more likely we are to survive. This is an ingrained habit from the dawn of time. But when we start to shift to finding the tiny simple wins, we start to see more and more proof that we can, in fact, survive this storm and come out stronger on the other side.

CELEBRATE THE SMALL STUFF IN ACTION

Imani: Stay-at-Home Mom of Three with No Energy

When Imani first started using #onewinaday she could barely find anything to be thankful for (aside from a new baby girl). She had no energy, a new medical diagnosis, and two older kids who were constantly at each other's throats. She was starting to believe that life was never going to get better, yet she decided to give the challenge a try. She began to notice small things, like her kids playing for a few minutes without a fight while she nursed the baby, her husband helping with bedtime when she was depleted, and tiny progress made in her own medical journey. Slowly, Imani regained her hope and positive outlook. This allowed her to have energy to face each day without starting from negative ten before she even set foot out of bed.

⌗ ACTION STEP: CELEBRATE ONE SMALL WIN

Your tiny next step is to take a pause right now and find one small thing to celebrate. **Hint:** you've made it to the end of stage one. This is a call for huge celebration, even if you aren't remaining calm *yet*, or you aren't surviving the storms like a pro *yet*. Where can you collect your wins each day? Many of our students have special journals, bulletin boards, or whiteboards where they collect wins. One student created a "wins scroll" and included her family in the project; the scroll was fourteen yards long last time I checked in with her. What will you use?

Note: Having a place to collect these moments allows you to revisit them when your days feel dark and you feel like you're losing hope. Simply head to your wins, look back at some of your first-ever wins, and you will notice just how far you've come in such a short time.

PUTTING IT ALL TOGETHER: YOUR RIDE THE STORM PLAN

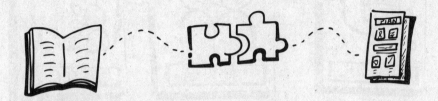

Congrats! You made it. You've completed the first stage in your journey of parenting a challenging child.

You've learned how to weather the worst days and stay grounded even when your child's behaviors knock you to your knees. You've even learned how to provide safety in the middle of the storm and shift your focus from problem-solving to staying curious so you and your child can emerge from the chaos connected.

I don't want to burst your bubble, but you ain't done yet.

You see, I'm not here to offer you theories and ideas you might be able to use someday. Instead, I'm all about actionable steps you can take to ensure a brighter future for your family.

I've included these summary sections in each chapter to remind you to slow down, process what you've just learned, and create an actionable plan you can use for your family today.

By reviewing, putting the pieces together, and creating a tangible plan you can practice out of the moment, you'll be ten times more likely to use the knowledge when you need it most. By writing out the plan on paper, you create pathways of connection in your brain that increase memory, retention, and your ability to implement the plan when your protective brain takes over.

A PLAN IS ONLY AS GOOD AS ITS PLANNING

For every plan we create, there are three distinct stages to keep in mind:

1. **Before:** the prep work needed before the next time
2. **During:** the core steps to remember and implement in the moment
3. **After:** the processing, tweaking, and recovery once the worst of this storm is over and before the next one

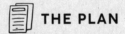 **THE PLAN**

Your **Ride the Storm** plan is created ahead of time so you and your family can follow it the next time fists start flying, cursing begins, or your kid starts to run away. This plan is designed to keep you and your family safe and allow each of you to get through the tantrum, meltdown, or outburst relatively unscathed. This plan is not for fixing, solving, or disciplining behavior. You aren't ready to do that yet. This plan is simply to get through the moment with more grace, connection, and understanding than you might have been able to in the past.

I've already introduced you to the parts of the Ride the Storm plan. Let's review:

1. **You: Stop, Breathe, Anchor:** In the middle of the storm, your own automatic stress response is heightened, making it near impossible for you to remain calm and grounded. This three-second exercise allows you to pause, activate the logical part of your brain, and stay present for your child. Your anchor is a thought, memory, or phrase that reminds you and your brain that you're safe.

2. **Connect: Moments of Safety:** In the middle of a storm, you cannot control anyone else or how they react. That's why it's imperative you check your own body for signals you might be sending inadvertently. By scanning your body in the middle of a tantrum, meltdown, or outburst and softening your eyes, jaws, shoulders, and voice, you begin to help your child's automatic stress response to calm alongside you.

3. **Understand: Get Curious Shifts:** Understanding the why behind a behavior or a storm is incredibly important; however, while your house is being battered is not the time for twenty questions. Instead, simply use one of the two shifts introduced in this chapter to get curious. Iceberg theory helps you look beneath your child's behavior to see what's really going on (allowing empathy on your part), while the "it's not about you" shift helps you remember that your child's behaviors are not attacks on you (removes resentment).

4. **Empower: Celebrate the Small Stuff:** Finally, after the storm has passed and you've emerged from the chaos, it's time to celebrate the small wins that are starting to happen. At first, these wins will be hard to see, but they will become your lifeline and create a strong foundation both you and your family can fall back on as you weather more storms in the future.

Riding Out the Storm

As soon as the storm starts, it's time to start your action plan.

1. **Anchor**

   Stop. Don't move an inch. Stop talking. This will ensure you aren't reacting in the moment and gives your brain the pause it needs to access your ability to calm down. Next, take your big, deep breath into your belly and out through your mouth to remind your brain that you're safe. Finally, activate the anchor you've chosen to use in this moment. If it's an image of your child, visualize them in your head as you breathe, allowing your automatic stress response to decrease just a tad.

2. **Scan**

   Now that you're calmer, scan your body for any residual remnants of your frustration. Soften your eyebrows, open your mouth to relax your jaw, exhale into your shoulders and feel them fall. Soften your body, lowering it toward your child, and quiet your voice.

3. **Shift**

   Finally, stay curious with your iceberg or it's-not-about-me shift. Remember that your child needs you and this isn't about you. Your child needs you right now to anchor, scan, and remain curious. Once the storm begins, these are the three steps that will play on repeat until the storm passes. Stop, Breathe, Anchor, scan your body for signals of safety, remind yourself this isn't about you, there is more beneath the surface, until the storm is over.

   Stop. Breathe. Anchor. *My child needs me (visualize as a baby).*
   Scan. *Soften my body.*
   Shift. *This isn't about me.*

Recovery after the Sky Clears

Once the tantrum, meltdown, or outburst is finally over, unfortunately your work isn't done. It's only natural to want to forget it ever happened, curl up with a Netflix show and a cup of your favorite beverage, and zone out. However, pretending the storm never happened is only going to pile the stress, worry, and intensity onto the next storm if you don't address it head-on. You have options here, and how long you take to recover is completely up to you. Don't feel the need to rush through this part of the plan.

1. **Celebrate the Small Stuff**

   Once you've had a moment to process your feelings and what just happened, your next step is to find the small win in the storm. Some of our students do this immediately following a storm, but that usually comes with practice and time. Don't feel bad if this is just too hard to do immediately following a big argument. The key here is to look for proof that your family can and will survive these storms.

2. **Tweak and Adjust the Plan**

   With every plan, not just Ride the Storm, it's so important that you don't lose all hope if things don't go perfectly. This is your reminder to not throw the baby out with the bathwater. Look back at your plan, specifically your action steps (anchor, scan, shift), and see what went well, what didn't work as well as you had hoped, and what is one small change you can make for next time. Do you need more practice for your anchor? Do you need a reminder to stop? Do you need to soften a different part of your body, move closer to your child, or say something different? This is where the plan becomes unique to you and your child.

3. **Rest, Restore, and Reconnect**

   Finally, after every major storm, rest and restoration is vital. This allows you and your family to weather many more storms together and rebuild connection and resilience. This might look like taking a break from big appointments, having a family movie night with takeout, or everyone going to their rooms for alone time to decompress. Restoration might include fixing any furniture or items that got damaged in the outburst, applying bandages to anyone who was hurt in the crossfire, or even removing items that could be a danger in future storms. In further chapters we will talk more about how to rebuild connection, but for now you can focus on small moments of affection like increasing hugs, sitting with your child as they play their favorite video game, or listening as they tell their long stories about dinosaurs even though you have zero interest.

PREPPING FOR THE NEXT STORM

The number one goal with Ride the Storm is safety. Because of this, before your next major blowup, it's imperative to do some of the prep work.

The most important thing to do before your next storm is:

Practice, Practice, Practice

While most of the steps in the Ride the Storm plan happen in the middle of fists flying and screams of *no*, practicing your action plan before the next time you need to be anchored and calm is imperative. Anchor, scan, shift: these are the three steps that you will need to practice out of the moment as much as you can. Many of my students like to practice every time they go to the bathroom. By practicing out of the moment, you start to create new connections in your brain, so this habit replaces the old habit of jumping to reactions. This new, calmer you becomes the norm the more you practice and prepare.

Remember,

STAGE TWO:
YOUR ENERGY RESERVES

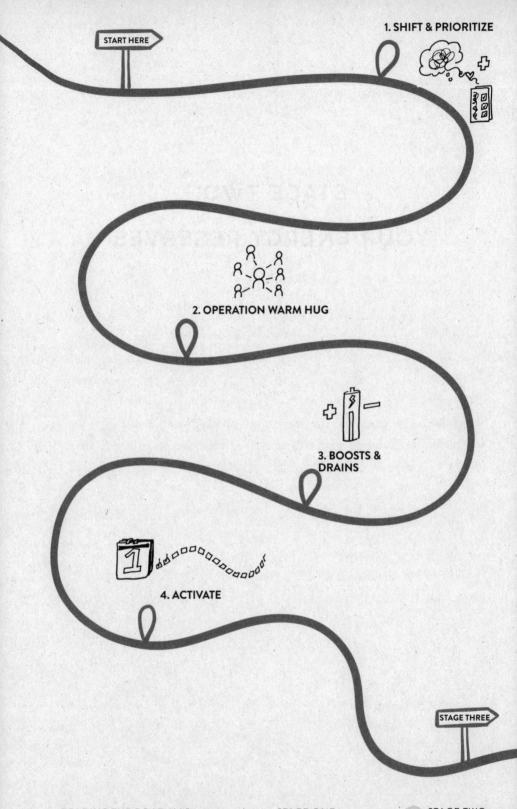

START HERE

1. SHIFT & PRIORITIZE

2. OPERATION WARM HUG

3. BOOSTS & DRAINS

4. ACTIVATE

STAGE THREE

YOUR CHALLENGE: HAVING ENERGY TO FACE ANOTHER BATTLE

"Should the cabin lose pressure, oxygen masks will drop from the overhead area. Please place the mask over your own mouth and nose before assisting others." If you've ever flown on an airplane, you've likely heard these instructions. But have you ever wondered why you're instructed to put your oxygen mask on before assisting others?

Quite simply, it's because your brain cannot function without oxygen. Much like a car can't operate without gas or your kids' latest gadget can't work without batteries, your brain needs to be fueled to let you not only survive but make decisions, stay calm, and have the capacity to help others.

As parents, especially parents raising challenging kids, we commonly find ourselves helping everyone else around us but forgetting about our own well-being. Self-care is for *other* people, not us. Yet, when we can't remain calm after the tenth argument in a day, find the energy to patiently try another strategy, or do anything but plop on the couch at the end of the day, we beat ourselves up for not doing enough. You aren't alone in this dilemma.

A GLOBAL PROBLEM

After nearly two years of parenting in a pandemic on top of dealing with already challenging behaviors beforehand, parents (especially moms) were completely depleted. While I know it seems counterintuitive to focus on you before taking on the challenge of understanding your kids and addressing the behavior you see, it is imperative.

The science proves it. Multiple studies both before and after the pandemic have shown that parent burnout is at an all-time high and it's not getting any better. In fact, parents with multiple children, children with ADHD or anxiety, or parents concerned that their child might have an undiagnosed challenge are at even greater risk of burnout. Parent burnout leads to a higher likelihood of depression, anxiety, and increased alcohol consumption. It's also tied to a larger chance that parents will fall back into old-way parenting (insults, shame, criticism, screaming, cursing, and even physically harming children—e.g., spanking).

Burnout doesn't just affect your behavior and ability to remain calm and present around your child. When you're depleted, the effects ripple into your child's behaviors. A study at Ohio State University even found that as burnout increased, so did parent reports of children's misbehavior.

COMMON CHILD BEHAVIORS ASSOCIATED WITH PARENT BURNOUT

I don't mention these behaviors to add guilt or stir up your catastrophizing thoughts. So if you saw the list above and thought *Great, it's my fault*, I want to stop you right now. It's quite the opposite. I want to drive home the importance of taking care of yourself. Until this point, you've been fighting an uphill battle, and for good reason.

I know you really want to skip this stage and get right to the nitty-gritty of how to handle challenging behaviors. But I know that if you don't slow down to take care of yourself first and you continue to be depleted, every struggle you want to solve (getting your kids to go to school without a fight, having siblings that want to spend time together, diminishing the aggressive outbursts, etc.) will be a hundred times harder.

The Dirty S-Word: Self-Care

Let's talk about the S-word: *self-care*. If you rolled your eyes in disbelief and thought *Great, just another "expert" telling me I need self-care and my child's outbursts will magically disappear*, I hear you. I used to roll my eyes too, until I realized that I had been fed a crock of lies about what self-care meant.

Despite what society would have us believe, self-care is not time away from your kids, bingeing on cake after the kids go to bed, or something that requires hours (that you don't have).

Self-Care Is Selfish

Before I dive into what self-care really is, I want to dispel the primary myth that is pervasive in today's culture about self-care: the belief that self-care is selfish. This couldn't be further from the truth. Going back to the findings from the Ohio State University study, when parents don't take care of themselves there are very clear consequences: increased depression, decreased empathy and connection in parenting, increased challenging behavior (from parents and kids). While many of us know the importance of self-care, we shrug it off and allow these lies that self-care is selfish to take over. We tell ourselves, "I'm fine. I don't need anything. I'm not burned out . . . yet." But the ramifications of ignoring our own health are bigger than many of us even imagine. They include a persistent sense of hopelessness, difficulty concentrating, and strains on relationships.

Self-Care During Survival Mode

If you're anything like I was, just a shell of yourself, all this talk of self-care might sound grand, but it seems completely out of your reach. You aren't alone. In fact, most of the parents I work with find themselves in this exact same conundrum. Logically, they know that self-care is good for them and their kids, but they don't know how to fit it in when they can barely sneak away to the bathroom for five minutes a day (and even then, a toddler comes in with them).

I've compiled a list of simple self-care practices you can do without adding more to your to-do list or taking more time away from your already busy schedule.

Simple Self-Care Practices That Can Be Done without More Time

This is a great way to get started. Because for now we need to keep it simple, so it doesn't feel out of reach.

⚠ CAUTION: RESIST THE URGE TO SKIP SELF-CARE

Despite my warnings, students try to skip the self-care piece all the time. But inevitably, they find themselves stuck in survival mode with feelings of failure for years (not just months). Once they slow down, come back to this piece to add to their energy plan, and focus on building the habits set forth in this stage, they make progress faster and easier than in years past. Suddenly they can remain calm, create plans that work with their children, and their family starts getting along like never before. One mom recently told me she actually gets more done and with less stress now that she has three kids (and a ten-month-old baby) than she did when she just had one child; all because of the plan I am going to walk you through in this stage.

📄 THE PATH FORWARD: YOUR FIVE-MINUTE ENERGY PLAN

When you're parenting a challenging kid, you need energy to make it through each new challenge. We've established that. As soon as you figure out how to survive one storm another comes around the corner. If you don't have the energy to stand back up, ground yourself, and get everyone to safety, all hell starts to break lose.

The Five-Minute Energy plan will give you more time and energy so you can weather any storm that comes your way (even category three storms). In the chapters that follow, I will break this plan down, one piece at a time.

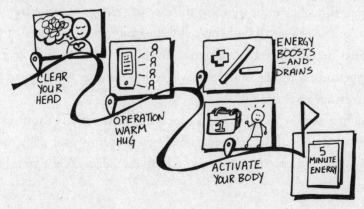

YOU: GET YOUR HEAD CLEAR

We'd all be fooling ourselves if we tried to pretend the only things causing chaos in our lives were related to our kids and their behaviors. The truth is, parenting isn't done inside some magical bubble where you're immune to the stressors of real life. You know, the piles of bills on the kitchen table, the never-ending loads of laundry, the last-minute project your boss just handed you—you name it, the list goes on.

Before long, the chaos of raising a family in our modern world combines with the stress of raising a challenging child and dread sets in, making it near impossible to get a moment of peace. And it shows, all over your face from the worry lines in your forehead to your clenched jaw. Soon, your kids start to notice Mom's not too happy. And they start to wonder, "Did I do something wrong . . . again?" We have to find a way out of this unsustainable stress, not just for our own sanity but for our children.

When you start the day thinking *I can't do this*, you feel angry and hopeless all day, and your behavior is surly and sluggish. However, when you shift your thoughts in the morning to *I can take today one step at a time* or *I can do hard things*, you'll find yourself feeling more hopeful and a little less frustrated. You'll notice an increased ability to remain calm in the storm for longer periods. Rippling from there will be more energy and hope to tackle all your struggles as a family.

The first step in your Five-Minute Energy plan will help you clear the garbage in your head by inserting small practices into your daily routine. This is done with two important tools, both intended to clear your head.

1. **Shift:** An internal head clearing of thoughts, worries, and stress that drains you and causes more damage than good.
2. **Prioritize:** An external head clearing of the to-do's, obligations, visual clutter, and things taking up space in our head.

THE INTERNAL CHAOS: SHIFT

Shift is the intentional focus on what's going on between your two ears: your thoughts. This can look different depending on how deep in the trenches you are, or how much background knowledge and experience you have with mindfulness practices. The good news is you can be a total newbie and still start to shift as soon as today.

While this can be done any time of day, the earlier in the day you can focus on your mental game, the better your day will go. It allows you to be open and receptive to using other tools you've picked up along the way, instead of forgetting to use them when you need them most.

Simple Shifts You Can Try Today

Grounding Exercises

Grounding exercises are some of my favorite shifts, and what I used when I first started out. Simply getting quiet and allowing myself to hear my own voice, the wind outside, or the birds chirping almost always calms my soul and helps me shift for the day. Here are some of my favorite ways to begin to ground your body and mind that don't take much skill or practice:

- Belly breathing (in through your nose, out through your mouth)
- Hand-to-heart breathing (from page 55)
- Standing barefoot on the ground
- Stretching to the sky and down to the ground
- Prayer or guided meditation (apps such as Calm, Headspace)
- Lying down on your back and focusing on your breath

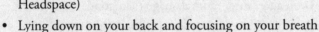

Affirmations

When you're first starting to shift, be sure to choose an affirmation that you actually believe, otherwise your brain will fight you on it and try to pull you back into your automatic stress response.

You might remember in Stage One you created an anchor to help you calm your nervous system in the heat of the moment and were introduced to an affirmation anchor. While these can be the same as what you use for your daily shift, most parents find that more of a mantra or guiding overall principle works better here. Different from an anchor, affirmations can change each day depending on the mood you're in. I love to keep a deck of cards with my favorite mantras and affirmations at my desk so I can pull one that feels relevant to the message I need most that day. Here are a few affirmations or mantras that Calm the Chaos parents have used to shift their internal chaos:

- Today is just one day.
- One bad day doesn't make me a bad parent, it makes me human.
- I am enough.
- I'm not a perfect parent, but I'm exactly the one my child needs.

Journaling

If you have a little more time to give to your shift, or writing is therapeutic for you, get a journal or a planner that you can write in each morning as you begin your shift. Here are a few simple prompts that don't take much time or effort to answer:

- Today I feel . . .
- I am grateful for . . .
- My intention today is . . .
- One new thing to try today is . . .
- One thing I can control . . .

Thought Swaps

In Stage Three, I will introduce you to the thought monsters and super swaps that you can use during your shift each day. Until then, here are a few of the most common swaps our students use when they're just starting out:

- My child *always* yells → my child *sometimes* yells
- Our children hate us → we are rebuilding our family
- I've got so far to go → look how much I've done already
- I can't do this → I just haven't done it yet

Visualizations

Your mind is a powerful tool. Closing your eyes and visualizing a result or overcoming an obstacle can be a simple way to start your day off strong.

Did you know your brain can't tell the difference between something you visualize and something that has already happened? That's why this tool is used by top athletes around the world before big games or events. They close their eyes, visualize the goal, the obstacles in the way, overcoming those challenges, and reaching their goal. The good news is you don't need to be an Olympic athlete to use this strategy. When my son was having multiple daily lengthy meltdowns, I would begin each day visualizing how I was going to respond the next time it happened. This allowed me to instinctually follow the plan I practiced in my head instead of reverting to old-way parenting in the moment. Here are a few scenarios you can visualize during your shift:

- Responding to an argument calmly
- Getting out the door without a fight
- Turning in a project you've been working on
- Opening your fridge to see the meals prepped for the week
- Ending the day with cuddles and good night kisses
- Picking up your child from school and they're happy

⚠ CAUTION

As you read this list, you might have nodded along and thought, *Seems easy enough. I can do this.* If so, yay! However, if you were immediately filled with dread because it seems near impossible to start your day on a positive note, there might be more going on under your "iceberg." It's easy for me to write this list and make it seem like these will whisk all your concerns and fears away. But that is not what I'm trying to say at all. I am simply sharing a tiny next step that can help you get started on your journey to remaining calm and helping your child do the same. It will be important to choose only one thing from this list to begin; otherwise, when the time comes to use or build this habit, you will find yourself feeling more overwhelmed than when you started.

NOT JUST FLOOFY NONSENSE

There's a known connection between your thoughts, feelings, actions, and results; in fact, they're interrelated. According to cognitive behavior theory, if you change one, you can change the others, which makes sense given the connection.

I guess you could say that *shifting* is the same as mindfulness. However, I'm hesitant to use that word. Often when parents hear the word "mindfulness" they associate it with being a calm Zen parent who can do yoga poses in the living room while their kids run circles around them. It can be easy for parents in the trenches to dismiss any mindfulness practices as out of reach, floofy nonsense, or just a buzzword.

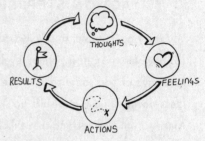

The problem isn't with mindfulness itself. Instead, it's the ideas and beliefs we've been fed about what makes "good" parents versus "bad" parents. This idea that you must always remain calm, never lose your temper, and be present for your children 100 percent of the time is simply unattainable.

Ripple Effects of Mindfulness

Mindfulness doesn't have to be all or nothing. In fact, it can be small moments throughout your day, such as a few quiet minutes before you wake the kids, a brief meditation, or a simple affirmation you speak to yourself in the mirror as you brush your teeth. The truth is mindfulness is a key ingredient to the "you" piece of the Calm the Chaos framework. I've already introduced you to several mindfulness tools (shifts) you can use to help you, even if you're in survival mode: freak-out timer; Stop, Breathe, Anchor; stay curious.

"I can't do this." "It won't help." "What's the point?" are common objections. And yet, every single time a parent hits rock bottom and they start the practice of shifting their thoughts at the start of their day, they always come back to tell me this was a lifesaver for them and their family. Not only are they able to slow their reactions but they're also able to connect with their kids (because they don't have the resentment or anger anymore), and they're able to problem solve and create plans because their head is clear of the trash that's been holding them back for so long.

ACTION STEP: SHIFT YOUR MINDSET

Your tiny next step is to simply brainstorm some shifts that feel accessible to you given the current chaos levels in your home. You can borrow from the list above or add some that you've tried in the past. Once you have a few ideas down, choose one shift you're willing to try for the next few weeks. Make sure it's something that takes only a minute or two a day, so it's easy enough to do it no matter what the day throws at you.

THE EXTERNAL CHAOS: PRIORITIZE

Now that you've begun your practice of shifting out of internal chaos, it's time to take a very honest look at your to-do list so you can tackle some of the external chaos. Here's the point: you can do anything you want in life, but you can't do it all at once.

By focusing on your own stress levels and prioritizing tasks, instead of treating them all the same, you will increase your ability to remain calm, make decisions in the heat of the moment, and remember your tools when you need them most (including your Five-Minute Energy plan).

I want to introduce you to the most powerful tools that will allow you to prioritize when everything seems like one big mess:

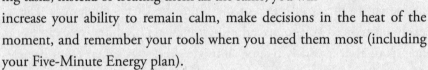

Brain Dump

When my brain feels like a bowl of tangled spaghetti, my very first action is to grab a piece of paper and my favorite pens and get everything down  onto the page. Think of this as dumping your purse onto the counter to see what you have and what you're missing. In the end, the gum wrappers and expired coupons will end up in the trash, the change will end up in the jar by the back door, and maybe only two pens will get to stay. That's exactly the purpose of the brain dump: it's about getting all the items crumpled together in your brain on paper, so you can see what needs doing now, what can wait, and what can get thrown away because, honestly, it's just not that important.

When you're ready to do a brain dump, simply grab a piece of paper, a journal, or the back of napkin (whatever you can find). Then set a timer for a short amount of time. Our students like to do one, three, or ten minutes depending on how much time they have. Setting a timer helps keep your catastrophizing thoughts at bay, so you don't spiral into feeling more overwhelmed. Remember, you're not making a to-do list yet. This is simply about creating an inventory of things that are on your mind so you can see them all in one place.

Organize the Mess

Now that you've dumped everything out in front of you, you might feel like there are so many things on the list that you simply don't know where to even begin. That's because our brains are designed a lot like filing cabinets. It likes to make connections and group items together to understand all the information it's taking in. To satisfy that urge, we're going to organize the items on your page.

There are several ways you can do this:

1. **By category:** home, work, school, kids, appointments
2. **By urgency:** urgent, important, no deadline
3. **By goals:** family, self, dreams, work

My favorite way to categorize is based on urgency and goals. Because I'm a visual learner, I use colored markers to highlight items that I want to group together. I start with items that are incredibly urgent (meaning they have a deadline of today or tomorrow). Then I find the items that align with my number one goal at this stage of my life (creating a family that works together, implementing a new energy plan, writing this book, etc.). Finally, I find the items that help me feel less stress (like taking a walk around the block).

Rocks, Pebbles, Sand

Perhaps you've heard the story of the professor who stood in front of his class with some rocks, pebbles, sand, and a jar. He proceeded to place the materials into the jar in different orders to demonstrate that more could fit if the rocks were added first. "If I'd started with the sand," he said, "there wouldn't have been room for everything else."

While there are different variations of this story, they all have the same message:

- The rocks represent our biggest priorities (what matters above all else)
- The pebbles represent other important things (deadlines and non-negotiables)
- The sand represents our daily tasks and to-dos (laundry and housework)

When picking our priorities, we must choose the "rocks" first; they won't fit later if we start with the less important tasks such as housework and appointments. This will make all the difference in the world for your stress levels and ability to get more done in less time. That's why the final step of prioritizing is to choose your top three priorities.

The Big Three

By choosing your top three priorities, you aren't saying the other things on your list aren't important; you're simply choosing the three that are most important for today. The rest can wait until tomorrow (or the next day). The tiny progress you make each day will compound. You'll get more done with less stress. Try to get everything done on your list and you end up getting zero done and feeling like a failure.

In order to choose your big three, look at your categorized list and ask yourself: What are three things that if you did today would help you feel like you made progress?

Note: There are many days where I simply don't have the energy or capacity to accomplish more than one priority in the day. On these days I love to ask myself, "If I do nothing else today, what can I do?" Can I let you in on a secret? Sometimes that one thing is rest.

Not-to-Do List

The sand in your daily jar represents the items that you can delegate to other members of your family, delete completely (go to paper plates to reduce dishes), or batch for certain days of the week. But one of the most effective lists you can make is a not-to-do list.

This is a list where you put things you vow to *not* do. This can be things like:

🧠 LET'S TALK ABOUT STRESS

This pervasive belief that parents *should* be able to run the house, handle the meltdowns and tantrums, fix dinner, cart kids to activities, pursue their own career, and still have energy to stay calm and pleasant is wearing all of us down. I truly believe that parents are phenomenal creatures capable of moving mountains. However, I also know that it's impossible to take on the never-ending to-do lists all at once without repercussions.

As a neurodivergent adult with ADHD, I spent my life struggling to take on the regular tasks of everyday living. I could barely keep up with the dishes or manage decisions. I could give you a mile-long list of challenges.

Once I became a parent deep in survival mode, my ability to do anything other than play defense against meltdowns was nonexistent. I thought something must be wrong with me, because I was led to believe that good parents are organized, clean, and keep the house running no matter what.

There are a lot of reasons why a person might struggle with organization or prioritization, such as being neurodivergent or having trauma in their past. However, the most pervasive reason so many parents struggle with these day-to-day functions, even if they aren't diagnosed with any difference, is *stress*.

The front of your brain (the prefrontal cortex) is the part that is responsible for your executive functions to operate properly. And when we are stressed, it disrupts the connections, making it near impossible to be organized, remember information, and work productively. If you're raising a challenging child, you are by definition stressed. Ever wonder why so many mamas leave their coffee in the microwave and then forget it? Yep: executive functions.

Executive functioning affects things like:

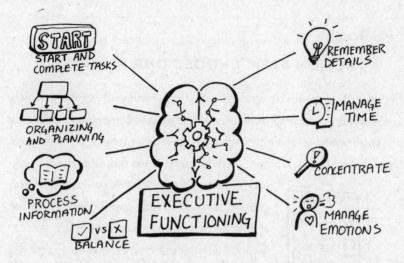

The good news is this means that you aren't broken because you can't get everything done. But you do need to reduce your stress to function better.

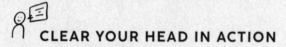

CLEAR YOUR HEAD IN ACTION

Giselle: Neurodivergent Mom of Autistic Teen

As a parent with ADHD and executive function challenges herself, Giselle was constantly overwhelmed. It didn't matter what she tried in the past, she couldn't follow through with plans she'd make and would have downward spirals where she couldn't get anything done for weeks at a time. However, when she started to clear her head of both the internal chaotic thoughts and external to-dos, life became easier. She began to start each day with a simple shift by looking at a note card on the cupboard that reminded her to breathe and use her favorite thought swap: "I get to, and that means . . ." By shifting from "I have to" as she looked at the day ahead, she was able to give herself the power of choice and control in her own life. Next, she would choose her big three priorities for the day, always including just one thing for her, one thing for her son, and one thing for the home. With these strategies, routines, and systems in place, she focused on doing what she wanted to do and regained a sense of control.

ACTION STEP: CHOOSE ONE PRIORITY

For your simple next step, grab a piece of paper and your favorite pen. Take two minutes to do a brain dump. You will be amazed by how much floods out of your brain when given the opportunity. Take a moment to notice what kinds of things make it onto the list. Is it to-dos, worries, stressors, big projects, or something else? Ask yourself, "If I only get one thing done today, what will it be?" Look at your list and choose the one item that you believe will help reduce stress and keep you moving forward. What is one priority you can choose for today?

CONNECT: OPERATION WARM HUG

"Help! I just feel so lonely and left out. No one gets me or my kid. And taking my kid anywhere is just too much work and management."

If I had a dollar for every time this sentiment was posted in one of my online communities, I would be a very rich woman.

Even before the pandemic and two years of lockdowns around the world, three out of five Americans reported feeling lonely and isolated, lacking in friendship. In fact, out of three hundred thousand parents I surveyed, 80 percent said isolation was one of their top parenting struggles (above meltdowns, aggression, defiance, and whining).

Why does this matter so much?

When connection is missing in your life, it can be hard for you to remain calm and think creatively to solve problems (both of which are vital if you wish to get ahead of the chaos caused by tantrums, meltdowns, and outbursts). That's why the next part of your Five-Minute Energy plan involves daily connection. It's the warm hug you need but don't know how to get.

So how do you go about grabbing those hugs?

NOT JUST PLAY DATES AND NIGHTS OUT

A quick Google search on how parents can get more connected yields several ideas, most of which feel out of reach when your kid is not like the rest of the pack. They can include such things as mommy and me classes, volunteering, play dates, and my favorite one of all: just put yourself out there. If, like me, this list leaves you thinking, *I don't ever leave my house, so I'm fresh out of luck*, I've got some great news for you.

Connection Can Be Simple

Connection and belonging can be small and simple. In fact, Dr. Edward M. Hallowell, psychiatrist and bestselling author of *Connect*, defines connection as "feeling a part of something larger than yourself, feeling close to another person or group, feeling welcomed, and understood." He goes on to state that a five-minute conversation has the power to make all the difference in the world. And I couldn't agree more. Those students who added daily connection to their lives (no matter how small or big) have seen an increase in their ability to remain calm, find creative solutions to problems, and feel energized when their days would be otherwise overwhelming.

Connection can be as simple as a:

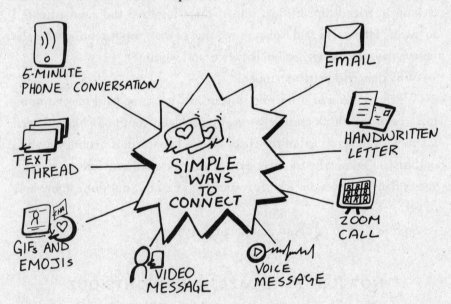

MASLOW HAD IT RIGHT

We don't simply prefer human relationships; we need them to survive. We humans are social creatures. This is a fact. Psychologist Abraham Maslow, who created Maslow's hierarchy of needs, and any number of psychological resources agree that belonging is a basic human need. Some would argue connection is as needed as food, water, and air.

As much as we might not like to admit it, we are hardwired for connection. We are shaped by our social interactions, and when our social bonds are threatened or severed, we suffer greatly. Unfortunately, our need for connection doesn't just affect us; our sense of isolation and the associated effects can affect our children and their long-term health and educational success.

By building moments of connection with your child, your spouse, a coworker, you also build trust, empathy, and emotional safety, which makes it easier for the other person to accept help, calm down, and problem solve. In later chapters, I will be sharing more ways to build connection both in the moment and out of the moment with your child and family. After you read these chapters, you will have far more ideas you can add to your daily connection so you can build trust little by little each day. But for now, I really want you to focus on small ways you can increase your feelings of belonging and connectedness in daily life, even if it's not with your children or partner.

Even Lone Wolves Can Connect with Others

If the idea of connecting with humans daily gives you hives, you might be an introvert. And that is totally okay. I get it; there are days where the energy of others feels too big to take on. But I want to reassure you, there are lots of ways to add your daily dose of connection, even if the energy of others makes you want to bury your head in the sand like an ostrich.

OPERATION WARM HUG IN ACTION

Alice: Reconnecting with a Spouse

After her twins were born, Alice felt like she'd become roommates (and not even good ones) with her spouse. When she tried to talk to her spouse about anything involving parenting, it almost always ended in a fight. This went on for years. To add to her stress, she wound up tiptoeing around her spouse. She knew her daily connection plan needed to include her partner if she was going to get any time and energy back into her life. Instead of looking for big date nights or large connection, she focused on tiny connections that could happen on a daily basis. She intentionally created little moments of safety and connection by thanking him for taking the dog for a walk, doing the dishes, or taking out the trash. She'd touch his shoulder when she passed him, she'd stop and give him her full attention when he talked, even when she was busy. She made him breakfast without being asked. Despite beginning with resentment, hurt feelings, and anger toward her husband, she started to rebuild their relationship one small connection at a time. Seeing the positives helped her to swap her thoughts, see he was on his own journey and doing the best he could with what he knew. This connection gave her something to draw on, changed how she responded to him, and enabled her to create a better partnership again.

ACTION STEP: CHOOSE TO CONNECT

Your simple next step is to find three ways that you can connect in under a minute. Start by brainstorming ways you can connect with others and feel a sense of belonging without leaving your house or joining every school committee.

- Who are some people you miss talking to (old friends, extended family, siblings, etc.)?
- Is there at least one person you can start your daily connection habit with (possibly a spouse or neighbor)?
- What are some ways you like to feel connected? Are you more of an extrovert that needs in-person connection, or are you more introverted and a text feels more your style?
- What have you done in the past that helped you feel connected? Was it a text chain? Sitting with your partner while you both read quietly? Or something else?

   Now that you've made your list, it's time to take action. I invite you to make three connections today—your style, your choice.

UNDERSTAND: ENERGY BOOSTS AND DRAINS

Look, I get it: when your kids finally shut their eyes and go the eff to sleep after a stressful day of work, getting meals on the table, arguing over homework, dealing with emails from the school, and battles over teeth brushing, all you want to do is plop onto the couch and numb with a binge-worthy series. This is your brain doing what it does best, trying to protect you (darn brain, keeps falling back to survival tactics).

Unfortunately, TikTok videos, social media scrolling, and Netflix bingeing are only a short-lived solution. Sure, at first we feel calmer and more relaxed, but really all we are doing is ignoring the real problem or numbing ourselves to pain. This is called a maladaptive coping strategy. You don't need another episode of *Stranger Things*; you need an activity that will help relieve your stress long term (adaptive coping strategy).

That's why the next step in your daily Five-Minute Energy plan is to *recharge* using small tasks that boost your energy reserves while removing draining activities that are sucking your time and energy dry.

YOUR ENERGY SOURCE

Much like solar panels and windmills build energy over time (so if the sun goes down or the wind stops blowing, you still get power), your energy is built with a consistent habit, which compounds each day. Sustainable energy—the kind that you can rely on the next time your child gets in trouble at school, hits their cousin at a birthday party, or you get in a fight with your partner over parenting styles—is born of small, energy-boosting activities and the removal of habits that drain your time and energy.

Boosts and Drains

Building up our energy reserves involves two important elements:

1. **Boosts:** small activities that make you feel good about yourself and energize you
2. **Drains:** activities or behaviors that suck your energy or make you feel worse than when you started

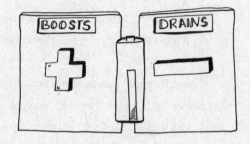

The key to making this strategy work isn't to copy all the ideas from this section of the book and act on them. Instead, I encourage you to truly understand your unique boosts and drains, so you can personalize your plan to rebuild your energy reserves.

Boosts

We often think of boosts and refilling our cup as spa days and weekends away. However, we need to find sustainable energy-renewing activities we can do, even if we are sitting in the same room as our children, that don't require us to remove ourselves from our everyday lives.

Psychologists have found five types of coping strategies that reduce stress and increase energy:

1. **Support:** getting help or advice, talking with someone who understands
2. **Relaxation:** resting and restoring your nervous system
3. **Problem-solving:** taking action toward a resolution of the problem
4. **Humor:** lightheartedness that brings joy and laughter
5. **Physical activity:** moving your body

Consider these categories when choosing your energy boosters from the list below. What you like will vary greatly from the next person based on your personality, biology, history, and preferences. I've included some of our students' favorite boosts. The goal is to find something that gets your body going, energizes you, or motivates you to tackle the day.

Simple Boosts to Add Energy to Your Day

Listen to music	Take a bath or shower	Cry it out
Talk to a friend	Play an instrument	Smile and laugh
Pet the dog	Play a game	Stretch your body
Get outside	Garden	Get a hug
Color, draw, or paint	Drink water	Clean or declutter
Cook a meal	Enjoy a hobby	Play with your kids

The key to finding a boost that works for you is to find something that can be done on a regular basis (which rules out hour-long bubble baths) and supports your well-being physically, mentally, and emotionally. Some of you will surely disagree with this next statement, but boosts aren't your cup of coffee in the morning or your wine after the kids go to bed. It's also not your excuse to eat your kids' Halloween candy or down a pint of ice cream. While you can find me enjoying any of those things, I have learned that they can't be things I rely on to bring me joy or energy. It doesn't mean you never get to enjoy these wonderful things. Instead, I want you to find something that truly restores your energy.

Drains

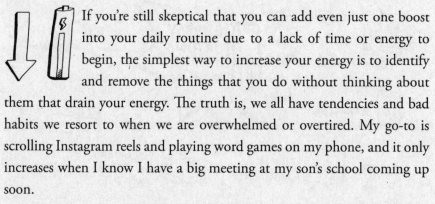 If you're still skeptical that you can add even just one boost into your daily routine due to a lack of time or energy to begin, the simplest way to increase your energy is to identify and remove the things that you do without thinking about them that drain your energy. The truth is, we all have tendencies and bad habits we resort to when we are overwhelmed or overtired. My go-to is scrolling Instagram reels and playing word games on my phone, and it only increases when I know I have a big meeting at my son's school coming up soon.

A drain can be anything from things you dread doing to things you do to avoid the real task in front of you. I've compiled a list from real parents of drains they've removed from their schedule. Many of these items were things they didn't even realize were draining them dry until they tried removing them for a week. The difference in their energy (and therefore ability to show up calmly for their kids) was astounding.

Small Energy Drains to Remove from Your Day

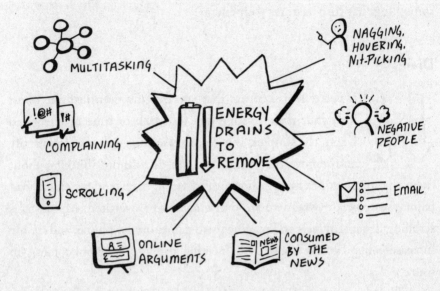

⚠ CAUTION: AVOID THE TEMPTATION TO ADD MORE

As you begin to find things that boost your energy, it can be tempting to add a ton of energy-boosting items to your daily schedule. However, I want to warn you against falling into this more, more, more mentality. This will only add to your guilt and shame of not doing enough, and that is the opposite of what we want at this stage of your parenting journey (heck, we never want to add more shame and guilt).

Your time and energy reserves are finite.

Every time you say yes to one thing, you're saying no to something else.

On the flip side, every time you say no, it gives you room for things that are a "hell yes" in your life.

You get to choose to focus on something that helps you create the family you've always dreamed of, such as connection time with your children, energy working through your next struggle, or helping your child build skills for their future. So, let's make it worth it.

BOOSTS AND DRAINS IN ACTION

Uma: Single Parent with Zero Support

Raising four young children on her own left Uma feeling spent. Any extra time she had (which was zero) was allotted to holding her breath for the next outburst. When she wasn't fighting over homework with her oldest daughter with ADHD, she was chasing her four-year-old with developmental delays that affected her speech and ability to toilet or dress herself. In between the chaos of the two older children, she was carrying or nursing her one-year-old. But then she began to add small boosts of outside time and checking in with her own body daily. This included trips to the playground where every child could find something to do, and she could check her own physical needs. She also realized there were small things that were causing more damage to her energy than helping. Surprisingly, the little help that she did get was more draining on her emotions. She found that she had to defend her parenting, explain her daughter's needs, and prep for hours for the help. Inevitably, her children would struggle even more. Once she realized this, she removed these "helpers" from her life, and the days started to feel lighter and easier to manage. This small boost of energy was just what she needed to start a small fairy garden with her kids, which rippled into more energy for connection time and gave her more anchor moments for chaotic eruptions with her kids.

ACTION STEP: CHOOSE YOUR BOOSTS AND DRAINS

Your simple next step is to choose some boosts and drains from the lists on pages 114 and 116 or brainstorm some new ideas for yourself. It might even be helpful to think about what you've done over the last few days.

- What tasks or items boosted your energy?
- What did you do that wasted or took away time?

Choose today to intentionally eliminate one habit that is draining your energy. Pay attention to how much time you save by removing this from your day. Next, make a point to add one activity that can be done in a minute or less that boosts your energy. This could be dancing, stepping outside, or drinking water. Whatever it is, try this new habit for the next week and see how it helps your energy reserves.

EMPOWER: AN ACTIVITY A DAY KEEPS THE MELTDOWNS AT BAY

Now, I realize you didn't pick up this book for health tips. But one thing I know now that I wish I did years ago is just how simple it can be for even the most burned-out parents to start a healthy habit. I know that when I started getting healthier, I had more energy, got better sleep, and was in a much better mood, meaning I could weather any tantrum, meltdown, or outburst that came our way.

By moving just a little each day or adding in small healthy habits, you can reduce anxiety, negativity, and fatigue, while increasing energy, memory, and your ability to remain calm and confident.

When you activate your body through movement or healthy habits, your body temperature rises and feel-good hormones (such as dopamine, serotonin, and endorphins) are released, which ultimately help you stay calm. In addition, the energy you gain from new healthy habits (even small ones) helps you keep up with the ever-changing challenges you face in parenting.

This means even when you feel completely depleted and are tempted to get sucked into an energy drain, you can move your body to give it the jolt it needs. Instead of hunkering down in bed, your head under the covers doom scrolling through your phone, you can jump-start your energy with any of the following, giving you far more benefit long term.

Simple Ways to Activate Your Body

Movement:	Non-Movement:
• Jog	• Drink more water
• Swim	• Take vitamins, supplements
• Garden	• Increase fruits and vegetables
• Dance	• Wind down with a book in bed
• Physical therapy	• Dedicated breathing exercises
• Increase daily step count	• Reduce screen time
• Stretch	• Reduce smoking or alcohol

BUT WHAT ABOUT THE KIDS?

If all this talk of movement sounds great in theory but you're still skeptical because your kids are bound to tackle you anytime you pull out a yoga mat, you aren't alone. I've compiled a list from parents around the world of ways they include movement in their day while involving their kids.

- Build and run an obstacle course with your children
- Have a dance party
- Race your kids to the end of the block and back
- Go for a family bike ride
- Walk the dog together

- Do jumping jacks, sit-ups, etc., as a challenge with your kids
- Play pretend animal games
- Have a family parade with costumes and music around the house

The goal is to move more today than you moved yesterday. That's it, plain and simple.

No need to set grand marathon goals, just add a minute of dancing, an extra push-up or jumping jack. At first, your progress is going to feel nonexistent, until one day you realize that you have more energy, are in a better mood, and can remain calm more often, all because you chose one tiny movement or healthy habit to activate your body.

ONE PERCENT A DAY KEEPS THE MELTDOWNS AT BAY

All this talk of building healthy habits can be overwhelming, as though I'm suggesting that in order to calm the chaos in your family, you've got to go all out. The goal, however, is to build a sustainable energy source that you can rely on time and again, no matter how busy you get. I don't want you to uproot everything; instead, I want you to do what I and so many of our Calm the Chaos students have done: change 1 percent each day.

That's it: 1 percent.

Sounds ludicrous, right?

A Little Goes a Long Way

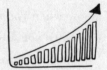

James Clear, psychologist and bestselling author of *Atomic Habits* (which has sold more than ten million copies), found that "if you get 1 percent better each day for one year, you'll end up thirty-seven times better by the time you're done."

In fact, Clear studied the difference between those who attempted to make one tiny change each day over time and those who made no change at all. The group that made no changes got further away from their goal, while the group that continued to make small shifts each day improved exponentially, even though at first the improvement was hardly noticeable. Clear also found that people who set a simple intention for their habit, like "when I [insert first activity], I will [insert habit]," were far more likely to see growth and create a long-lasting habit than those who attempted to create a new habit without a set intention.

This is important for two reasons:

1. You can make tiny changes each day and change your life.
2. You can create a sustainable habit by setting a clear intention.

We've had thousands of parents take on the challenge of activating their body one day at a time. Each day they add a little more time, one more rep, another lap, or an extra bottle of water, and wind up feeling so much more successful.

CREATING A DAILY ACTIVATION HABIT

Step One: Choose One Activation

Start by picking one small activity from the list on page 120 that you feel comfortable doing for one minute today.

Step Two: Set an Intention

Choose when you will do this new habit. Will it be:
- when you walk in from dropping off the kids at school?
- while you make dinner?
- right before you hop into bed?

Once you know when you will do your one activation habit, write out an intention that looks like this: When I . . . , I will . . .

Examples:
When I *get home from drop-off*, I will *do one minute of dancing.*
When I *am ready to get into bed*, I will *stretch for one minute.*
When I *take my kids to the park*, I will *do one pull-up on the monkey bars.*

Step Three: Do More Tomorrow Than You Did Today

Now that you have your activation and you know when and where you will do it, it's time to start the incremental changes. This means adding a minute, a lap, or a rep. Go ahead now and decide what you will add each day. This is about building momentum and solidifying the habit in your brain. While it feels like almost nothing at all, this is the step  that will have the biggest impact on your energy levels over time. One student recently told me that when she started doing this, she added one minute of playtime with her kids outdoors; now she has room and time to add full workouts with her kids or beside her kids.

The growth is exponential. I encourage you to trust the process.

Here's the cool part: science backs this up. In fact, several studies have been done tracking the effect of exercise, physical well-being, and small amounts of movement have on parenting and mental health. The overwhelming consensus was that while thirty minutes of light movement a day was ideal, any increase in movement and decrease in sedentary behavior had huge effects on the overall well-being of parents.

ACTIVATE IN ACTION

Louie Lynn: When You Despise Exercise

After having her fourth child, Louie Lynn was completely depleted. She felt unhealthy and moving her body hurt. Her doctors ordered her to exercise, but despite knowing movement was important, Louie Lynn refused because she believed that meant picking a sport, pounding the pavement for hours at a time, or joining a gym. None of these sounded appealing or easy to do with four kids under four. However, shifting her focus from long, drawn-out exercise to short bursts of movement one minute a day allowed her to think creatively about what movement could look like for her. She started small with one minute of yoga stretches a day, adding a minute as she got comfortable, one week at a time. Now she and a friend keep each other accountable and meet online for daily thirty-minute yoga sessions that she can do with her kids in the same room. This small, daily movement has boosted Louie Lynn's energy in a way no other exercise had in the past. She now has enough energy and ability to focus on showing up for her kids as the mom she wants to be.

ACTION STEP: CHOOSE ONE ACTIVATION

Your simple next step is to take a look at the lists on page 120 or brainstorm your own lists of possible activations.

1. Think about your body and what has felt empowering to you in the past.

    Do you need to start with movement or no movement?
    Do you need an activity you can do with your kids around?
    What is speaking to you most right now?

2. Next, choose one activity and commit with an intention.

    When and where will you do this activity?
    How much will you add each day?

3. Finally, I encourage you to find a way to keep track of your progress. I track my activations in my planner, but if that's not available, I use a simple Post-it note.

    If you want a fun way to track your one-a-day habit, I've included the same tracker that our students use in the bonus pack that you can download at www.calmthechaosbook.com/activate. Once you fill it out, post on social media or email it to me. I want to celebrate your tiny changes and your commitment to your own health.

📑 PUTTING IT ALL TOGETHER: YOUR FIVE-MINUTE ENERGY PLAN

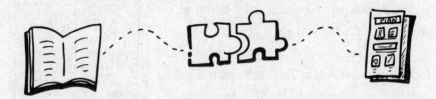

Woot woot! Way to stick to it.

You just completed your second stage in your journey of parenting a challenging child (even if you were tempted to skip this stage completely). You learned how you can:

- finally put yourself first for maybe the first time in years.
- stop trying to balance all the spinning plates without everything crashing down.
- add small habits (and remove harmful ones) to your daily routine to boost your energy.

But as you already know from the last stage, knowing and doing are two different things. So before you can officially move on to stage three, there is something you must do: create your written action plan. Your personal Five-Minute Energy plan, to be precise.

📑 THE PLAN

Let's face it, no matter what parenting stage you're in, there will always be something that requires your attention. Building your energy reserves now with these small daily habits ensures that when the next big fight or unexpected crisis arises, you have everything you need to make it through without completely burning out or losing your cool.

Don't worry so much about getting a perfect plan or even doing all four of the steps in your Five-Minute Energy plan just yet. The most important thing is that you carry this intentional self-care forward, tweaking and building on your action plan as you go.

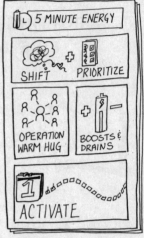

The unique aspect of this plan is that you're focusing solely on *you*. This entire plan is a deep dive into applying the Calm the Chaos elements to connecting, understanding, and empowering yourself daily.

You might have noticed that the plan included two parts for the *you* piece (internal and external head clearing), and that's for good reason. If you're overwhelmed, both parts will help you stay grounded and find clarity. As a reminder, here are the four steps we've covered so far in the Five-Minute Energy plan, organized using the You-CUE framework to make it easier for your brain to remember.

1. **You: Get Your Head Clear**

    Shift (internal): If all else fails, and you struggle to implement anything from this stage, this one habit can radically change your life. It's a great way to begin your day, but it can be used anytime you start to notice your thoughts racing or your mind feeling like jumbled gobbledygook. We discussed several ways to *shift* your mindset that you can use by simply pausing and taking a minute to say your affirmation, or whatever mindset shift feels best to you.

    Prioritize (external): When our to-do list sits in our head, it can feel overwhelming and overpowering. The weight of the list alone can make us want to crawl under the covers and binge the latest series everyone's been talking about. However, doing a brain dump, sorting our tasks, and choosing just the most important things for each day can help keep us on our feet and away from Netflix. *Prioritize* with one big brain dump at the beginning of the week and then simply choose your big three (or big one) each morning. This reduces feeling overwhelmed and helps you move forward even when it feels like the list is just too much.

2. **Connect: Operation Warm Hug**

   Connection is a basic human need just like water and food, and yet so many parents feel isolated and disconnected from those who are supposed to be helping them. We discussed several small ways to connect daily with family, neighbors, and even your own partner that don't include leaving the house or any prep work ahead of time. By sending a quick text, leaving a voice message, or sitting beside someone while they do their thing, you reduce your own stress and increase the likelihood that you will be able to remain calm during the next squabble with your kiddo.

3. **Understand: Energy Boosts and Drains**

   We spend so much time trying to understand what our children need that we ignore what drains or boosts our own energy. However, when we take time to explore and experiment with small habits that build our energy reserve, we don't feel the need to escape from our family to take care of ourselves. The task of self-care becomes much more doable and accessible. Finding small ways to eliminate energy drains throughout the day also allows you to give your children more patience and understanding in the middle of the storm.

4. **Empower: An Activity a Day Keeps the Meltdowns at Bay**

   If you want to have enough energy to take on the next tantrum, meltdown, or outburst, finding small ways to activate your body each day is key. An activation can be anything that helps you feel energized, builds momentum, or increases your physical health. It's a small focus on your own physical well-being that can be built using tiny 1 percent changes each day. At first, this movement feels small and inconsequential, but as you continue with the habit it becomes your driving energy source. Soon you will have enough energy to do things with your family you never thought possible.

PUTTING THE PIECES TOGETHER

1. Before: Choose Your Plan

The good news is you've already done the heavy lifting for the prep work if you did the action steps in this stage. If you haven't done them yet, no worries; I've got you. In order to make your plan, choose one tiny habit for each of the steps in the plan.

 Shift: What will you do each day to shift your mindset? Choose a category and then get specific with what you will do or what phrase you will use.

 Prioritize: Which task management tool will you use to prioritize your day?

 Connect: Who can you connect with each day? Choose one person to start. What can you do to connect with them, even if you can't leave the house?

 Recharge: What is one small habit you can add to your day that will give you more energy? What is one thing you can remove from your day?

 Activate: What small movement or physical activity will you do each day to activate your body? How long or how many reps will you begin with? What will you add each day?

2. During: Following Through

If you've ever set a New Year's resolution or tried to deploy a self-care plan based on an infographic on Pinterest only to find yourself completely abandoning ship just a few days in, you aren't alone. In fact, this is just your brain working just like it was designed.

This brain function can be a pain in the rear, but it doesn't mean this plan can't work for you. Give yourself permission for this to be less about doing everything all the time, and more about building a habit, little by little. Here are a few tips for continuing your Five-Minute Energy plan even if you're completely overwhelmed:

1. Celebrate how many days in a row you *do* follow through.
2. Start back where you left off if you miss a few days.
3. Try just doing one part of the plan a day.
4. Spread the plan throughout the day.
5. Create a reminder that works for you.

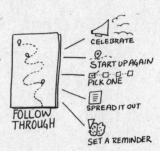

3. After: Tweaking the Plan When You Fall Off

As with every plan along your journey, it's important to remember that nothing is finite or set in stone. There is flexibility in your plan. After you've attempted your Five-Minute Energy plan for a few weeks, it's a great time to check in with yourself and how things went.

Questions to ask:

- Was there anything that felt easy to implement?
- What got in my way of doing it daily?
- Is there a better time of day?
- Can I try a different activity?
- Can I extend the time or add a new step to my plan?

Remember,

STAGE THREE:
THE CALM
AT THE CENTER OF
THE STORM

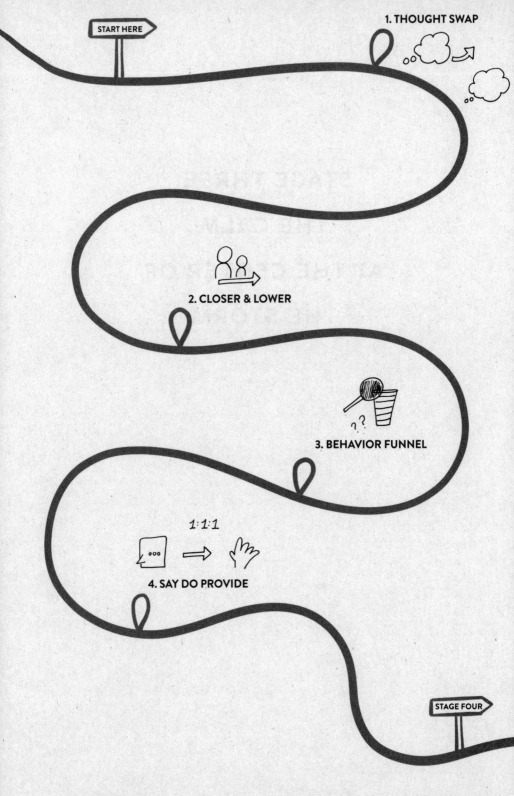

START HERE

1. THOUGHT SWAP

2. CLOSER & LOWER

3. BEHAVIOR FUNNEL

1:1:1

4. SAY DO PROVIDE

STAGE FOUR

YOUR CHALLENGE: DEFUSE THE CHAOS WITHOUT ADDING FUEL TO THE FIRE

"Just shut his door and don't engage. He'll learn to calm down on his own."

This was advice from a therapist on how to handle my son's epic meltdowns in the moment. I was willing to try anything. Despite working with my son and countless professionals for the past five years, I was still struggling when things were at their worst. When his screams subsided, I thought, *It must be safe to enter.* As I slowly peeked in, I found a scene straight out of a horror movie. In desperation, my son did two incredibly extreme and dangerous things. First, he opened the window of his second-story bedroom and attempted to jump out, and then he placed a plastic bag over his head to make the screaming stop. He wanted the screaming to stop as much as I did.

I replay this scene over and over thinking how badly this could have ended. In that moment I knew I needed a *new* plan for "in the moment" that kept not only me and my other kids safe but my son safe as well. The system I created took too many tears, too many holes in the walls, and too many lost years, but this In-the-Moment plan exists. Even better, it works.

WHEN NOTHING WORKS

When your child doesn't calm faster but instead gets worse in the heat of the moment, you're left with trying another ineffective technique or throwing out your plan and starting all over from scratch. You may even resort to the old way of dealing with chaos. I know I once did, particularly after trying everything else.

Traditionally, parents and professionals have leaned heavily on controlling and managing behaviors in the moment to force compliance, teach self-control, and encourage better behavior. Parents have been counseled to punish the child for the unwanted behavior, lecture about what is right or wrong, seclude or isolate to teach a lesson, or reward for compliance. When all else fails, parents like you feel they must resort to yelling, screaming, and being firm to get their child to do anything they ask.

Sure, with these methods, you're going to see behavior changes in the short term, but at what cost?

Unfortunately, using these In-the-Moment strategies doesn't solve the immediate problem and leaves you feeling like you've tried everything but nothing works. It also doesn't help children build the skills they need in life to be resilient, happy, and successful adults. Nor does it serve the relationship between the child and parent, which isn't good for you or your kids long term.

There's one big, vital piece that's missing from these ineffectual old-school or trending approaches: you need to become your child's safe place to have big emotions, tantrums, outbursts, and "unacceptable" behavior (without judgment or fear).

What your child needs most in the heat of the moment isn't more strategies, fixes, or discipline; instead, your child needs to feel seen, heard, and understood.

These old-school attempts to calm the chaos only serve to disconnect the child from the parent. That's why I call these disconnected actions.

🧠 JUST CALM THE EFF DOWN

When your child is screaming at you, not listening to your request to clean up, or fighting with their sister for the tenth time that day, it's not uncommon to want to scream, "Just stop. Calm down already." Unfortunately, if telling someone to calm down worked to calm them down, you and I wouldn't be working through this book together right now, would we?

During any stressful situation, talk, rational or otherwise, can't be accessed by your child's brain. If you remember, we talked a little about your  child's automatic stress response in the first stage, Surviving the Storm. This is important to discuss here, because in the moment, even if you're remaining calm and cool, your child is still in fight or flight, and unable to access any logic or reasoning.

There are any number of strategies and tools designed to teach children about their emotions, how to self-regulate, and mindfulness techniques to use in the moment. And for good reason: when a child can recognize and regulate their own emotions, they're far more equipped to handle challenges in their life than if they don't have this skill.

Unfortunately, in the moment is the worst time to try out these strategies. The truth is all the best strategies and tools in the world are useless if your child is not calm or feeling safe enough to access them.

⚠ NOW IS NOT THE TIME

You can remind yourself that in the heat of the moment is not the time for teaching, solving, or fixing. Save the teaching and skill building for the moments when you and your child are both calm, connected, and safe (physically and emotionally). In this chapter, we will focus on getting the bomb defused before coming up with a preventative action plan for next time.

Remember, this is about taking baby steps forward. You don't have to completely overhaul your parenting overnight to see success. Simply commit to swapping one disconnected strategy for a more connected one. You can do this.

📑 THE PATH FORWARD: YOUR IN-THE-MOMENT PLAN

You have a Ride the Storm plan to find your calm, but let's be honest, that only gets you so far. So, the challenge becomes:

- How do you get your kiddo calm, safe, and deescalated *before* you run out of steam?
- How do you connect when anything you say or do makes your kid throw things at your head?
- What do you say that doesn't get used as ammunition?
- How do you keep yourself and your other kids safe while you wait it out?
- How do you figure out why the heck your kid has turned into a mini version of the Hulk?

One of the biggest difficulties when dealing with challenging behaviors is that even the best laid plans can fall short when shit is hitting the fan. Whether you're dealing with little fires everywhere or dangerous meltdowns, tantrums, or outbursts, you need a solid In-the-Moment plan to defuse the situation without making it worse.

That's where your In-the-Moment plan comes in.

By the end of this stage, you will have a plan that will allow you to help your child calm down faster and easier without adding more chaos to an already stressful situation. Whether you're dealing with a child refusing to put their shoes on or a child screaming in the middle of the Target parking lot, you'll be able to use this plan to remain calm as well as help your child calm down. In the sections ahead, I will break this plan down one piece at a time.

YOU: SLAY THE THOUGHT MONSTERS

Milk, toilet paper, and diapers. That's all you need from the store after you pick up the kids from school. You want to make sure this trip doesn't end like the last one, with one kid being carried out in a football hold, and the others trailing behind wailing as if you'd tortured them, so you attempt to warn them. "Hey, guys, we're stopping at Target. But it's just a quick trip. In and out."

You no sooner move your shopping cart forward than your middle one exclaims, "Mom, can we please look at the toys?"

Shrugging off the request, you grab the milk and then the toilet paper, but now it's time for the real test. The diapers. Right next to the toy aisle.

The pleas persist.

Do you stick to your guns—in and out—or do you give in to avoid the ensuing tantrum?

Fast forward and now the toddler is crying for the baby doll and pulling on your shirt, trying to stand in the cart. The middle kiddo is having a full-on tantrum right in aisle three, kicking and all. The oldest blurts out, "You're the worst mom ever. You *never* let me get any games."

STOP RIGHT HERE

Let's pause this scene right here, before you spiral into an explosion. Even if you keep your cool (or hide your rage), this is no longer a quick trip. Accept that first, then tread lightly so you don't end up derailing your whole day.

I get it. You're trying to keep everything moving in the right direction.

But I assure you, if you don't take the time to defuse the bomb right here, you might never make it out of the store, or if you do, your whole day will be shot because you'll be replaying this cataclysmic event and dealing with the associated fallout.

Before diving into how to defuse your kid's behavior, let's start with the first step in your In-the-Moment plan. As with each of the plans I share with you, we start with *you*, because you are the linchpin that holds it all together. Before you can get anybody else back on track, you have to ground yourself, check in with your own thoughts and feelings, and calm yourself. This will ensure you don't go into battle mode already triggered and about to explode yourself. This way, you can access the helpful tools you've already learned.

You might remember from the Ride the Storm plan that it's imperative to start with the Stop, Breathe, Anchor technique to calm yourself. What I'm about to share is the next iteration of an anchor. Since you've had enough practice with a variety of anchors, you're ready to expand into thought swaps.

CHANGE YOUR THOUGHTS, CHANGE YOUR ACTIONS

In order to change your actions, you have to start with changing your thoughts or feelings in the heat of the moment that derailed everything to begin with. You'll hear me repeat this time and again. This is key because if you're stuck believing that your kid is the reason you can't ever go anywhere, or that your child always has a tantrum, you're far more likely to feel resentful, angry, and fearful, which in turn makes it extremely hard to show up with empathy and compassion.

So how do you change your thoughts when everything is moving so fast?

Thought Monsters and Super Swaps

When your child is melting down and you can feel the piercing glares of onlookers, you first want to clear your head of any thoughts that might make it harder to engage with your children with empathy and compassion. We do this with two important tools.

Thought monsters: Disempowering thoughts that rob parents of empathy, patience, and joy.

Super swaps: One of the best ways to slay the thought monsters is to create a swap. They're the more empowering versions of thoughts that allow you to shift from frustration, resentment, and negative emotions to empathy, compassion, and hope.

How to Swap Your Thoughts

As with many of the tools I'm sharing with you in this book, this is most effective when you practice this exercise while you're calm and quiet. Many of our students use their shift time during their Five-Minute Energy plan to swap their thoughts using thought monsters and super swaps. I'll use the example of the Target meltdown from earlier to show how to do this swap after the fact.

Step One: Identify Your Thoughts

When you think of the latest explosion or storm that you've had to deal with, what thoughts flooded your mind? Go ahead and jot down the first thought that comes to mind.

Example thoughts:

1. *Great. Here we go again. This always happens when we go to the store.*

2. *My kids are so disrespectful.*
3. *Everyone is just glaring at me. I bet they think I'm a terrible parent.*

Step Two: Name a Thought Monster

Look over the list of thought monsters (found in the chart on page 142) and find one that represents the thoughts that you're having most often.

Example thought monsters:

1. Always and Never Beast
2. Negative Nelly
3. Judgy McJudgerson

Step Three: Call on a Super Swap

Now that you have your thought monster, look through the list of super swaps and find one that combats your monster the best.

For example:

1. Fact Finder Freddy
2. Not Yet Yeti
3. Wah-Wah Warrior

Step Four: Swap Your Thought

Finally, with the help of the super swaps by your side, make a slight adjustment to your original disempowering thought for something more empowering and helpful, such as:

1. *After school is not a good time for shopping trips with all three kids.*
2. *My kids still need help making plans for the store.*
3. *My family needs me, and I can ignore the onlookers.*

Common Thought Monsters and Super Swaps

Getting clear now about the common thought monsters that creep in during your family's most challenging moments allows you to be prepared and not caught off guard. In addition, I'd like to introduce you to the most common super swaps parents use to combat the debilitating thoughts that take over, especially when the bomb is about to explode. Finding one super swap to use in your time of need can be like having a sidekick who tags along with all your family struggles.

THOUGHT MONSTERS	SUPER SWAPS
Judgy McJudgerson: Fear of what onlookers might think Thought: "What will they think?" Feelings: Shame, embarrassment, guilt	*Wah-Wah Warrior:* Other people's opinions are not about you Thought: "This isn't about me." Feelings: Empowered, hopeful, proud
Always and Never Beast: Thinking in absolutes Thought: "My child always does this." Feelings: Resentment, anger, despair	*Fact Finder Freddy:* Finding proof of what is working Thoughts: "Sometimes," "When this happens" Feelings: Hope, calm, patience, curiosity
Cyclone: Everything is out of control and spiraling Thought: "I can't take it anymore!" Feelings: Overwhelmed, frantic, anxious	*DJ Break Down:* Breaking ideas into smaller chunks Thought: "I can take it one step at a time." Feelings: Empathy, self-compassion
Shoulda, Woulda, Coulda: Constantly second-guessing your decisions Thought: "I should be able to . . ." Feelings: Regret, self-doubt, shame, jealousy	*Progress Princess:* Focus on what is going well, small progress Thought: "I'm still learning." Feelings: Joy, confidence, hope
Negative Nelly: Looks for the worst-case scenario Thought: "My child can't, won't, doesn't." Feelings: Sadness, resentment, anger, fear	*Not Yet Yeti:* Highlighting how far you've come Thought: "They can't do this . . . yet." Feelings: Empathy, connection, hope

 **NEUROSCIENCE EXPLAINS IT ALL**

There is no denying that your mind is a powerful machine. Thought monsters and super swaps are so effective due to three concepts based in neuroscience.

1. The Lemon Effect

Did you know that simply imagining a scene or something familiar can affect your behavior? Here's what I mean:

Close your eyes and imagine a big, juicy lemon. Now imagine the lemon is peeled and sliced in half. Next, I want you to see yourself taking a gigantic bite out of the lemon. It's sour and juicy. Picture the bite in your mouth. Did your mouth just water?

My guess is yes. That's because just by thinking of the lemon's tartness, your body started to react.

Now here is the part that relates to thought monsters. When you focus on old thought patterns and beliefs such as

- I can't;
- I'm the worst;
- this will never get better;
- everyone will think I'm a terrible parent;
- my child is so disrespectful,

your body will begin to react based on your thoughts. How do you feel when you think, "I can't" or "my child never"? My guess is you feel hopeless and a tad resentful. And when you feel hopeless, your actions will likely be to give up or stop trying new things. When you feel resentful, your actions will most likely be disconnected and you will be less willing to listen to and empathize with your child.

2. Ruts and New Pathways

The good news is that the opposite is true. If you can swap your thoughts, old beliefs, and stuck patterns, you can start to shift your feelings and therefore your actions. Your brain creates these "ruts" or pathways when you think the same thoughts over and over or do the same action on repeat. This is your habit brain taking over when problems arise. This causes you to get stuck and unable to see a way forward.

However, by swapping your thoughts and actively choosing a new thought, you create brand-new pathways in your brain. One of our students realized: "If I can teach my child bad habits, that must also mean I can teach them good habits." Choosing new and empowering thoughts is where resiliency and hope are built.

3. You Aren't the Problem, the Problem Is . . .

Finally, one of the most powerful reasons that super swaps work both in and out of the moment is because of something known as narrative therapy. The idea is that if you can remove yourself from a problem, thought, anxiety, or fear, it suddenly becomes much easier to identify and tackle head-on. By acknowledging the thought or fear, giving it a fictional name such as Always and Never Beast, and then consciously choosing to call on the super swaps to help you create a new thought, you're helping your brain process difficult and deep-rooted beliefs and thoughts. You're separating yourself from the problem, which removes blame, shame, self-doubt, and anxieties and makes it so much easier to play with the concept in a nonthreatening way.

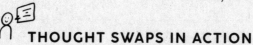

THOUGHT SWAPS IN ACTION

Maya: Morning Hyperactivity Due to ADHD

Maya was struggling with her son's extremely hyperactive behavior in the mornings, pre-ADHD meds. He would touch everything in sight, wouldn't listen, said mean and hurtful things, and caused stress for the whole family. Maya had the Negative Nelly thought monster taking over, which in turn left her seeing her son as mean, disobedient, and out of control. She felt insensitive and unkind and wasn't proud of how she saw her son.

She knew she needed to kick Negative Nelly to the curb if she was going to be able to show up with kindness and patience for her son. She decided to call on Fact Finder Freddy to see what her son needed in the mornings when his meds hadn't kicked in yet. She created a new thought: "Without meds, my son is not regulated, his brain is struggling to process, and he is not able to do this himself . . . yet." This allowed her to remember in the moment that he needed her help and guidance and therefore show up with more support and understanding during these rough mornings.

ACTION STEP:
SWAP ONE THOUGHT MONSTER

Your simple next step is to examine the old thoughts and beliefs that come up in the heat of the moment. I encourage you to choose just one explosion for now; you can always do more examples later.

Once you've looked at the disempowering and negative thoughts that creep in during the worst moments, choose one thought monster that matches this thought so you can externalize the thought and remove it.

Finally, choose one super swap to call on to help you make an empowering switch that you can use in the moment the next time your child refuses to get off their game system, put on shoes, or eat the dinner you made.

If you'd like to print a poster of the thought monsters and super swaps, I've included them in the toolkit that comes with this book. You can download them at www.calmthechaosbook.com/tm.

CONNECT: DEFUSE THE BOMB

In the movies, when the hero is trying to disarm a bomb before it detonates, rarely do you see them talking to the bomb or trying to reason with it. Okay, you never see them do this. Instead, the hero takes small, precise, and quick action; they keep all words and movements to a minimum. The number one goal is to defuse the bomb, or at the very least, minimize the damage it will cause if they can't get to it in time.

You'll want to approach your child's challenging and often explosive behaviors the very same way.

Jumping to strategies and tactics while the kids are still "armed" is the primary trap I see parents (and even professionals) fall into. Again, there's a place for emotion coaching, skill building, and problem-solving, but I can assure you, while your child is whaling on their brother is *not* that time.

The goal in the heat of the moment is to defuse the situation without adding more fuel to an already volatile situation.

DISARM YOUR OWN BODY

I want to remind you of the importance of checking your own body and the signals you might be sending during any challenging moment. In Stage One, we discovered how to create moments of safety in the worst of the storms. During a tantrum, meltdown, or outburst with your child, these still apply. Consider this your way of disarming yourself in the moment before attempting to connect with your child, give them support, or help them through their tough moment.

As a quick recap, this would mean that you are:

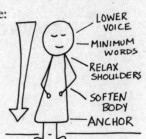

- Softening your body
- Relaxing your jaw or shoulders
- Lowering your voice
- Keeping words to a minimum
- Anchoring yourself with your thought swap

Right now, your child's stress response is heightened, meaning their senses (sight, sound, touch, etc.) are all overstimulated. I'll be sharing more about how senses play a role in challenges in the next chapter, but for now, just know any additional noise, input, or stress coming from you would feel like a scratchy sweater on an already sunburned back. By disarming yourself, you're limiting the chances that you might further trigger your child (and therefore find yourself in a power struggle) beyond the current level.

GET CLOSER AND GET LOWER

We've already covered the importance of connection, even in the middle of conflict. But how do you do that when your child is calling you names, slamming doors in your face, or hurling the TV remote at your head? We'll learn how in the next part of your In-the-Moment plan: **get closer and get lower.**

Get Closer

I'm not proud to admit it, but for a long time I was a yeller. I believed that to get my kids to listen, do anything I asked, or stop fighting, I had to raise my voice. I was raised by a yeller, and my mom was raised by a yeller. It was in our bloodline, or so I was told. For a long time, I believed that there was no other way than to be this way. But boy, did I hate it. One afternoon, my throat throbbing from screaming so loud, I sat on my couch and realized I had to do something different.

That's when I remembered my days in the classroom. If a child struggled to listen to instructions, I never would have thought to yell at them. If a child was touching another child, I would never scream from outside the classroom to get them to stop. No. Instead I would move my own body and get closer to them.

I would quietly walk over to the child struggling, crouch down beside them, and check in to see how I could support them. Why then with my own kids was I turning into the wicked witch?

I decided to give this magic teacher trick a try.

- When my kids started squabbling, instead of yelling from the kitchen to settle down, I got closer.
- When my child refused to get ready for school, instead of screaming from the top of the stairs to hurry up, I got closer.
- When my son refused to get off electronics, instead of yelling from the other room to get off or else, I got closer.

And guess what? It worked. Even without changing what I said or did once I moved closer, 90 percent of the time the behavior shifted, and the yelling wasn't necessary.

I started to teach this to our Calm the Chaos students, and they saw the same results. However, when I share this strategy on my social media, the comments are always the same:

- If I get closer, I'll get hit.
- This doesn't work with all kids, my kid's too old.
- Getting closer just makes things worse.

I get it. This seems so simple that it can't possibly work. Honestly, you've probably tried this one way or another and had some of these same struggles. So let's just address some of the common arguments against getting close in the moment.

⚠ WHY GETTING CLOSER DOESN'T ALWAYS WORK

Look, I've been there. I've moved closer to my daughter when she was throwing herself onto the couch because she didn't want to go to school, only to get kicked in the leg. If I took this one incident and assumed that getting close didn't *ever* work, I would be missing a huge opportunity.

Just like we talked about in the last section with the Always and Never Beast, when we focus on something never working, we miss the small opportunities and nuances that *do* work.

Typically, there are a few reasons getting close might not work . . . yet.

In many cases, you might need to revert to a Ride the Storm plan. In the next stage, we'll be talking about skill building out of the moment to get ahead of these extremely dangerous situations. But for now, know that if this is the case, it doesn't mean getting close doesn't work. Ultimately, I want you to learn that there is a way to make getting closer work in your unique family. It might take some iterations and tweaks, but it can and does work.

CHALLENGE	ANTIDOTE
Too upset: When the parent or adult trying to get closer is upset themselves, this can be extremely triggering for a child already in disarray or spiraling into frustration.	**The antidote:** Disarm your body and Stop, Breathe, Anchor before approaching your child.
Too many words: When you get closer and ask questions, lecture, or give ultimatums, you're simply adding more chaos to an already volatile situation. Your child can't access their logical brain to answer, and worse, the added interrogation can send them further into a spiral.	**The antidote:** Stop talking. Just listen.
Too close: If you're getting kicked, spit on, hit, or having things thrown at you, move farther away. When a child is overstimulated, dysregulated, or stressed, having their personal space encroached upon can feel the like the walls are closing in, and they will do anything to push back.	**The antidote:** Come into the same room. Stay farther than arm's length away. The key is to not yell from upstairs, the kitchen, or the other room. Move into the same area as your child (but not in their personal space).
Too dangerous: There are times that getting closer can be dangerous for you or your child. If you have a child who runs after you, throws things, or runs when upset, getting too close could set off a ripple effect of even more dangerous behavior.	**The antidote:** Safety is the main priority. Instead of being right next to your child, try sitting near the door, or just on the other side of the door with the door open. Use a pillow or something soft as a barrier between you and your child. Remind your child, "I want to help, but it's not safe yet."

Get Lower

Another reason getting closer doesn't work in the moment is because, without realizing it, we often tower over kids (which only increases their stress responses). Think about the last time you tried to get your child off their electronics. Picture them sitting on the couch or the floor. In all likelihood, you were standing over them (possibly with your hands on your hips). Or imagine your children getting ready for bed, rolling on the floor refusing to put their pajamas on. Were you standing over them giving them "mommy eyes"? If so, you're not alone. We all picked up leftover remnants of authoritative parenting habits over time; it would be impossible not to. But it's imperative to shift away from this drill sergeant stature and lower your body to your child's level.

Unless you're dealing with a teenager, it's most likely that your child is much smaller than you are. When you enter an argument or battle over socks or going to school, your standing body feels overpowering and intimidating to your child, which will increase the likelihood that they will fight back, run away, or argue.

However, by lowering your body and sitting near your child, you immediately disarm yourself, become a safe and inviting person, and appear as more of an equal to your child (at least in size). This is less threatening and much more inviting, which means your child will be less likely to be combative or defensive.

Simple Ways to Get Lower:
- Squat or crouch down
- Get down on the floor
- Ask your child to stand up
- Sit beside your child while they play
- Sit against the wall with your legs apart

If you're getting older like me and your bones crick and crack at every bend, it's okay to sit on a bench, chair, or couch. Often parents and grandparents take this step so literally that they miss the opportunity to make their body smaller and less threatening. The key is to find a way to disarm your body even more by getting shorter while finding a way that works for you and your unique situation.

BREAKING BAD HABITS

You're reading this book because you've encountered some chaos in your family, whether it's common parenting struggles such as arguing over schoolwork, electronics, and chores, or more challenging struggles that include school trouble, meltdowns, and aggression. This means that up to now in your parenting, you have likely encountered fights and arguments with your children. Like it or not, both you and your children have developed habits of communication, even if it's not the most connected kind.

In short, the patterns of communication in your family have built up a wall of distrust. You don't trust that strategies will work, that your child will work with you, or that they want to work together with you. Your child doesn't trust that you will follow through with remaining calm, working with them through their emotions, or that they won't get in trouble one way or another.

By implementing closer and lower, you're ensuring that you rebuild and strengthen the trust between you and your child. This will take some time and some work outside the moment (which we will discuss in the next stage). For now, while you're still trying to defuse things in the heat of the moment, you need a simple way to connect that doesn't break the trust further or push your children away even more. If you remember, we are continually working to build the magic five-to-one ratio both in calm, connected times *and* in conflict. By moving closer, you instantly connect and provide your presence for your child, which makes a massive difference in the trust and relationship.

CLOSER AND LOWER IN ACTION

Leslie: Running and Hiding Before School

Like clockwork, as soon as it was time to leave in the morning for school, Leslie's son would run away from her and hide. He was determined to miss school yet again, but Leslie needed to get him there, or at least closer to it. She knew he was scared and needed to know he was safe, and that getting too close would trigger a meltdown. She started by simply moving into the same room he was in, softening her body, and then climbing into whatever space he had squeezed himself (usually under the bed). She kept her words to a minimum and would just rub his back and sit with him. This was drastically different from what she used to do: yell and chase him to get into the car with threats of what would happen if he didn't. Eventually sitting with him under the bed turned to sitting by him on the couch and checking in with a thumbs-up or a thumbs-down about how her son felt about school. Over time this small connection point became the backbone for their "go to school" plan.

ACTION STEP: GET CLOSER AND LOWER

Your simple action step is to make a reminder for yourself to move closer. For me this is a Post-it note in my kitchen next to the sink, or by my computer where I'm working.

Find a place where you notice you yell from the other room, reprimand without getting closer, or shout warnings. The note can be as simple as "Get Closer" as a quick reminder you can see in the heat of the moment that will help you follow through as you build this habit.

UNDERSTAND: DIG BELOW THE SURFACE

If you've ever asked a kid, "Why'd you do that?" only to be met with a blank stare, you aren't alone. As parents, we want answers, and we want them fast. Unfortunately, our children don't always have the answers. They're still learning how and why they do what they do, just as much as you are. So if your kids can't let you in on the secret behind their baffling behavior, who can?

You.

If you've ever seen the memes of the icebergs on social media, you've likely noticed twenty to forty options of what could be going on under the surface.

I don't know about you, but this just leaves me more overwhelmed. How the heck am I supposed to figure out what the behavior is telling me when there are just so many opinions and options? It's like trying to choose a cause of the behavior from thin air. Enter the behavior funnel.

THE BEHAVIOR FUNNEL

The behavior funnel is a unique system you can use both in and out of the moment to help you get a better understanding of why your child is doing what they're doing. Think of this system much like sifting pans that you might use if you were panning for gold.

In the heat of the moment, you will use this more like a mental checklist as you quickly assess how to help your child calm down as soon as possible. Out of the moment, you can slowly work to uncover the unmet needs or challenges that are contributing to the outburst, tantrum, fight, or meltdown.

The more you use the funnel, the more second nature it becomes in decoding your child's challenging behaviors.

Bear with me while I go all scientific on you. You'll appreciate why throughout this section. According to my research and experience, there are typically six causes (or missing needs) of all behavior that lead to stress and chaos in families.

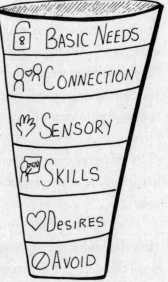

1. **Basic Needs:** Food, water, sleep, warmth, shelter, sense of safety
2. **Connection:** Sense of belonging and acceptance to a group or individual; positive social connections with other humans
3. **Sensory:** Sensory needs are either not being met or overwhelmed; this is the way your body interprets and interacts with the world around you
4. **Skills:** Social, emotional, cognitive skills that help an individual be successful and meet the expectations placed upon them
5. **Desires:** Innate and strong preferences that drive behavior such as interests, obsessions, or likes
6. **Avoidance:** An extreme dislike or disinterest in a topic or item

In order to use the behavior funnel, it's imperative that you go through each of these possible missing needs one level at a time. Each of the levels have been listed in order of most likely to least likely root causes, starting with basic needs. By using the system in order, you're sure to pick out the cause before going too far down the list or jumping to conclusions.

Let's take a deeper dive into each of the root causes of behavior.

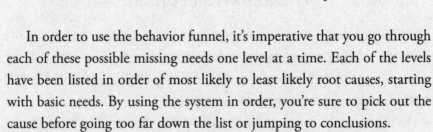

Basic Needs

Think of basic needs as anything your body needs for survival. If you've ever bit your partner's head off because you were hangry or didn't sleep well the night before, you have most definitely experienced the effects of not having your basic needs met. The same is true (if not more so) for our children.

Basic needs that affect behavior are:
- Food
- Water
- Sleep
- Warmth
- Health
- Toileting
- Body temperature
- Physical comfort

BASIC NEEDS

One of the most overlooked basic needs that not just children but all humans have is the need for safety and security. And after collectively going through a global pandemic together, every human's most basic need for safety and security has been severely tested. It will take years to truly unravel the effects and trauma of the uncertainty, unpredictability, fear, and worry born during that time.

So often parents will tell me, "My kids are safe. They have a roof over their heads, we feed them healthy foods, it's definitely not a struggle with basic needs."

Yet if your child is nervous to be themselves, scared of a punitive consequence, anxious about how their day will unfold, unsure if the day ahead will be good or bad, or uneasy about their surroundings and environment, they're definitely going to exhibit outward behaviors.

The truth is, if a child senses danger (perceived or real), they will act out in any way possible to remove themselves from the source of pain or worry.

Questions to Assess Basic Needs:

- Has my child had anything to drink or eat lately?
- Is my child tired or coming down with something?
- Is my child too hot or too cold?
- When was the last time my child went to the bathroom?
- Is my child worried or afraid of something?
- Is my child in any pain?
- Does my child fear the outcome or consequence (getting in trouble)?
- Does my child know the plan for the day?
- Did something unexpected or unplanned happen?
- Is my child uncomfortable physically or emotionally (anxious)?

Connection

Humans are social beings. (We got into that in Stage Two.) We need connection and a sense of belonging to survive. You will see me repeat the concepts of safety and connection throughout this book, because it's easy to overlook these needs in search of a deeper, more complex answer to why things are going wrong. While it's easy to assume that you aren't spending enough one-on-one time with your child, and that's what's creating the problem, there may be any number of factors—some related to you, some to others—causing the behavior.

Connection Factors That Affect Behavior

Connection is less about time spent together and more about how that time together makes each person feel. Connection isn't just about how you and your child are interacting, it's also how connected your child feels to other people in their lives. For example, do they have a trusted friend at school, a safe person at daycare they feel comfortable with, or a good relationship with their siblings? By all means, check yourself, but then zoom out to look at connection factors that could be related to your child's behaviors. This could include family, friends, authority figures like a teacher or coach, or even neighbors. Hint: for teenagers and older children, a lot of this connection (or lack of) could be online and through social channels and harder to pinpoint.

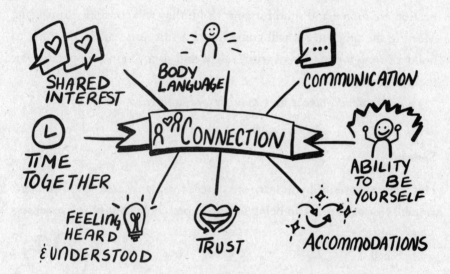

Questions to Assess Connection Needs:
- Is my body sending signals of safety?
- Am I open and inviting?
- Am I present and truly listening?
- Has my child had an argument with anyone lately?
- Does my child have a person with whom they share an interest?
- Have I been busy or less available lately?
- When was the last time they were yelled at or got in trouble?
- Can they express themselves without judgment?
- Do they have a teacher they trust?
- Does my child feel like their concerns are being heard?

- Is there someone they haven't seen in a while?
- Has my child struggled with a peer or friend recently?

⚠ **Note:** if a child has been adopted, is a foster child, or has suffered childhood trauma, they will be lacking tremendously in safety and connection even if you're providing them with an ideal environment with the most empathetic and caring interactions.

While there is most likely more under the surface, until safety and connection are rooted and solid for your child, they will continue to struggle. Meeting the other needs will come, but I assure you, taking the time to build a strong foundation of trust, safety, and connection is imperative for these children.

When in doubt, take it back to safety and connection.

Sensory

How many senses did you learn we have? If you answered five, you aren't alone. Most of us grew up being taught in preschool about the five senses:

- Sight
- Smell
- Taste
- Touch
- Hearing

We were taught these are basic ways our body takes in information from the world around us. We might have done some fun taste tests or experiments with textures to that end. But that's where the lesson ended.

What if I told you there are a lot more than five senses, and they aren't just how we take in information but how we interpret and interact with the world around us?

⚠ Parents with a child diagnosed with autism, ADHD, sensory processing disorder, or trauma usually understand the role senses play in their child's behaviors. In fact, they'll often jump straight to sensory as the unmet need, missing safety, and connection. Those who haven't been down this road usually miss sensory issues and sum it up as, "My child is just being a kid."

This is why I have included a very basic and oversimplified explanation of sensory needs in the form of questions about your own body:

- How do you feel after a day of being touched nonstop by your children?
- What happens after being surrounded by constant noise?
- Do you prefer sitting in the back of the car or do you have to sit near the front because you get carsick?
- Can you get to the bathroom without stubbing your toe in the dark?
- How does your mood change when the counters are completely covered?
- Do you work better with or without music or background noise?

All of these scenarios and reactions can be tied to your sensory systems and how you interact with your environment.

But let's go one level deeper, because that's how important this stuff is. This is what your child in chaos may be responding to without you being aware.

The Most Well-Known Senses That Affect Behavior

Tactile: physical sensations or touch (clothing, socks, hair, teeth, food, mess, water, etc.)

Auditory: noise (music, crowds, talking, background noise, electronics, etc.)

Visual: sights (lights, wall decorations, clutter, sun, crowds, TV shows, video games, etc.)

Olfactory: smells (perfumes, cooking, people, buildings, outside air, etc.)

Gustatory (oral): tastes and oral sensations (flavors, chewing on pencils, texture of foods, etc.)

Three Lesser-Known (But Extremely Important) Senses That Affect Behavior

 Vestibular: movement (running, spinning, swinging, car rides, roller coasters, bike riding, etc.)

 Proprioceptive: body awareness (pressure, jumping, squeezes, hugs, pushing, leaning, bouncing, etc.)

 Interoceptive: internal cues (emotional regulation, bathroom needs, body temperature, hunger, thirst, etc.)

Your child's body, as well as your own, can either be over- or under-sensitive to these different sensory inputs. This will result in two different behaviors:

1. **Avoiding:** refuse to do certain tasks or activities (like putting on socks in the morning or going into large, noisy crowds)
2. **Seeking:** actively or impulsively being drawn to activities or tasks that provide this input (even if they're unwanted behaviors, like climbing the side of the stairs or jumping on the couch)

Questions to Assess Sensory Needs:

- Is there too much/not enough noise?
- Are there strong smells?
- Is the scenery too bright or busy? Too dark?
- Has there been a lot of movement? Or long periods of no movement?
- Are you introducing new foods? Is the food the same as always?
- Is there a need to push, pull, or lean?
- Is there something uncomfortable on their skin?
- Do they have to get wet? Messy? Dirty?
- Is it loud? Quiet? Are there sudden noises? Chatter?
- Is the space closed in or wide open?

Side Note

At this point, parents almost always have an aha moment. Their whole life flashes before their eyes and they think, *Oh*, that's *why that bothers me. That's why I've always done that. Huh.*

Just knowing there are more than five senses and how they play a vital role in your child's behaviors will allow you to show up with more empathy, compassion, and understanding for your child (and grace and forgiveness for yourself).

Skills

Dr. Ross Greene, author of bestselling book *The Explosive Child*, is known for saying, "Kids do well, if they can."

If a child doesn't have the skills to meet our expectations, then they will act out or behave in ways we might consider inappropriate or unacceptable. In recent years, many more parents are aware that children with challenging behaviors aren't acting out because they want to.

Now for the caveat: I have seen many well-meaning parents, teachers, and even therapists jump to skill building when a child is simply not ready. We usually have to go back a level or two in the unmet needs order.

If a child's need for a sense of safety and security isn't being met, it doesn't matter how many skills they have.

In addition, if a child is over- or understimulated by sensory input, it will be hard for them to access their skills in the heat of the moment.

For this reason, I've placed skills fourth on the behavior funnel.

Most parents have expectations for children that aren't in alignment with their child's cognitive (thinking), emotional, or developmental age. Beyond books like *What to Expect When You're Expecting*, parents aren't given developmental milestones to use as a guide. Not to mention that all children are unique in their development and might be outliers in any one or multiple areas of development.

For example, I've had many parents come to me frustrated that their two-year-old can't sit for thirty minutes at the dinner table. Did you know attention span is typically calculated as age plus one minute? With this calculation, a toddler can be expected to have the attention span of three minutes. In short, you might be expecting way too much of your children for now.

There are many "missing" skills that are related to challenging behavior.

Basic Skills That Affect Behavior

The majority of challenging behaviors can be solved and decoded with the first four levels: safety, connection, sensory, and skills. However, the issue may lie deeper, which is why we've got two more layers in the funnel.

Desires and Avoidance

Has your child ever done something completely out of character because they wanted something so badly—maybe an award or recognition, a special toy, or a bag of candy? That's because all humans have desires and interests.

The same can be said about avoiding things that your child simply doesn't like. Think about a child who refuses to wear anything blue or won't go to a party because they hate clowns. It's human nature to avoid pain or discomfort, even when it comes to a strong preference. I would say this is even more true for children who are neurodiverse or labeled by others as strong willed.

Desires That Affect Behavior:
- Causes that are important to you: animal rights, the environment, etc.
- Strong belief system: believing that everything should be fair
- Special interests: trains, dinosaurs, Lego, robots, princesses, etc.
- Strong innate preferences: introvert/extrovert, active/quiet, messy/orderly
- External motivators: winning a prize, pleasing others, moving up in a sport
- Internal motivators: prefers to be alone, perfectionism, curiosity

One of the reasons rewards have been so prevalent in parenting and behavior change techniques is because the desire was believed to be stronger than whatever was driving the behavior. Unfortunately, this emphasizes compliance versus getting a child's needs met and understanding where the behavior was stemming from in the first place. Over time, children will lose motivation over the reward and the need is left unmet.

Questions to Assess Desires:
- Does my child have a plan in their head they haven't told me about?
- Is this a transition to a nonpreferred activity?
- Is there something they love that they're missing out on?
- Do they have any choice in this situation?
- Is their opinion being heard?
- Do they have a strong preference here?
- Is there a special interest driving this behavior?
- Do they have a strong belief about this?

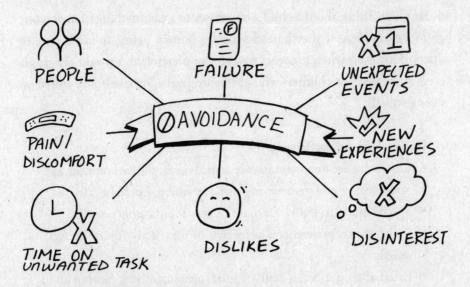

Avoidances That Affect Behavior:

- People: kids on the playground picking on them
- Failure: missing a basket in gym class
- New things/experiences: going to a new school
- Unexpected event: fire drill or substitute teacher
- Pain or discomfort: getting wet or dirty or wearing itchy sweaters
- Time doing something they don't like: sitting in church
- Dislikes: lima beans, smell of Grandma
- Disinterest: reading, playing with Lego, dolls, etc.

Questions to Assess Avoidance:

- Does my child prefer something else?
- Do they have a favorite flavor, color, character?
- Is my child afraid of anything?
- Does my child have interest in this subject?
- Does this drain my child?
- Is this difficult for my child?

Hopefully, you can see how both desires and avoidance overlap a ton with the other layers of the behavior funnel. Which leads to the next question, no doubt: So how do you know what the *real* cause is?

The way you avoid making the mistake of jumping to conclusions is to ask why:

- Why does my child want this so badly?
- Why do they want to avoid this at all costs?

Nine times out of ten, you will be led right back to the top of the funnel: safety, connection, sensory, or skills.

That's the beauty of the behavior funnel. Even if a child is struggling because of desires or avoidance, you will likely catch the cause early on, because you will be looking for the real reason using a process of elimination. Not only will you know your child is avoiding a task but you will also know why. Knowing this will allow you to solve the problem when everyone is calm.

HOW TO USE THE BEHAVIOR FUNNEL
IN THE HEAT OF THE MOMENT

If you're wondering, "Dayna, how in the world am I supposed to do all that while my teenager is telling me to get a life or slamming the door in my face?"

The answer is simple. You aren't.

The truth is, in the heat of the moment, you won't have time, nor will you recall all of these questions. And remember, your child can't access their thinking brain in the middle of an argument or outburst, so asking questions right now will only add more chaos to the mix.

Instead, your focus is on meeting the needs that are easily identifiable, starting with basic needs.

Seven Questions to Ask Yourself in the Heat of the Moment

- Is my child hungry or tired?
- Do they feel safe?
- Are they feeling disconnected?
- Are their senses overloaded or underwhelmed?
- Is there a skill they might be missing?
- What are they really wanting right now?
- Is there something they're trying to avoid?

Remember, the key is not to problem solve right now. Here we are identifying the actual problem or problems. Simply make a quick assessment so you can empower yourself with a plan for what to do and provide (the next step in your plan).

By recognizing the underlying need (even if you miscalculate), you will be able to show more empathy and compassion in the moment, which will make it even easier to soften your body, provide moments of safety, and remain calm through the storm.

⚠ CAUTION: DON'T JUMP TO CONCLUSIONS

It's worth repeating. I can't tell you how many times I've seen parents jump to the bottom of the funnel. After all, it's habit to think kids are pushing our buttons and doing things just because they do or don't want to.

Most of the In-the-Moment challenges can be solved or decoded using the top three layers: safety, connection, and sensory. Because even if there are lagging skills or desires or avoidance, you most likely won't be able to solve those in the moment because skill building and problem-solving happen when everyone is calm and regulated.

BEHAVIOR FUNNEL IN ACTION

Jen: Meltdowns over Bath Time

When Jen first started trying to understand why her girls refused bath time, she was at a loss. She was sure they didn't want take a bath simply because they wanted to play longer or didn't want to stop what they were doing. She thought they were old enough to take a bath on their own (they were five and ten) and didn't think she should coddle them just to get them to get clean. When it came time for baths each night, she would find herself frustrated by the extensive battle to get the girls into the tub. However, when she slowed down and used the behavior funnel to assess what was under the surface, she quickly realized there were sensory needs and skills missing that were at the root of the bath-time struggles. In the moment, this allowed her to be calmer and more empathetic toward her girls' refusal. She then created a plan with the girls for how they could build the skills needed to clean themselves independently and lower the sensory overload. She realized this needed to look different for each girl, even though they were both autistic. One wanted bath time to be more fun with mermaid stories and diving for jewels along with swimming goggles to keep the water out of her eyes. The other found bathing a sensory nightmare with tangles, soap smells, and temperature transitions that set off sensory alarms.

ACTION STEP: GET CURIOUS

Think through the last time you had a battle with your child. What behaviors did you see above the surface? Was there yelling, hitting, kicking, name calling, refusal?

Using the behavior funnel, starting with basic needs and safety, ask yourself questions about what could be under the surface and then move down the funnel one layer at a time, stopping when you've found something insightful. This will give you a starting point for understanding and having empathy for why your child is struggling. When you have this new information, is there something you can do differently next time this type of outburst happens?

- Is there a way you can help your child feel safer or get their basic needs met (like bringing snacks to the school pickup line)?
- Is there a way to build connection before the next outburst or show compassion for the missed connection?
- Is there something you can do to remove sensory overload in the heat of the moment, like turning off all noise and lights?
- Is there a skill you could work on before your child needs to use this skill in the future?
- Is there a personal preference that makes it easier to understand your child's behaviors and that you can make a plan for?

It's important to remember that now is not about solving the problem but about understanding so you can respond with more empathy, compassion, and calmness in the heat of the moment. In the next chapter, you will start to work with your child to build skills, problem solve, and even rebuild trust and connection. For now, focus on gaining clarity on why your child is doing what they're doing.

If you'd like to print out the behavior funnel so you can keep it handy in the middle of your next storm to quickly assess your child's needs, you can download it at www.calmthechaosbook.com/funnel.

EMPOWER: SAY AND DO THIS

Let me guess. You know what you *should* do in the heat of the moment, but actually doing it is a completely different story, right? I get it.

At this point, you've most likely read enough books, listened to enough podcasts, and spoken with enough experts to know the *best* way to respond to your child.

But when your child starts arguing with their sister over candy, and one gets hit and the other starts crying, everything you've ever learned seems to slip away, completely out of reach. All you're left with is rage and frustration.

In this moment, it doesn't matter how many popular parenting scripts you've saved, the only thing coming to the tip of your tongue is, "How many times do I have to tell you? That is not okay!" Or worse, "What's wrong with you?"

I've got great news for you: *You are not a failure, nor is something wrong with you.* This is 100 percent normal.

I've said it before, but it bears repeating: in the heat of the moment, your brain decides it's going to take over and completely override any sense of logic you might have normally relied upon. Your ability to recall and remember what you *should* do shorts out, causing you to revert to old habits and behaviors.

That's why you need a plan that is so easy you don't have to think to implement it in the moment. You need something short and sweet that is both easy to remember and simple to tweak (so you don't have to stress over getting it perfect).

This is where the last step in your In-the-Moment plan comes in: 1:1:1.

WHAT TO SAY AND DO IN THE HEAT OF THE MOMENT

Knowing exactly what to say and do ahead of time will allow you to face any situation with confidence and calm. Deciding before the storm arrives what you will do when all hell is breaking loose will help your brain stay on track instead of reverting to instinct. Think of this much like performance athletes practicing and perfecting the same plays long before the big game. Even though they don't know exactly what the other team is going to do, they've set themselves up for success by creating automatic moves and responses they can rely on in the heat of the moment.

Instead of feeding you a bunch of things you "should" or "could" say and do, you are hereby empowered to choose what will work best with your unique family and situation, so the next time your child is talking back, lying, or being rude, you know exactly what you can say or do to defuse the argument quickly.

Your 1:1:1 is made of three simple parts:

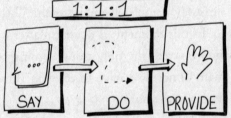

- one thing to say
- one thing to do
- one thing to provide

Let's walk through each of the parts, complete with examples, and then you can create your own list so you can start practicing as early as today.

Say This

If you're like most of the parents I work with, your first instinct in the moment is to go into fix-it mode. You might enter a situation asking a ton of questions, trying to assess what is really happening, what your child needs, and how to get to the bottom of the chaos.

For others, the main goal is to end the chaos as soon as possible before being triggered themselves or setting off a ripple effect within the rest of the family. To prevent that from happening, parents are willing to say and do almost anything to get the behavior to stop. Either way, instead of defusing the ticking time bomb in front of you, it just makes things worse.

Common Phrases That Can Cause More Harm than Good:

- Stop
- Why are you doing that?
- How many times have I told you?
- You hurt my feelings
- I'm so disappointed in you

- Be good
- You're fine
- It's not okay to . . . (hit, kick, spit, etc.)

While these phrases are a mix of seriously negative and not so negative, they all fail to help in the moment. They don't work because, in the middle of a storm, neither you nor your child can access your logical thinking brain and so problem-solving and fixing don't work. In fact, without your child having access to this part of their brain, your voice sounds a lot like that of Charlie Brown's teacher: "Wah-wah, wah, wah, wah-wah." If you've ever been upset and someone insists on talking at you, you know that this feels like nails on a chalkboard. Instead of calming you down, it has the opposite effect. The same is true for your child.

Yes, it's your job as the parent to teach and guide, but what children need most in the heat of the moment is to feel seen, heard, and understood.

But how do you help your child feel seen, heard, and understood while avoiding lengthy conversation? We employ simple connected scripts.

Simple Connected Scripts

When your nervous system is overloaded, scripts help your brain know what to say. Scripts have become extremely popular in the parenting world, with "Say this, not that" memes. Unfortunately, these scripts are often used as a one-size-fits-all solution or as part of an arsenal that can't be remembered in the moment. What I am suggesting instead is to find one script to use that works with you and your unique situation. Practice it out of the moment (during your Five-Minute Energy plan) and then tweak it after you see how your child responds to that particular script.

When crafting a connected script, I like to use the following guidelines:

1. Minimal words (fewer than ten words)
2. Void of your own emotions or judgments (angry, sad, disappointed)
3. Mirrors what you see (only what you can see from a camera lens)
4. Neutral language (doesn't use "always," "never")
5. Sentence starter (just a few words that can be used with different situations)

Here are some real connected scripts our Calm the Chaos parents have used with great success. See if they give you ideas for your own.

Common Connected Scripts for 1:1:1

- I notice you're struggling with (insert what you see happening)
- I see you're (insert what you see)
- I hear that you (insert what you hear them saying)

The key here is to choose just one phrase that feels right for you and your family and keep it simple to start. Most of the parents I work with start with "I notice" combined with simply stating that they notice their child is struggling. This keeps words to a minimum, doesn't allow a lot of room for assumptions, and simply lets your child know that you see and hear that they're having a hard time.

As you use these phrases more and more, you can elaborate and get more advanced. In fact, once you've moved to the next stage, you will revisit your 1:1:1 and create a connected script that allows for more input and feedback from your child and creates a dialogue before things get too bad. However, when you're first starting out, I recommend keeping it as simple as possible and only using one phrase.

Do This

The next part of your 1:1:1 is to establish what you will do in the middle of the storm. This is where things can really go off the rails if you aren't cautious. I want to remind you: the goal in the moment is not to change the behavior, it's to defuse the situation and understand what's hiding behind the behavior.

What your child needs more than punishments, rewards, or isolation is the time and space to process their frustrations and emotions.

The easiest way to accomplish this is with a tool you already learned earlier in this stage: **closer and lower.**

The simplest action you can do is to simply move near your child so you become their trusted calm space, even when you can't get right beside them. While there, don't do anything except soften your body and wait it out. The key is to stay as quiet as possible to not add more input and stress to the situation.

Sometimes this wait can feel like an eternity, especially if you're already late for work, or you have glaring eyeballs on you in the checkout line of the grocery store. But I assure you, you will spend far less time defusing the bomb by doing nothing and simply holding space for your child in the moment than if you try to reason, threaten, or force your child to change their behavior.

As you get more advanced, and you've got a simple In-the-Moment plan that is working with your unique child, you can start to create new action plans with your child. I'm not going to go a ton into how to do that here because doing so requires your child's buy-in and trust, which happens ahead of the moment, but here are some options you might choose for your *do*:

- Remove breakable items from the area
- Remove any other children from the room
- Soften your body
- Wait it out calmly

Provide This

The final piece of your 1:1:1 is deciding which tool you can provide in the heat of the moment.

I'm not talking about all the tools and gadgets you might have collected over the years to help with the meltdowns, tantrums, schoolwork battles, and more. I used to have a closet filled to the brim with all the latest and greatest calm-down tools such as stickers, stress balls, timers, fidget toys, and fancy calm-down posters.

Look, I get it. These tools have a lot of great qualities and I'm a sucker for a good calming tool when I see one. Yet these are probably not working for you right now because your child is missing the skills needed to benefit from these tools in the moment. When your child is already screaming at the top of their lungs, there isn't a single fidget toy in the world that will calm them down.

The most powerful tool you can provide your child in the heat of the moment is *you* and your calm presence.

Remember, the goal in the moment is to defuse the situation. The simplest tool you can use is your own body language. That's how you provide your child signals of safety.

By using closer and lower (beginning on page 148) combined with softening your body to create moments of safety (page 84), you can become this calm presence for your child.

Your body language, your energy, your sense of groundedness are key to reducing chaos. Then, you need to help reduce the stress in your child.

PROVIDE A SAFE PLACE

This is a slightly advanced tactic, but if you already have some buy-in from your child, you can set up spots—either in the house or out in public—that your child can escape to when overwhelmed or frustrated. We talked a lot about you and your presence being the safe place for your child, but if you have a teenager or a child who prefers to be alone or gets overly emotional with people near them, having a safe place your child can go to in the heat of the moment can be a lifesaver. This is simply a nonpunitive, nonthreatening location the child helps create that gives them the space and room to calm down in the moment. These spaces don't need to be fancy, cute, or even a whole room in the house.

Possible Locations for a Safe Place:
- Behind a chair, couch, or table
- In their own bedroom
- In a corner with pillows and blankets
- On the couch at the opposite end from other family members
- A huge cardboard box with cushions inside

We had safe places in every room in our home during our most turbulent times. This is an advanced strategy because, if you haven't built the safety and trust yet, a spot like this can seem punitive and threatening to a child, despite your best intentions. The very tool intended to create safety becomes a source of frustration and disconnection.

I mention this option because for those of you with children who run away or want to get behind furniture when you get closer and lower, you may want to establish a location (or several locations) that are calming for your child beforehand. If this strategy is going to be used, it has to be introduced and practiced many times ahead of the moment.

As you build more In-the-Moment plans with your child, you will want options for other great tools you can provide in the moment. Below is a list of simple tools real families have used to provide safety and calm in the heat of the moment. Make sure you introduce each one to your child when everyone is calm, and practice using them multiple times before they're needed.

BASIC NEEDS	CONNECTION	SENSORY BREAK/INPUT
Deep breathing	Hand on heart	Deep pressure
Water	Hold hand	Lights turned off
Snack	Hug	Sounds turned off
Bathroom break	Lap to sit in	Soft blanket
Safe place	Listening ear	Weighted blanket
Pillow to hit	Your presence	Space to run

As with each of your options in your 1:1:1, I recommend you keep your provide as simple as possible to start. I've given you a lot of options to choose from, but it's always best to start with the simplest option, especially if you're still dealing with dangerous behaviors and challenging blow-ups.

A Simple 1:1:1 Plan You Can Implement Today:

Say: I notice you're struggling

Do: Move closer and get lower

Provide: Moments of safety (your calm presence)

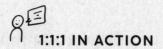

1:1:1 IN ACTION

Aleix: Strong-Willed Child Trying to Parent Sibling

Aleix is the father of two little girls with big personalities. His eight-year-old is known for trying to parent her little sister. Aleix believed she did this because she was trying to be the center of attention. When her sister would get frustrated and have a crying fit, the eight-year-old would swoop in and try to mediate. Instead of helping, she would insult her sister. Aleix just wished his daughter would let him parent in the moment. Realizing she simply wanted to help her sister without knowing how, he created a 1:1:1 for the eight-year-old.

> Say: I hear your voice is getting louder. I notice you would like to help your sister.
> Do: Take a break together with the older daughter.
> Provide: A safe place to cuddle and talk to Dad about her worries for her little sister.

Not only did Aleix empower his daughter by giving her the space to be heard and understood, he was able to minimize the spiraling chaos that was happening when both children got involved.

ACTION STEP: YOUR 1:1:1

Your simple next step is to create a simple 1:1:1 for a common struggle you're dealing with in the moment.

First, think about the last time you got into an argument, broke up a fight between your children, or dealt with a massive explosion from your child.

Second, choose one phrase you can say in the heat of the moment that will keep you calm and disarm your child. This should be validating of their emotions and help them feel seen, heard, and understood. *Hint: the simplest phrase is "I notice."*

Next, choose one action you can take in the moment that will create connection and allow your child time and space to process their emotions and frustrations. *Hint: the simplest action is to move closer and lower.*

Finally, choose one tool you can use in the moment to help your child calm down faster and help them know they have you as their safe place in any storm. *Hint: the simplest tool is your calm presence.*

Ninja tip: write out your 1:1:1 and place it somewhere you will remember it the next time your child begins to struggle.

📄 PUTTING IT ALL TOGETHER: YOUR IN-THE-MOMENT PLAN

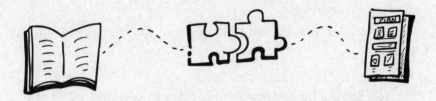

Way to go! You've made it more than halfway through your journey! Okay, this journey is never completely done, but your progress is worth celebrating. Time to do a little dance.

Even if there are still days you feel like hiding in the bathroom or you're still losing your cool a few times a week, there is reason to clap and dance. As parents, we don't celebrate our progress as much as we should. Consider it a huge win!

📄 THE PLAN

Just like your Ride the Storm plan, your In-the-Moment plan is created ahead of time so you don't have to think twice about how to defuse the next argument, fight, or meltdown.

Your In-the-Moment plan is designed to help you respond with empathy, compassion, and understanding, even if it still feels like the explosion came out of thin air.

This plan is simply meant to keep you and your child connected through the chaos, without adding more fuel to an already volatile situation. By knowing exactly what to say and do in the heat of the moment, you will become your family's calm in the middle of the storm. By implementing this plan, you will notice that the explosions have less intensity, happen less often, and don't destroy everything you've worked so hard to build up to this point.

As always, the focus is less on getting the plan perfect and more on having a plan that you can tweak as you go, starting with the simplest one and building over time as you gain more understanding of your child's unmet needs, how they respond to various phrases and actions, and what works with your unique family.

I've already introduced you to the parts of the In-the-Moment plan. Let's review:

1. **You: Slay the Thought Monsters:** Entering any situation with a negative outlook, especially one with a ticking time bomb on the brink of explosion, can be catastrophic. That's why it's imperative to check the thoughts swirling in your head before entering any argument or chaos-causing battle with your children. By simply recognizing the thought monster wreaking havoc on your confidence and swapping it out for a more empowering one (super swap), you can now have the calm and confidence to handle even the most stressful situations with your nervous system intact.

2. **Connect: Defuse the Bomb:** The number one goal in the heat of the moment is to disarm the other person with minimal damage. It's hard to do this by yelling from the other room or behind a closed door. With two simple movements (closer and lower) you can better assess the challenge at hand. This will not only allow you to be more present in the moment but give your child the connection and attention needed when they're struggling the most.

3. **Understand: Dig Below the Surface:** Your child can't tell you what's wrong, especially in the heat of the moment. So how in the world are you supposed to find the source of the chaos? The behavior funnel simplifies the science of your child and their behavior so you can quickly assess and attain the underlying cause, even if they don't have the words to tell you. Considering the six causes of behavior—basic needs, connection, sensory, skills, desires, avoidance—you can ask yourself a few simple questions to gain a deeper

understanding into your child's frustrations, making it even easier to defuse the situation.

4. **Empower: Say and Do This:** Finally, having a plan for what to say, do, and provide in the heat of the moment will be vital in diminishing the damage from any argument or fallout. You'll naturally be able to stay connected and show empathy and understanding in a way unique to your family.

PUTTING THE PIECES TOGETHER

Now that we've reviewed the different pieces of your In-the-Moment plan and pulled out the most essential steps in this stage, let's put the pieces together to make a plan that you can use for the next argument, fight, or meltdown.

Before: Prepping for the Next Explosion

The primary goal in the moment is defusing. To ready you for the next explosion, we must prepare you and your family.

Before your child's next outburst, tantrum, or meltdown:

1. Swap Your Thoughts

Think about what thoughts race through your head when an incident occurs. Do you feel like it always happens, resent that it feels like it's being done out of manipulation, or have guilt around how you should have responded? Identifying the common thought monster and swapping it before the next time can be incredibly helpful. Which super swap will you call on so you can remain calm in the chaos?

2. Identify Small Warning Signs

Getting clear on when and where to use your In-the-Moment plan is important. You want to have warning signs that help you identify the best time to use the plan for maximum benefits. After all, the later you enter a stressful situation, the harder it will be to calm down your child and remain calm yourself.

This will be an indicator for your brain to engage the In-the-Moment plan. You can add this to your plan using a statement like this: "When (insert warning sign) happens, I will use my In-the-Moment plan."

Think about the incident we talked about in step one. What were some of the early indicators? What happened first? Don't worry too much about seeing these signs clearly right now; we will do a lot more of this work in the next stage. For now, simply identify one indicator that lets you know it's time for you to use your In-the-Moment plan.

3. Practice, Practice, Practice

I recommend you create your plan out of the moment, before you need it. Then practice so your skills are sharp when it's time to defuse the ticking time bomb.

I would recommend using parts of the In-the-Moment plan daily as new ways of interacting. Here's what I mean:

- **Closer and Lower:** When it's time to get the kids for dinner, instead of calling from the kitchen (even though everyone is playing happily), walk over to the other room and sit beside them. Watch them play their game for a bit, and then let them know dinner is ready.

- **I notice, I see, I hear:** Use these phrases throughout your day instead of only when your child is upset. This way, your child gets used to hearing the statements when things are happy or neutral, at the very least, and doesn't immediately associate them with negative interactions. Daily repetition also ensures that these phrases become more natural to your way of speaking and therefore easier to use when the stakes are high.

- **Behavior Funnel:** Start to notice when certain factors affect family behaviors. Do certain people get hangry when they haven't eaten? Does your toddler get fussy when they have a wet diaper? Do you get edgy when you haven't talked to a friend in a few days? Do you avoid certain activities because you don't have the skills needed to be successful? Do you have strong preferences that guide your decisions in your day to day? The more you use this detection skill in everyday life, the easier it will be to use during difficult situations. I wouldn't be surprised if you start to use the behavior funnel to understand why the heck the cat is zooming ninety miles per hour around the house at 8 p.m.

During: Defuse the Bomb

Chaos erupts! It's go time for your In-the-Moment action plan.

Repeat until the bomb has been defused.

The key, while your child is destroying their bedroom, yelling obscenities, or charging at you with anger, is to hold the course and repeat steps one to four until the chaos is defused.

I want to give you permission to walk away for a minute to anchor and get back to your calm and grounded presence if the intensity and duration is just too much and you feel your blood boiling. Your 1:1:1 would look like this:

Say: I need a minute; I will be right back.

Do: Take a short walk out of the room or to the other side of the room.

Provide: yourself with deep breaths and your anchor.

After: The Repair Work

Once the bomb has either been defused or detonated and both you and your child have calmed down, repair work is needed before the next big explosion. Don't worry about doing this immediately following the incident or struggle. You can give both you and your child the time and space needed to cool off. Sometimes that might mean that this work happens the next day.

Rest: Giving everyone involved time and space to breathe and reset is important. If your nervous system is still feeling in danger or on alert, it will be hard to do any reconnection or repair work needed. Give yourself and your child the permission to take all the time needed (even if this means you don't discuss the blowup until the next day or so).

Reconnect: Once you can see that both you and your child have returned to a calm and grounded demeaner, it's time to reconnect and repair. I do not believe in perfect parenting. In fact, research shows you only have to get it right 70 percent of the time. It's how you show up and make sense of the other 30 percent that matters most. That's why reconnecting and repairing the relationship is imperative after any struggle, no matter how big or small.

Reassess: Take a moment once you've reconnected with your child and repaired any hurt feelings or breakage in the relationship to reassess the root cause or unmet needs that contributed to the blowup. This information will help you reassess your 1:1:1 plan and how you can better support your unique child through their struggles.

Remember,

you've got this!

STAGE FOUR:
NO MORE STORM CHASING

1. CHAOS CAUSER

2. MAGIC RESET BUTTON

3. BEHAVIOR SPIRAL

4. HUDDLE, HUDDLE, HUDDLE

STAGE FIVE

YOUR CHALLENGE: DO AWAY WITH THE WHAC-A-MOLE PARENTING APPROACH

It was my son's first day of eleventh grade at a brand-new high school in a brand-new city. He got into a fight, and it wasn't pretty.

Another suspension.

Another principal.

Another meeting with a team around the table.

Only this time, things were different. No one was talking consequences or discipline.

"Mrs. Abraham, this happened in an instant. But after reviewing your son's account of the events, the tapes, and testimonials from witnesses, we can see the buildup and exactly where things went south. Let's put some things in place so this doesn't happen again."

Sitting in that office, I could hardly believe my ears. Just a few short years ago my son was being treated like a wild animal while everyone threw their hands in the air. Now, school administration was listening, learning, and, more than anything, willing to create solutions to prevent this from happening in the future.

Obviously, the process of getting to this point took work. But the good news is it's the exact work you've already been doing so far (Ride the Storm, energy, and In-the-Moment planning). With this foundation, my son and I were able to become a team that worked together. We were able to unravel the events that caused so much stress at home and school, and together we created plans that prevented the outbursts in the first place.

I call them Ahead-of-the-Moment plans because if you can catch a problem before it explodes, you can make life easier for all involved, particularly your child. By creating Ahead-of-the-Moment plans and unraveling incidents with my child, I was able to empower him with a language and tools to use when I wasn't around (like detailing the fight at school).

We'll build your Ahead-of-the-Moment plan in this chapter so you can finally get in front of your family's biggest chaos causers, whether it's school suspensions, outings to the grocery store without tantrums, or simply getting your kids to stop fighting you tooth and nail over homework.

But before we get to creating these plans for your biggest challenges, we have to address a huge elephant in the room.

THE D-WORD

For far too long, discipline has been touted as the ultimate solution for parenting. In many ways discipline has become synonymous with parenting. Which would explain why the number one question parents ask me is "How do I discipline my child?"

But before I go there . . .

What Is Discipline?

Seems like a straightforward question, right? Except when I asked three hundred thousand parents, teachers, and therapists for their definition, I received three hundred thousand different answers. Sure, there was some overlap, but there were far more nuances and conflicting definitions.

Instead of asking "How do we discipline?" we should be asking "How do we raise children who have compassion for themselves and others?"

If you recall, when I first started this journey with my son, I had two goals:

1. For him not to hate others for not understanding him.
2. For him not to hate himself for not being like everyone else.

In order to make this a reality, it was clear I'd need a new lens for approaching discipline. One that allowed my son to understand the concerns of others around him when he struggled to fit in (or acted out) and also gave him the understanding and compassion to love himself for his behavior and how he navigated the world around him.

Disciplinarian versus Guide/Mentor

There's a saying in the business world that goes something like this: there is no such thing as failure. Try something new and you get either the results you want or the lesson you needed at the moment. A good business mentor won't tell you what you should and shouldn't do; instead they'll give you a framework and some guidelines, coach you through the hurdles and mindset blocks, and cheer you on from the sidelines. After the results are in, they'll sit with you and debrief. Despite a win or a loss, they'll ask what went well. What could be done differently in the future? Postgame, a sports coach will do the very same thing. Because this way, the player(s) will be able to internalize the lessons without remaining dependent on the coach to provide a list of to-dos.

Parenting can be done the same way. What would happen if guiding your child was less about showing and telling what they should or shouldn't do, and more about working together—offering guidelines, creating plans that work, debriefing after an incident?

How would the child benefit from an open-ended exploration with a trusted partner, as opposed to being handed a checklist of tasks and requirements?

That's exactly what I'm suggesting children (especially the most challenging ones) need most.

Instead of teaching children *what* to think and do, we must teach them *how* to think and problem solve.

Why?

Imagine your child being able to:
- advocate for their own needs and wants without yelling or arguing
- problem solve through an argument on the playground over who should get the play structure first
- show compassion for a friend when they get hurt or are throwing a fit
- create a plan around electronics that makes both you and them happy with the outcome
- get ready in the morning for school without any reminders or nagging
- understand their own emotions, triggers, and sensory preferences in such detail they can stand up for what accommodations help them be successful in the classroom

All of this and more is 100 percent possible. In fact, these are just some of the real-life examples from our Calm the Chaos families.

We've established that, until this stage, there hasn't been any room for problem-solving or skill building. You've been busy creating safety (physical and emotional) for your family, regaining your own energy to weather violent storms, and finding simple connected ways to disarm and defuse arguments with your children.

But now it's time to stop playing defense and start proactively getting ahead of the storms, so they're less intense and fewer in frequency. In order for the chaos to get better, you need to be able to:
- understand the root of the problem
- problem solve with your child
- build skills to get ahead of the challenges

📑 THE PATH FORWARD: YOUR AHEAD-OF-THE-MOMENT PLAN

With the steps in this chapter, you can finally stop playing parenting Whac-A-Mole, solving one problem after the next. Instead, you will be able to help your child build the skills needed to problem solve and communicate their needs without having to yell, hit, or bite, avoiding the fight altogether.

Whether you're trying to finally have peaceful mornings before school, you want your teenager to actually clean their room, or you want to get ahead of the after-school meltdowns once and for all, this plan is for you. In the sections ahead, I will break down this plan one piece at a time:

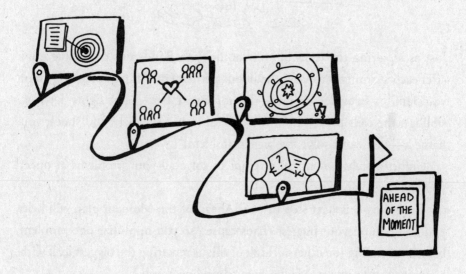

# YOU: CHOOSE YOUR CHAOS CAUSER

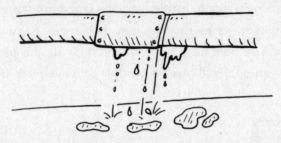

Just as repairing the leaks in your home with Band-Aids or bubble gum after each storm fails to keep the floods permanently at bay, patching all of your family's struggles at once—the homework battles, the fights between siblings, the calls from school, the refusal to put on socks and shoes, you name it—just won't solve the bigger problem.

Unfortunately, when you attempt to solve all your problems at once, you end up solving none.

That's why this next step in your Ahead-of-the-Moment plan will help you home in on your biggest chaos causer, so you minimize one problem before addressing the others. Think of this as repairing the biggest leak with new pipes and cement. Maybe even rebuilding a wall.

YOUR BIGGEST CHAOS CAUSER

In order to make progress and start calming the chaos in your family, you have to slow down and choose one struggle to focus on. It can be hard at this stage to know where to put your focus; many more challenges will pop up and try to distract you. And believe me, as an ADHD adult, I understand distractions. I also understand a sense of defeat, feeling overwhelmed, and constant stress.

When you're considering which challenge to focus on, consider the one that is the root cause of all the other chaos. We call this your number one chaos causer.

"What about all the other things?" you might ask. "Do I just let them go? But how?"

I've got you. I've used this process in my own family, with my business, and even in writing this book. Countless families have used this method to reduce feeling overwhelmed and start seeing results instead of spinning in circles.

This process will help you identify your biggest chaos causer so you have time and space to do things you never thought possible. It's just three simple steps:

Step One: List

Make a list of all the struggles, stressors, and chaos causers happening in your family right now. At first, you might think of the big ones such as:

- hitting
- screaming meltdowns
- self-harm
- sibling fighting

This is completely normal. Your brain is wired to remember things that cause pain. However, these aren't happening in a vacuum. There are other things going on in your home that add to the chaos and stress of your everyday lives. This list should contain a mixture of extremely big struggles and even small annoyances. In fact, I would have you stretch yourself to think of things that aren't specifically about the children.

Anything is fair game with this list. The goal is simply to get it all out on paper instead of rattling around in your head. In your mind, you'll see the problems as one gigantic lump, as opposed to line items you need to address individually.

Here are some chaos categories to get you thinking:

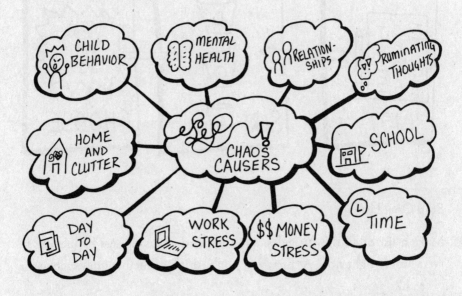

Tip: I like to set a timer when I make this list, because it can be tempting to let it grow and grow. That list will start to feel so big and heavy that it'll be hard to move forward. If you know you can overthink or get sucked into the abyss of being overwhelmed, do yourself this favor.

Step Two: Sort

Once you have your list, sort the items into categories. You might remember doing something like this in the Ride the Storm plan when you identified your storms. While this is similar, you now have more knowledge, understanding, and connection, so you can address these challenges from a different perspective. While there might be overlap, don't worry too much about the similarities.

For this step, I want to introduce you to a filter called DQA. This stands for the three types of chaos causers that you likely have on your list:

D: Dangerous: puts you, your child, or others in harm's way

Q: Quality of life: lowers the mood, energy, and connection in your family

A: Annoying: frustrating but not life-altering or hurtful to others

Here are some common chaos causers (sorted for you):

D: DANGEROUS	Q: QUALITY OF LIFE	A: ANNOYING
Hitting	Lying	Whining
Self-harm	Negative self-talk	Repetitive noises
Drug use	Picky eating	Inappropriate jokes

Step Three: Choose

Finally, choose your biggest chaos causer from the list you compiled. But how do you choose when there are so many options?

First, I want to assure you that you can't get this step wrong. No matter what you choose, you'll make progress with your family. Simply by choosing, you'll minimize frustration, even if you don't go after the perfect one. Here's a simple way to determine your first selection, perfect or not.

Trust Your Intuition: Look back at your list and see if there is one struggle that jumps off the page at you. One that is so obvious you feel it in the pit of your stomach. You can't go wrong by trusting the instincts you naturally have as a parent. I want to empower you to lean into that feeling and knowing.

Dangerous: If you have any challenges in the dangerous category, this is where I suggest you start. Because addressing a dangerous chaos causer first will have massive ripple effects in other areas.

Now that you've narrowed down your list to your biggest chaos causer, you can focus your time and energy as you work to create Ahead-of-the-Moment plans.

But what should you do about everything left on the list?

⚠ PUTTING BLINDERS ON

Yep. That's right, put those blinders on, friend, and only look ahead at the one focus. That doesn't mean you ignore everything else; it simply means 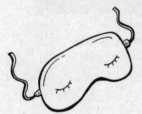 those other issues don't get your time and energy right now. For example, if I'm starting a new healthy habit of exercising regularly, I'm not going to stress over drinking a gallon of water, eating vegetables at every meal, or sleeping seven-plus hours a night, because I'm focusing on building a different (but related) habit. I'm going to focus on my step count or working out for half an hour, three times a week. The same is true with your chaos causer.

Tracking Progress

We've already talked a lot about how important it is to focus on the progress you're making, the small wins, and the tiny steps you're taking instead of focusing on going from zero to done in a matter of days. This is more important at this stage than ever before, as you work to create and tweak your Ahead-of-the-Moment plan for your biggest chaos causer. In fact, it's so important I've created a system that allows you to see the progress you're making as you move forward.

Before you can know how much progress you've made, however, you must first know where you're starting. This is why we need to identify your baseline.

A baseline is simply a tally of how often your chaos causer is currently happening, giving you a clear picture of where you currently are on your journey.

Think of any goal you set for yourself—budgeting, weight loss, running a marathon in a certain amount of time, finishing a book by a certain deadline, you name it. All of these goals are best accomplished when you know your starting point. From time to time during the process, you can look back and quantify the gains you've made, which will keep you motivated. The same is true for your chaos causer. It can be easy to feel like nothing is working, no change is happening, or you're taking one step forward and two steps backward. However, having a reference point can give you all the proof you need that things are actually changing. Good old Fact Finder Freddy can use this information to combat the Always and Never Beast.

FIND YOUR BASELINE

① GET CLEAR

② TRACK

M T W TH F SA SU

③ REVIEW

Get Clear

What does your chaos causer actually look and sound like? Remove any emotion or judgments and instead get clear on what is happening through the lens of a camera. What do you see, hear, or otherwise notice happening during your chaos causer? For example, if you chose meltdown as your chaos causer, what is happening during a meltdown? You might list things like hitting, yelling, running away, throwing items, etc. What you want to avoid is writing down items like disrespect, rudeness, or being mean, because these terms are impossible to track. We're looking for a very clearly defined behavior or action to track.

Track

Now that you're clear on what you're tracking, simply take note each time these actions happen. I like to look at an entire incident of a chaos causer, say a meltdown, versus looking at the pieces, say how many times a child hits in one meltdown. The goal is to get a baseline account for how often your chaos causer is happening in one week. If the chaos causer is also something that happens at school, you can ask the teachers and administration to let you know how often they're seeing it happen as well. I tend to focus on one location at a time, because the reason for a given incident can vary greatly, and I'm looking to manage the variables.

A word of caution: no one wants to feel like they're being judged or watched closely, so do this work discreetly without making a huge deal of it to your child. Please, for the love of everything human, don't shout out, "There's another fight with your brother, now that's ten times this week." This is counterproductive given the goal at this stage, which is to build trust and connection.

Review

After you've tracked for a week, you now have a baseline measurement. As you begin the work in this stage, the number might actually increase (this is totally normal, as you and your child are both learning new skills and building trust). It's also entirely possible (and likely) that you won't see much change at all in the beginning because the work you're doing is cumulative. After you create your Ahead-of-the-Moment plan and implement it a few times with your child, you can debrief and look at your baseline to determine what's working and what's not.

MULTITASKING IS A MYTH

As busy parents, we are inundated with more and more things we should do each day, leading us to believe the only way forward is to multitask to get it all done. However, just as we have covered in the Five-Minute Energy plan about prioritizing, science has shown us the importance of focusing on only one thing at a time. One study by psychologist Dr. David Meyer found that switching between tasks and focus actually costs time. In fact, shifting from one focus to another reduced productive time by as much as 40 percent. I don't know about you, but as a busy parent with a ton on my already full plate, I need as much time as I can get. Once I started to home in on just one challenge at a time, our entire family felt lighter and less stressed. Problems became far easier to solve.

CHAOS CAUSER IN ACTION

Kylie: Mom of Eight with Multiple Challenges

As a mom of eight, Kylie was utterly overwhelmed by the interrelated struggles, from her defiant seven-year-old to her anxious middle two kids to her non-verbal seventh child throwing himself to the floor and refusing school. How could she choose one and ignore the needs of all the others?

She was multitasking so much that she never breast-fed sitting down. Kylie realized that if she was going to get ahead of any struggles in her family, she would need to get a handle on her youngest's dangerous desire to get into everything. If Kylie took her eyes off the child for even a second, she would get into cabinets and the teenager's things, including razors and glue. As soon as Kylie chose this as her biggest chaos causer, the other children started to notice as well. The whole family banded together to solve the problem. Focusing on one struggle meant they didn't just find a temporary solution and move on.

ACTION STEP: CHOOSE YOUR NUMBER ONE CHAOS CAUSER

Your tiny next step is to find your number one chaos causer using the process outlined in this section.

1. List all the stressors currently adding chaos to your family.
2. Sort the stressors into three categories: dangerous, lowers quality of life, or annoying.
3. Choose your number one chaos causer and put the blinders on.
4. Find a baseline for how often your chaos causer is actually happening in a week.

CONNECT: MAGIC RESET BUTTON

Parents are always asking me about consequences, boundaries, and rules to help them get ahead of their chaos causers. Unfortunately, this is the wrong place to start, especially for our most challenging kids. After all, they spend much of their life getting into trouble, being yelled at, or told to stop whatever it is they're doing. And let's not talk about the number of furrowed eyebrows or crossed arms they encounter on a daily basis.

This leads children to believe "I'm bad," or worse, "I'm broken."

We can break this cycle, but not with more rules and boundaries that they're already struggling to follow. Instead, we can take it back to connection.

This does not mean:
- creating special one-on-one time
- praising the good and ignoring the bad
- rewarding the behavior you want to see more of and doling out consequences for the behaviors you want to see less of

Each of these tactics has some major flaws.
1. One-on-one connection time is only a sliver of the entire day. This can leave children feeling like they're worthy only of small bits of time with their parents.
2. Parents are left overwhelmed trying to fit in one-on-one time with every child, every day. On top of their already busy schedule, they feel guilty when they can't give undivided attention for fifteen to thirty minutes each day.

3. Some parents aren't natural players, meaning sitting and playing with their child or doing an activity of the child's choosing is actually a drain. And let's be honest, there's only so much Fortnite a parent can hear about.

4. When we praise the good and ignore the bad, we leave children assuming the other parts of them are somehow broken. In addition, children can feel drawn to hide or lie about the parts that don't get praise because they seek the approval of their parents.

5. Ignoring the behavior you don't like doesn't make it go away. The child isn't learning any new skills or ways to problem solve to avoid these challenges in the future. Not to mention, many children will only escalate their behaviors if they don't feel like the parent is listening to their challenges.

6. Rewarding positive behavior teaches compliance and leads children to seek external approval from others instead of being motivated internally by their own goals.

7. Punishments teach fear. A child doesn't learn alternative solutions, communication skills, self-regulation, or problem-solving by being grounded or losing their computer keyboard for the night.

Instead, it means creating small moments of true connection in between the storms through:
- validation
- acceptance
- communication

I've found that building positive interactions out of the storm is key for getting ahead of any chaos causer and building a solid relationship of compassion, empathy, and understanding. These are the tiny moments that happen as you walk past your child and lay your hand on their shoulder, text your teenager about a shared interest, or ask about a heated topic without judgment. Each of these tiny moments builds the necessary trust for your child to come to you when they're in trouble, accept help in the middle of a storm, and problem solve when things don't go their way.

Connection is such a pivotal piece of getting ahead of any chaos causer that it's the second step in your Ahead-of-the-Moment plan. It works so well that our families call this step "the magic reset button."

THE MAGIC RESET BUTTON

If you remember from the Behavior Funnel, connection and belonging is vital for successful relationships. There, you read about the magic five-to-one ratio, which points out that for every one negative interaction, you need five positives. This step is about building that reserve of positive interactions to offset the negative that will inevitably happen during a storm.

The shifting of this ratio is the reset your child needs, and the key to less chaos in your household.

The Silliest Request Ever

When I first discovered the magic reset button, it was simply a theory I had. At that time I couldn't drive to the grocery store without being called back home to deal with a massive explosion. And even when I was home, my husband and my son couldn't be left in the same room together alone, as they would set each other off like dynamite. Something had to change. I wondered what would happen and if it was possible to manufacture the five-to-one ratio between the two. I was homeschooling at the time, so I decided to make it a homeschool requirement for my son to find one positive interaction between him and his stepdad each day. And then here's where it got fun: I required my son to take this notebook to his stepdad and ask him what he noticed, as well.

Every day, each of them had to find one positive interaction the other person had. At first, they noticed things like my son opening the peanut butter jar for his sister, or Papa helping turn on the electronics. They were extremely tiny gestures. But it worked like magic. Soon my husband and son were talking about things other than the one positive interaction a day. They were working together with Lego and fixing computer parts. And best of all, when a storm came, my son accepted help from his stepdad, allowing my husband to create new memories of working with my son. Now, almost ten years later, my husband is actually the one who gets my son out of bed, turns off electronics, and holds space when he's struggling. My son ends every night with a side hug telling his stepdad, "I love you, Papa."

Two Types of Connection

There are many ways you can build this magic five-to-one ratio to reset your family's connection and get ahead of your biggest chaos causer. Over the last ten years, we've identified two distinct types of connection that rebuild trust and communication.

> **Planned Connection:** Dedicated time with each other.
> There is no denying that doing activities together builds a strong bond and connection. Setting aside time out of your busy schedule to build these memories can be vital when it comes to building your base level of trust and compassion as a family. These activities don't have to be every day, nor do they have to cost any money. It's simply about finding small moments to spend time together without the stressors of the day-to-day humdrum.
>
> **In-Between Connection:** The small interactions throughout the day.
> When we hear the word *connection*, we typically associate it with activities or time spent together. However, I would

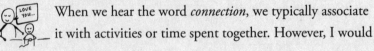

argue that most of the foundation of a relationship is built or broken in these in-between moments. The huffs and puffs when you enter your teen's bedroom to find they didn't pick up that water bottle after three days; the disappointment when a report card comes in with below-average grades; and the full name called when you've hit your limit. I always knew when my mom was angry when I heard "Dayna Carol," I didn't even have to see her face or be in the same room to read between the lines. If we can send so many signals when we're frustrated, what can be possible if we set an intention for how we respond, communicate, and interact on the fly?

Building a foundation of trust and empathy between two people is more than just spending time together. If that was all we needed, all families would be tight-knit and full of compassion and empathy after going through a global pandemic and lockdowns.

My goal is to show you how to build your days with both types of connection so you too can create this deep connection with your child, ultimately building a foundation a trust and compassion so both you and your child will be open to problem solving your biggest chaos causer. Let's take a look at some examples of both types of connection, so you can find what works best for your unique family and time constraints.

PLANNED MOMENTS	IN-BETWEEN MOMENTS
• movie night	• pat on the back in passing
• walks or hikes	• sitting beside them
• dance parties	• validating big emotions
• game night	• showing interest in their likes
• story time	• putting down phone
• zoo or museum trip	• texts throughout the day
• volunteering together	• helping them with a chore
• family vacations	• following a routine with them

Connection When You Have Zero Time

I can't tell you how often I hear parents ask me how to connect when they have one child who takes all the attention and they barely have a second to work or clean. They feel like they're constantly pouring into their child's connection bucket, but it's never enough. For this, I suggest both intentional connection or time beside each other.

Here are a few play-beside-me activities you can try if you aren't able to dedicate time away from the house or from your obligations. In fact, when I wrote this section, I had a child home from school who was getting connection time beside me quietly just by being in the same room.

- While you cook dinner, let your child pull up a stool and play on the counter next to you.
- If you need to work on the computer, have your child draw, paint, or create next to you.
- Move to the same room as your child and have them play on the floor while you fold laundry or do whatever you need to do.
- Let your child watch their favorite show with headphones on while you get in thirty minutes of work or attend an important meeting.
- If your child makes too much noise playing beside you, give yourself or them noise-reducing headphones so you can still work in the same room.

WHAT YOU FOCUS ON GROWS

By now, it's no secret that I am a huge fan of tracking and collecting information, especially when it comes to wins and progress. We have enough people and outside sources telling us all the things we are doing wrong; having a list of things going well is like a secret weapon on bad days where you start to believe the voices. The same is true when it comes to positive interactions.

The five-to-one ratio isn't meant to feel like another thing to keep track of, add to your list, or rearrange your entire day around in order to accomplish. It does not require you to keep track of positive interactions so closely that you keep five hair ties on your wrist so you can move them back and forth to track them. Instead, it's about looking for interactions throughout the day and realizing that there are some naturally occurring positives that are worth celebrating.

When it comes to building up connection moments ahead of your next storm, it's vital to notice these positive interactions. These moments start to become your new anchors for when you're in the heat of the moment and need something to remind you that your child isn't out to get you. And while these moments seem small and hardly noteworthy, I promise you they'll compound over time and have a huge effect on your mood, stress levels, and chaos causers.

There are many ways to track positive interactions, but the easiest way is probably to grab a blank notebook, or maybe one of those cute one-line-a-day journals from the local bookstore. Keep this as the place your family will document your positive interactions. The aim is to find one a day.

Our Calm the Chaos families once took up the challenge to tally all the small moments that happen in a day for one week. When they did this, together as a community we collected more than a hundred thousand tiny moments of positive interactions between family members. Before even getting to the problem-solving and skill-building part of the Ahead-of-the-Moment plan, chaos causers started to disappear.

Can you just imagine the ripple effect this would have on your community or even the world, if every human had just one positive interaction a day with each person in their life?

MAGIC RESET BUTTON IN ACTION

Rachel: Negative Nelly Stole Her Will to Connect

Rachel found parenting three neurodivergent children as an autistic woman extremely draining. She was constantly fighting thought monsters about her kids and their behaviors. Connection time and one-on-one time had become transactional, which meant that her kids were always left wanting more of her (which she didn't have left to give). However, when she started noticing small moments of connection and became intentional with her in-between moments, she started to swap her thoughts about her children and actually enjoy spending time with them. It worked so well to combat Negative Nelly that she has since used the magic reset button to get her spouse on the same page by noticing moments of appreciation and connection between him and the kids and to build connection between her ten-year-old and five-year-old who were struggling to get along due to social emotional delays of the younger sibling. Now, anytime something starts to feel off balance or stressful in her home, she takes it back to connection and finds proof of what's working versus what's not.

ACTION STEP: POSITIVE INTERACTIONS JOURNAL

Your tiny next step is simply to find a notebook or journal to keep track of your family's positive interactions. Starting today, notice at least one small moment of connection between you and your child or someone else in your family (partner or sibling). If you don't think your children will join in on the fun yet, I encourage you to do this by tracking on your own but still be intentional about creating these tiny moments each day. Later in this stage, I will share how to get your children on board with recognizing and creating small moments of positive interactions.

UNDERSTAND: UNRAVEL THE BEHAVIOR

"I hate you. You're the worst parent ever. Go away."

No parent ever dreams of hearing these words, yet they're far more common than we'd like to admit. One minute you're asking your sweet, loving eight-year-old to pick up the Lego bricks and get ready for bedtime, the next minute you're being screamed at. It stings. You want to lash out and say, "How dare you talk to me like that!" But you've been trying to do things differently since picking up this book, so you simply *breathe*, which doesn't lessen the sting, unfortunately. Before you can even muster a response, arms start flailing and toys start flying at your head. Your child is angry, and there's no backing out now.

At this point, the only thing you can do is ride out the storm with the plans you've already made in hand and wait for the screams to stop. But when the dust settles, how do you shake this awful feeling of disconnection between you and your child, the one who once would hop into your lap and give you nose kisses, telling you how you're the best parent in the world? Thought monsters start to fill your head:

Why is my kid so mean?
Where did I go so wrong?
Where in the world did this come from?

If you're like most parents, your answer to the last question might be, "It just came out of nowhere."

But I want to let you in on a secret:

There is always buildup, and it's our job as adults to get really good at detecting it long before the point of no return. There are always clues, and I'm going to show you how to find them.

While this can be extremely frustrating, I want to give you hope that it really is possible to see the storms approaching before they hit. In this step of your Ahead-of-the-Moment plan, you will use two tools to understand your biggest chaos causer and finally get ahead of the outbursts, tantrums, or meltdowns before they turn into hurricanes.

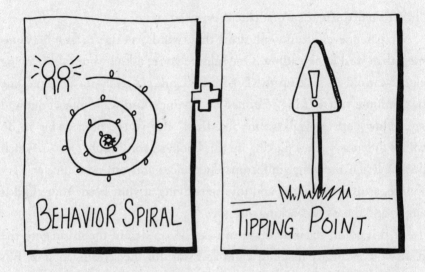

BEHAVIOR SPIRAL   TIPPING POINT

1. **Behavior Spiral:** A systematic tool for unraveling your family's most challenging situations to gain a deep understanding of where and how you can effect change in the future.

2. **Tipping Point:** Identifying the point of no return in any situation, where anything said or done will only make things worse. When you can pinpoint this moment on the behavior spiral, you will know when to implement your Ahead-of-the-Moment plan for maximum efficacy.

THE BEHAVIOR SPIRAL

Instead of jumping to conclusions, making assumptions, or problem solving in the moment, it's time to be a sleuth who can spot the warning signs long before things escalate, before you reach the point of no return.

Remember, the number one goal ahead of the moment is to build a solid foundation of trust and connection. Assumptions and jumping to conclusions only lead children to feel more unheard, misunderstood, and dismissed, no matter how hard you try to show them you're there for them.

When we looked at the iceberg theory (pages 67–69) and the behavior funnel (pages 155–56), we dispelled the myth that behavior is simply manipulative, mean-spirited, or just because a child does or doesn't want something.

In this section, I'm going to show you how you can unravel your child's biggest chaos causers without a PhD in child psychology or child development.

The ABCs of Behavior

As a teacher for more than twelve years, I was well versed in the most common method for understanding and addressing problem behaviors in the classroom: the ABCs of behavior. This method dates all the way back to the work of B. F. Skinner and is globally used by therapists, teachers, and behavior analysts to dig deeper into the underlying cause of behavior. There are three core parts to this method.

1. **The Antecedent:** What happens before
2. **The Behavior:** How the child responds (behaves)
3. **The Consequence:** What happens after (the positive or negative reinforcement)

In the classroom, I saw flaws in this methodology. I found myself looking deeper, beyond the expressed behavior in front of or behind a partic-

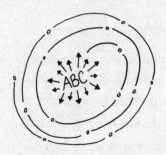

ular outburst, because I knew there had to be so much more at play besides the child's not wanting to do something.

I couldn't help but wonder what we're missing. What happens if we look at more than just the moment right before and after an incident? What if we could catch the buildup to the storm sooner, when we could actually affect the outcome before it's way too late?

The behavior spiral replaces looking at behavior in a vacuum with looking at the buildup to the tantrum, meltdown, or outburst. This gives parents and children so much more to work with when trying to create trust, problem solve out of the moment, and create plans that will work for everyone involved moving forward.

Let's take a look at how to use the behavior spiral with your biggest chaos causer.

Start with the End in Mind

Let's start in the middle of the incident.

Imagine your biggest chaos causer as the middle of the storm. (You've already done similar work in the last section.) Look at a specific incident, something that happened recently, like the last time your kids fought and ended with someone bleeding, or the last time your child screamed, "I hate you," and kicked the wall. Whatever the chaos causer, think of the last time the behavior happened.

Now, assuming you can report only what you see through a camera lens, what happened during the middle of that storm?

- What were they doing with their body?
- Was your child scowling, scrunching their shoulders, flinging their arms?
- Was your child storming off, staying in one area, refusing to leave?
- Was your child throwing items, hiding, or hitting?

- What were they saying?
- Was your child screaming, calling you names, using negative self-talk?
- Who was involved?
- Was it just your child, or was there another adult, a sibling, someone else?
- Where was your child?

You'll be using this information later when you have a conversation with your child and attempt to problem solve or build skills out of the moment. But for now, tuck it away. And note that your child is most likely not aware of what is happening to their body in the middle of the storm (often children even black out or say they can't remember the worst of the storm).

Spiral It Out

Next, backtrack and identify what incidents led up to the storm. Don't worry too much about getting all the details when you first start out, especially if the incident happened when you weren't in the room. The good news is the better you get at using this method, the easier it will be to put the details together from different sources (partners, siblings, friends, etc.).

Start by drawing a spiral like the one you see here and lay out the incidents that you can remember along the path. At first, you might only remember one or two parts of the spiral, and this is okay, as well. Start with the details you remember or already know.

What happened right before the center of the spiral? At this point, it's also important to write down what was said or done by the others involved. For example, did you tell your child to stop? Did a sibling take a toy? Did your child run away? Think of as many details as you can, working backward to when things appeared to be calm.

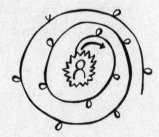

Most parents start their spiral where they got a negative reaction. For example, "I took my child's keyboard, then he yelled at me to give it back." They insert everything that happened after they took the keyboard leading up to the hole in the wall. However, they often resist going even further back: What happened before the keyboard was taken? And what happened before that? What other players were involved? What actions or statements may have affected their child leading up to the negative reaction?

To dramatize what I mean, one Calm the Chaos mother was at a loss because her son got sent home from school for hitting another child. The natural focus was on why her child hit another student. When I walked through the spiral with her, we saw so much more leading up to the punch:

- Her son didn't want to go to school
- He'd told Mom, "I'm nervous about the big storm today"
- Another teacher kept him in a small class to help him calm down
- Taught him how to make his first paper airplane ever
- Child appeared calm
- Integrated into the full classroom
- Another student made fun of the airplane
- Child threw the airplane at the other student
- The other student refused to give the airplane back
- The teacher asked the child to put away the airplane
- The child threw the airplane
- It hit the other student
- The teacher assistant removed the child from the class
- The other student laughed
- On the way out of class, the child punched the other student

Can you see the buildup? There was so much under the surface. By the time the assistant removed the child from the classroom, it was too late, the child was boiling, ready to explode.

⚠ NO EXCUSES NECESSARY

I want to be very clear: this isn't about excusing behavior, it's about understanding behavior so we can help everyone involved create a better solution in the future. The behavior spiral is a tool to help identify the buildup to challenging behaviors and pinpoint the triggers and point of no return (tipping point). This allows us, the adults, to foster and guide the children we love to self-awareness, compassion, problem-solving, and skill building with an Ahead-of-the-Moment plan before the tipping point.

Find the Tipping Point

 The tipping point, aka the point of no return, is that moment in the spiral when no amount of talking, problem-solving, threatening, or cajoling will stop the outburst. Any attempts to stop the behavior from happening after this point simply make things worse and add fuel to the brewing fire.

Being able to identify this moment on a behavior spiral is a complete game changer. That's the moment when your Ahead-of-the-Moment plan can have the most effectiveness. This tipping point is rife with clues that tell a parent they should move to using their Ride the Storm plan or In-the-Moment plan.

The work of identifying the tipping point is done out of the moment, when you're calmly reflecting on the last incident or outburst. Start with your spiral and then zoom out looking for where things started to go off the rails.

It's common for parents to choose the behavior as the tipping point. For example, when your child starts to kick and scratch, when they refuse to come down for breakfast, or they won't put their socks on for school. However, at this point it's already too late.

Instead, find a spot higher on the spiral when your child is still responsive to feedback, during a lull or quiet time before they've engaged with something that will cause them frustration if interrupted, or right before they get physical. You'll be making an educated guess the first time you choose this moment. It simply gives you a starting point from which to experiment, create an Ahead-of-the-Moment plan for, and then tweak after you implement.

Let's look at another spiral I did recently with a parent struggling with morning and bedtime routines with her five-year-old. According to her spiral, their mornings went like this:

Get out of bed

Go to the bathroom

Brush teeth

Get dressed

Refusal to go downstairs for breakfast

Based on this spiral, the mom was struggling to see a tipping point, which is incredibly common because our minds like to think in generalizations, omissions, and absolutes. This mom was only seeing general big-picture steps in the plan, but if we break down the morning even further there are missing details. A few questions I always ask when helping parents detail their spiral more include:

- What happened between points A and B?
- What did you say after step three?
- What did it look like between this and that?
- You say that he (insert behavior); what was happening right before that? What did you say or do?

When I asked these questions about the morning routine, the mom revealed that after getting dressed, her son picked up a toy and started playing. No matter what she said after this point, he was lost and stuck. He refused to go downstairs, and it became a game of tug-of-war.

This moment between brushing teeth and refusing to go downstairs is the tipping point; the moment where her son grabbed a toy. Imagine how much smoother this could be if they had a plan for what to do when he wants to play with a toy? What if he could take the toy with him to breakfast? How would this one small tweak ripple through the morning?

Now the mom has options. This lull in the morning was the breeding ground for chaos and the tipping point she could use as a starting point for the Ahead-of-the-Moment plan she creates with her son.

What Now?

You might be wondering:

- What do I do once I find the tipping point?
- How do I avoid passing the point of no return?
- What do I do in the heat of the moment when I notice we are at the tipping point?

Again, you've already done this work, for the most part. In the heat of the moment, when you notice the tipping point, you will implement your Ahead-of-the-Moment plan we're building in this stage. And if you pass the point of no return, no worries. Simply revert to your In-the-Moment or Ride the Storm plan.

After the dust settles, do another spiral and tweak your Ahead-of-the-Moment plan to move it earlier. For example, if you thought you could wait until your child started grunting to implement the plan but things only got worse when you tried to get your child to move to their calm space, try getting them to move to their calm space earlier (like when they first tell you they're tired and can't get dressed).

In the next section, we will talk about how to involve your kids in this process and get them to use the plan you both create. For now, I want you just to focus on finding the details in the spiral, the center, and the point of no return.

With each Ahead-of-the-Moment plan, tweak, and iteration, you will be able to move the tipping point further and further away from the middle of the storm, allowing you to intervene much earlier. In fact, the more you do these spirals, the more you'll start to notice patterns that emerge. For instance:

- When your child has a plan in their head but doesn't tell anyone
- Loud noises and environmental overload
- New people or changes in plans
- Feelings of being unheard or misunderstood
- Being made fun of or left out (or a fear of being left out)
- A groggy voice or furrowed eyebrow
- Hyperactivity just before getting incredibly rigid
- Anxiety or fear over something that is happening later in the day
- School ending or starting

In conjunction with the behavior funnel (pages 155–56), you can start to identify and help your child become more self-aware of their own triggers and warning signs—because remember, they aren't usually aware of these things. Don't expect to become a master at this overnight, or for your child to magically recognize and regulate a future storm because you had one conversation. While this is work that happens over time, it's well worth the practice. Not only will your child be able to calm down faster and easier in the future, they will also have the skills to articulate what sets them off and what they need to be successful. Every single time you trust the process, you build their trust in you.

🧠 THE BRAIN'S WARNING SIGNS

If you've ever blown a gasket and completely lost your shit on someone, I bet I don't have to explain the science behind why this method works for getting to the root of a challenge with your child or finding warning signs.

If you were to use a spiral, anyone could easily tell that your fit wasn't actually because of spilled milk on the floor at bedtime.

I would guess that if the only thing that had happened today was that your kids spilled milk, you wouldn't actually have yelled. Instead, your brain and body have been storing pent-up energy and frustration all day, with each moment on the spiral adding more fuel to the fire, until finally you couldn't take it any longer.

The same is true with your kids' behavior.

I want to remind you of the automatic stress responses we talked about early on in the book (fight, flight, freeze, fawn). These responses are the brain's natural way of dealing with and mitigating a perceived threat.

By spiraling out incidents and outbursts after they happen, you can start to identify patterns and triggers (what sets off the stress response) before they build up to an epic explosion.

As you look back at the spiral, what warning signs do you spot? Be on the lookout for two types of triggers:

Lava triggers: things that both build up over time with multiple exposures or when combined with other stressors (such as being touched out, changes in plans, making mistakes, being told no)

Snap triggers: things that immediately send you or your child into fight or flight (such as a sudden loud noise, being hurt, a smell or sensation from a memory)

As you notice and recognize the warning signs (both slowly simmering lava triggers and instantaneous snap triggers), you will become more compassionate, empathetic, and understanding of yourself and your child. This will only further deepen your foundation of trust and connection needed to get ahead of your biggest chaos causer.

As a bonus, as you start to identify these triggers and tipping points, you can share them with your children out of the moment. This is the empowering part of the framework, when you help your child gain language to explain their frustrations and buildup before they reach their own point of no return (more on how to do this in the next section).

BEHAVIOR SPIRAL IN ACTION

Maritza: Trouble in School

Maritza was getting called three times a week, leading to at least one suspension a week. Her son was on the verge of being expelled. Whenever Maritza saw the school's phone number on caller ID, she picked up her keys and answered with, "I'm on my way." Maritza realized she was getting called at the same time of day to pick up Albert, which led her to ask her son what they were doing in class before he went to the office. The class was doing writing. Just talking about writing with Mom got him all worked up. Turns out the spiral looked something like this:

1. It's writing time.
2. Albert would say it was boring.
3. He would refuse to do his work.
4. The teacher would threaten the office as punishment.
5. Albert got out of his seat and touched other kids.
6. The teacher threatened to send him to the office: "You're going to get in trouble if you don't sit down."
7. Albert would walk aimlessly around the room.
8. The teacher started following him: "Sit down."

9. Albert would knock off the markers on the white board as he passed.
10. The teacher said, "That's it. Time for you go to the office."
11. Albert would throw anything near him at the teacher and try to run away.
12. The teacher would call security.
13. Security grabbed Albert.
14. Albert would hit security.
15. Maritza would get called.

Once Maritza saw this spiral out time and again, she took what she found to the teacher and principal. Everyone agreed to get Albert help with his writing and stop threatening discipline as a means of controlling him. This discovery allowed Albert to thrive in school, helped the teachers to feel successful, and, best of all, ended the troubling calls. In fact, there wasn't even one call home or bad report for more than five straight months.

ACTION STEP: SPIRAL OUT BEHAVIOR

Your simple next step is to create your first behavior spiral using your chosen chaos causer, and to think about where the tipping point for incidents like that might be. Choose an incident that recently happened involving your child and the challenge you're focused on. It's important to do this during your downtime before the next storm arrives so you can have time and energy to get ahead of the struggles and involve your children.

Step One: The Center
What did the outburst, argument, fight, or meltdown look like in the heat of the moment? This is your center of the spiral. Remember, at this point it's best to look at everything through a camera lens and be as specific as possible, instead of "he was mean." Use language such as "he kicked the wall."

Step Two: Spiral It Out
Draw a spiral on your paper and work backward to note the buildup to the center.

I've included a spiral template you can download for free if you go to www.calmthechaosbook.com/spiral. It isn't imperative to get every single detail, but be sure to include actions and reactions from everyone who was involved, even if it was nonverbal body language.

Step Three: Find the Tipping Point
Take a look at your entire spiral from start to finish and see if you can find a moment where you could have intervened or done something different to affect the outcome of the incident. Again, there is no need to get this part perfect; it's simply a starting point that you will use as you work with your child to create a plan for how to handle things differently in the future.

EMPOWER: HUDDLE, HUDDLE, HUDDLE

Most parents try to get ahead of challenges in their family using one of the following methods:

- Setting new rules and consequences for breaking them
- Praising the good things happening (but ignoring the challenges)
- Lecturing about what is appropriate or not
- Getting clear on expectations
- Forcing children to apologize and make up

In all approaches, the parent is the number one speaker, and children are to "learn the lesson" needed so it doesn't happen again. However, if the main goal ahead of the moment is to create trust and connection between you and your children, then lectures, sit-down meetings, and unilateral decisions handed down from on high anytime trouble brews won't serve that end.

What I'm about to suggest is probably the most radical thing I've suggested so far in the book. Are you ready?

Instead of creating the solutions for your children or imposing new rules and regulations, I want you to have a meaningful two-way conversation with your children. Think of these as family meetings that actually work to build trust and solve issues.

I know, I know. This is unheard of. It means that you have to trust that your children actually have something valuable to bring to the table, that they have ideas to solve the problem you might not have thought of, and, get this, they might even teach you something.

That's what becomes possible with the next step in your Ahead-of-the-Moment plan: family huddles.

WHAT IS A HUDDLE?

A huddle typically has a few key components:

- **A facilitator or leader.** This is typically the parent, but it can also be a child once they're experienced in huddling as a way of communication and problem-solving.
- **The heard and valued voices of all involved.** These don't have be spoken-word voices if you have a nonspeaking child or a toddler with minimal words.
- **A central problem or focus.** Instead of trying to solve everything at one time, keeping the conversation centered around one key goal can help everyone stay on the same page.
- **An open and inviting conversation.** The conversation is not heated with emotion, full of judgment, or decided upon before it begins. Everyone's ideas are welcome.

The goal is for huddles to become the way your family communicates and solves problems together.

Getting Started

Unlike the typical family meetings where kids receive parental lectures, huddles can be informal and short. They can be configured differently depending on who's involved. Since this is a collaborative approach, huddles are most effective when you can have buy-in and willing participation from other members of the family. For now, you only need to involve the people who are affected by your number one chaos causer.

The Basic Structure of a Huddle

While huddles can take on many forms, it's a good idea to have the basic structure of a huddle in mind when you head into it. In fact, it's the same structure I used in the classroom so everyone got a chance to voice their concerns, while staying focused on a topic.

The step-by-step approach goes like this:

- **Celebrate:** Start every conversation with wins and celebrations. This can be a personal acknowledgment of something that you're excited about, proud of, or want to share with others. These can be silly and fun and are often the basis of most early huddles.

- **Identify focus:** Each huddle typically has one main topic of discussion. This can be a problem (sibling fighting), a future event to plan for (Grandma coming to visit), or simply something fun to brainstorm ideas around (games we can play together as a family).

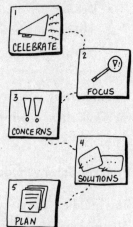

- **Concerns:** Leave room in every huddle to address concerns, worries, fears, or frustrations. Here, each participant has a chance to have their opinions heard in a safe environment. Even when you're doing a light and fun huddle, you can practice bringing up concerns (like, "What if we all get bellyaches from too much ice cream?").

- **Solutions:** This is a space for each person to share an idea or solution they have, no matter how out of this world it is. This gives children a safe place to play with and share ideas in a nonthreatening way. There are no bad ideas during a huddle.

- **The new plan:** Finally, huddles end with a new plan of action or plan for next time. Often, in huddles you're creating the same types of plans that you're working on in this book: In-the-Moment, Ahead-of-the-Moment, and, eventually, Family Success. Sometimes the plan becomes a list, a visual, an agreement, a new routine, or a schedule.

Four Types of Huddles

Now that you have a basic understanding of how to introduce a huddle and the structure, I hope you're starting to feel a little more comfortable with the idea of having your very first huddle. To help you feel even more comfortable, let's take a look at some huddles and the best use for each type.

- **Problem-solving:** Creating a plan as a family to solve a problem together
- **Brainstorming:** List building or idea creation, typically about ideas for play, chores, outings, etc.
- **Skill building:** Focused modeling and conversations that teach vital skills
- **Debrief:** Retroactive huddle to review a meltdown, tantrum, or outburst and how a plan worked, what to adjust, and how to move forward with a new plan

I'm betting you have questions about structure in each of these, so let me break them down further.

Problem-Solving Huddle

This huddle is the go-to style for getting ahead of your biggest chaos causer. All problem-solving huddles start with connection and compassion. Going back to our structure, start by celebrating wins before you bring up any challenge or problem to solve. (Remember, if your child is dysregulated, this is not the time to conduct a huddle.)

It can feel uncomfortable to bring up a hard topic or a past struggle, especially if you're worried it will set your child off again. A good way to offset this is to introduce the idea that you'd like to talk later, so they have time to gather their thoughts and ideas. Here are a few ideas for getting the conversation started:

- Are you ready to talk about earlier yet?
- I've noticed you've been struggling to . . .
- I'm wondering how we can solve . . .
- This worries me because . . .
- When this happens, it has this effect . . .

It's important that everyone gets a chance to share their ideas on how to solve the problem. When you first start this style of problem-solving, it's not unheard of for children to suggest old ways of handling behavior: time-outs, taking things away, grounding, spanking, etc. They're simply using the scripts they've been programmed to use. That's why these conversations are so important at any age.

After each person's concerns have been heard and ideas have been shared and processed, it's time to create a plan for the next time this problem arises. A simple plan for next time can be:

When X happens (I get angry), I will do Y (go to my safe place).

When X happens (Mom notices my face scrunch), she will do Y
     (pause and remind me of my safe place).

Brainstorming Huddle

This is one of my favorite types of huddles. It's an easy way to ease the family into having discussions about a common topic and a great place for you to model turn taking, listening to other people's ideas, and working together as a family. I always suggest these types of huddles to families that are struggling to connect, get siblings to get along, or get a kid to buy in to the process. Kids have been so used to "getting in trouble" that these types of huddles build trust and a foundation of belonging. This type of huddle simply comes up with ideas for a common interest.

Some fun topics to brainstorm together as a family:

- Games to play on game night
- Outings we like to do together
- Lunch box items we can pack independently
- Ways to help out around the house
- Where to go on family vacation
- Volunteer or random acts of kindness ideas

Skill-Building Huddles

Often these huddles happen after a problem-solving huddle or a brainstorming huddle as a way to build skills around a particular issue or concern. For example, if you're working on morning routines but a child lacks organizational skills to plan their morning, you might work on a skill that helps them get through the morning with ease. Or perhaps you'd like to help your child learn and practice skills needed to self-regulate and calm in the middle of an outburst.

These huddles are a great place for connection, games, role playing, and modeling by the adults. Children learn through stories, active play, interactive games, and scenarios. Skill-building huddles should be fun, light, and easy. If it becomes a stressor, it's time to take a break. If coming up with activities to teach skills isn't your thing, my book *Superkids Activity Guide* has more than seventy-five unique skill-building activities that are fun and easy to do with kids, each designed to help you and your child navigate challenging times of the day.

Common skills to teach in skill-building huddles:

- Breathing techniques
- How to ask for help
- How to communicate when things make you angry
- Calming exercises
- What to say or do when X happens
- Initiating play or conversations

Debrief Huddle

In each of the plans, we've talked about the importance of debriefing after a storm or an argument. This huddle is perfect for conducting that debrief with your children and eventually others involved, such as a teacher. In this type of huddle, you're reviewing what already happened and how things could be tweaked in the future. For instance, if you were debriefing the problem getting to the breakfast table with your child, you would have reviewed each of the data points you listed and elicited their feedback.

Some things to look for in a debrief huddle:

- What is working really well in the plan?
- Was the tipping point earlier or later than expected?
- Did everyone have the right supports in place?
- Did the In-the-Moment plan work to defuse the situation?
- Is there new information now that you didn't have before?
- Do you notice any triggers you didn't notice before?

Introduce the Idea

One of the hardest parts of running huddles in your family is simply starting them. Anytime we want to try something new and unfamiliar, our mind tries to trick us into believing it won't work or it will end badly. Don't worry, this is just your mind trying to protect you from the unknown.

A few simple ways to introduce huddles to your family could sound a little like this:

- "I learned this new activity for families. Want to give it a try?"
- "So, I've been thinking, I want to include you more in decisions we make around the house. I've got an idea."

Here are some simple tips on how to run huddles for the first time from our Calm the Chaos families:

- Keep it relaxed, positive, and fun
- Think short and sweet when you first start
- Include nonspeaking children and keep them engaged
- Begin with wins and celebrations in a fun way before solving problems
- Allow children to pass if they don't want to talk
- Try huddling over dinner
- Be willing to ditch the name "huddle" for teens that might think it's a silly name
- Start with a fun problem to solve: "What kind of ice cream should we have?"

🧠 HOW DARE YOU TALK BACK TO ME

I get my fair share of parents who come into my programs worried about their child's back talk and disrespect. Most of these parents grew up being taught that children are to do as they're told and be seen and not heard. Yet as adults, many of these parents (especially women) find that they struggle to speak up for their own needs and wants, advocate when things aren't how they want them to be, and find themselves constantly people pleasing. It takes some time for them to see back talk as a way to advocate for themselves instead of a mark of disrespect. No parent wants their child to fall into the same trap they're stuck in.

Speaking up, asking questions, sharing concerns, or arguing a point don't come naturally. In fact, I know a lot of adults who could stand some skill-building huddles on having productive and compassionate conversations. We have to teach children the art of listening to other people's concerns, sharing their own thoughts and ideas with compassion, and remaining open to ideas and solutions they don't agree with.

Dr. Ross Greene, bestselling author of *The Explosive Child*, has been doing this work for decades with some of the most challenging children. Numerous studies have been conducted on the effect of collaborating and involving children in the problem-solving process versus using a unilateral approach to behavior in which parents dole out solutions and punishments they deem appropriate. Involving children collaboratively in the problem-solving process reduces aggression, improves parent-child relationships, and increases academic behavior and social skills in children ages four to eleven.

HUDDLES IN ACTION

Danielle: Teenager Using Drugs, Failing School, and Addicted to Electronics

No matter what punishment Danielle tried, nothing worked for her teenager. She couldn't find anything that he cared enough about to matter, even when she took away the one thing he loved: electronics. The problem was her son was clever enough to comply until the punishment was lifted and then go right back to doing the thing that landed him in trouble. Everything she was trying was just pushing her son further away, and since he was already sixteen, she felt like time was running out. She introduced huddles (but called them something else that didn't sound childish to her teen). They talked about what made the class and teacher hard for him. He revealed that the noise of the ceiling fans, other kids scraping their chairs, and how the teacher yelled when something wasn't to her liking caused him to be on edge and made it hard to focus. This was compounded by the isolation resulting from removing lunch time with peers. When the teacher grabbed his backpack from his lap, he was even more triggered. Knowing these details made it easier for both of them to problem solve and create a plan with the school. And while this wasn't the only huddle they had, it was the start of what would become their new way of solving problems and rebuilding connection.

ACTION STEP: PLAN YOUR FIRST HUDDLE

Your simple next step is to identify which huddle you want to try first. If this is your first time doing a huddle, I recommend introducing the idea first and then starting with a celebration huddle in which the whole family simply shares wins from their day. All you have to do is decide when and where you'll have your first huddle, and then have fun. However, if you're ready to brave a full huddle, here are a few questions to think through before you jump in.

1. What topic do you want to address?
2. What time and place will be best to do your huddle?
3. Who will need to be involved in your huddle?
4. What are some wins you can bring to the table?
5. Why is this topic important?
6. What concerns do you have already?
7. What possible solutions can you suggest?
8. What will you do to get your child in the right mindset for a huddle?

PUTTING IT ALL TOGETHER: YOUR AHEAD-OF-THE-MOMENT PLAN

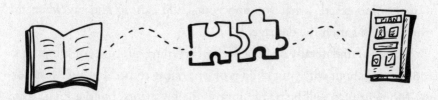

The fact that you've made it this far is a testament to what an amazing parent you are. Sure, there are still things you'd like to do better, get ahead of, or tackle as a family, but you're doing the work to get there.

By continuing to move forward, you've learned how to:

- Focus on the most important thing for you and your family
- Build a solid foundation of trust, acceptance, and connection with each member of your family
- Spiral out challenging events, so you can gain more clarity, remove assumptions, and discern the needs of each member of your unique family

Seriously, this is the hard stuff. You're breaking generational cycles, shifting huge paradigms, and choosing a new way forward with your family that takes each person's needs and desires into account. This is world-changing work you're doing.

I know you might not feel like it right now, but trust me, the sky's the limit.

In this section, we're going to build out your Ahead-of-the-Moment plan using all of this awesome momentum you've built.

Keep going, friend. The plan we're about to put together is one of many that will move you closer to raising children who are seen, heard, and valued for who they are.

📝 THE PLAN

The Ahead-of-the-Moment plan is created before you actually need it. The goal is not only to recognize the warning signs of an impending storm but to determine exactly what you and your child can do and say when the storm hits to soften the damage.

Instead of unilaterally making decisions, doling out rules, or jumping to conclusions about why your child is or isn't doing something, an Ahead-of-the-Moment plan will help you unravel the behaviors, build a foundation of trust and acceptance, and teach your child life-changing skills.

As with everything we do around here, the focus is on progress not perfection. Don't attempt to get the perfect plan on the first go. Instead, realize that you're building habits and skills of communication, problem-solving, and trust over time with every iteration of your Ahead-of-the-Moment plans.

I've already introduced you to the key elements you need to create an Ahead-of-the-Moment plan. Let's review:

1. **You: Choose Your Biggest Chaos Causer:** Trying to solve everything all the time is not only exhausting, it also doesn't work. You end up solving nothing at all. That's why it's absolutely mandatory to focus on your number one chaos causer. It doesn't mean that you will allow or ignore everything else going on in your family. Instead, it gives you intense focus. Most of your attention can be given to the challenge that is wreaking the most havoc on your family right now. By identifying your primary chaos causer, you can rest easy knowing that you're doing the absolute best you can with the energy you have.

2. **Connect: Magic Reset Button:** By building up the positive-to-negative ratio and taking it back to connection out of the messy moments, you allow your child to see that you aren't simply there to nag, criticize, or judge their actions. They'll begin to trust that you

truly do have their best interest at heart. This base level of connection makes it easier to have conversations, unravel challenging situations, and find a solution that works for everyone and their unique needs.

3. **Understand: Unravel the Behavior:** The behavior spiral allows you to unravel your child's most challenging moments to find the buildup as the storm brews. Using the behavior spiral, you can find the tipping point (or point of no return) where surviving the storm is the only option. Not only will you be able to start to understand your unique child and their needs, you will also start to see the cause and effect of your reactions and other factors that you might have missed before.

4. **Empower: Huddle, Huddle, Huddle:** Finally, getting your kids on board and helping them create change doesn't happen with a top-down approach. Instead, you need a process for open and collaborative communication that results in skill building, more connection, and, ultimately, change. Huddles give you and your family a framework for hard conversations so you can build the problem-solving muscles needed for lifelong success.

You can have the best strategies, planning, and coaching in the world, but when it comes down to it, if you and your child don't feel a deep level of connection and trust, it will be impossible to make progress. Remember, when we talk about connection, I'm not talking about more time spent together. Instead, I am referring to the quality of interactions, the signals you're sending, and the energy exchanged between you and your child.

PUTTING THE PIECES TOGETHER

Now that we've reviewed the elements you need to create your Ahead-of-the-Moment plan, let's put the pieces together so you can make a plan that works to get ahead of your child's tantrums, lying, stealing, or whatever chaos causer is plaguing your family.

In order to get ahead of even the most challenging behaviors, you must first:

1. Gather

The good news is you've been doing this the entire chapter. You've been gathering information to help you gain clarity and insight into your family's biggest challenges so you can not only get ahead of your biggest chaos causers but help your child when they're struggling the most. It's important to gather everything you've dug up under the surface and any clarity you've gained in one place before you try to huddle with your kiddo. Just a reminder of the steps to gathering and understanding the problem in front of you:

- Choose your focus using the DQA method to find your family's biggest chaos causer (page 199)
- Spiral out the last incident using the behavior spiral and find the tipping point (point of no return)
- Identify early warning signs using the Behavior Spiral, so you can be prepared and see the storms coming a mile away
- **Bonus:** Dig beneath the surface using the behavior funnel (page 155)

2. Connect

Building trust and rapport is key to getting a child to work with you and problem solve. Remember, this is done through both planned connection and in-between connection (page 208). I would argue that the connection made between moments is the most important at this stage for letting your child see you're on their team.

Even if your kid tells you no, go away, or I don't want to talk when you try to huddle, you can still build trust and connection. Join them in play, while they're watching their favorite show, or while they're between activities just to show you care.

Some simple reminders for strengthening the connection:

- Limit the nagging
- Pay attention to your body language
- Talk about nonconfrontational and lighthearted topics
- Show interest in their activities
- Ask open-ended questions about their day
- Celebrate the small stuff

3. Plan

In order to truly get ahead of your chaos causer, you'll need to break the barrier and talk with your child in a huddle. Instead of showing your child or telling your child the new way of doing things, I encourage you to ask questions, listen more than you talk, and be willing to make a plan you already assume is going to fail. Allowing your child to make mistakes is part of the learning process and gives you something to come back to afterward to adjust and work through together.

You can use any of the huddle types ahead of the moment to create a plan with your child. Before you need to solve for a serious problem, I encourage you to use a brainstorming huddle (page 231) and allow your child to do most of the planning and solutions when you first start. This helps your child see you mean it when you tell them you want them to have a say in how to solve problems as a family, and that you want to listen to their needs more intently.

Once you've huddled with your child, it's time to create a plan that both you and your child can agree on. The plan is simply what each of you will do at the tipping point to attempt to head off any big storms or blowups.

The easiest way to make this plan is to think of three things:

1. **When to use the plan:** Together identify when each of you will know it's time to use the plan. This could be when you pick them up from school, when they feel their body getting tense, or when you notice their voice getting louder. Use your tipping point and spiral to help you identify this moment together.

2. **What you will do:** Consider planning your own 1:1:1 (page 172) for what you will say, do, and provide when you notice the warning signs, so your child is prepared and in agreement with how you plan to help.

3. **What they will do:** Create a 1:1:1 plan with your child for what they can say, do, and provide themselves when the spiral is ramping up.

4. Practice

Finally, as with all your plans, you want to practice and play with the plan as much as you can before you actually need it. This makes it easy to remember in the moment and natural to follow. This might also require skill-building huddles (page 232) to help your child learn the new skills needed for their 1:1:1 plan.

Note: Make it fun and playful to practice these skills and run through these plans. Children learn through stories, concrete examples, and modeling. This is simply another way to build connection and trust with your child.

DURING: READY, SET, ACTION!

This is it, the moment you've been waiting for: getting ahead of your biggest chaos causer. When the moment comes, it's time to put everything you've worked so hard for into action. This is usually early in the spiral or around the tipping point. When you first start out, don't be too alarmed if you find yourself attempting your Ahead-of-the-Moment plan a little too close to the center of the spiral. As you implement and become more proactive, you'll get better at moving out your tipping point and jumping into action sooner rather than later. The best part is that as your child has practice with these plans, they will start to use the Ahead-of-the-Moment plans without you and your guidance.

There are three key parts to your Ahead-of-the-Moment plan in action:

1. Recognize

It's important to recognize and notice exactly when the spiral is starting. Notice what this looks like and sounds like. How will you know that the Ahead-of-the-Moment plan is needed? It could be a time of day, an activity that is stressful, or simply a behavior you notice as a precursor to a big storm. As soon as you recognize this signal, it's time to jump into action.

2. Jump into Action

At the tipping point, what will you say, do, and provide to support and coach your child? This is your time to remember your Stop, Breathe, Anchor (pages 52–53) so you remain the calm in the storm even when things are starting to ramp up. Have you planned to move closer and lower? Do you have a phrase you and your child practiced? Will you grab or bring a tool (like food or water, a sensory item, calming resource, etc.) for your child? This is the time to take your steps to help your child.

This is also when your child will attempt their own say, do, provide plan that you've agreed on beforehand.

3. Be Prepared for the Worst

Just as it takes time for you to form new habits, the same is true for your child. Remember, their brain is still developing, so it might take more time than you imagine. Don't assume just because you made a plan for ahead of the moment that your child will magically follow through the first time. If you notice that things aren't working, remain calm using your strategies, and simply revert to one of the following plans:

- **In-the-Moment plan:** the plan you made to move closer and lower and defuse the situation
- **Ride the Storm plan:** the plan you created early on to simply remain the calm in the storm and get everyone to safety

Having a backup (or a few backups) will help you and your child stay connected through the entire ordeal. This is not the time for ultimatums, bribes, or power struggles. Simply get through the moment, and afterward you can address where things went off track.

AFTER: CELEBRATE AND RECALIBRATE

Now that you've made it through a spiral with your plans in your hand, you can see what works and what doesn't. As with every plan, repair work and debriefing is needed. Before you jump into any tweaking or problem-solving, however, take a breather and let the dust settle. Then start with connection and celebration. Nix the nagging, reprimanding, and "I told you so," no matter how much you want to. Right after an incident, feelings are as raw as an open wound. Be cautious with your and your child's emotions.

Reconnect through activities and interactions that have nothing to do with the chaos causer.

When everyone has come back to a safe and connected place, you can huddle over what happened.

Celebrate what worked.

This is also a great time for brainstorming, skill-building, or problem-solving huddles. When tweaking the plan, I encourage you only to tweak one small part, be it the tipping point, what you say, what they do, what tool is used, or something else. Don't attempt to change everything at once.

Remember: 1 percent change is all you're aiming for.

And, as always,

STAGE FIVE:
BUILDING A
STORM-PROOF
INFRASTRUCTURE

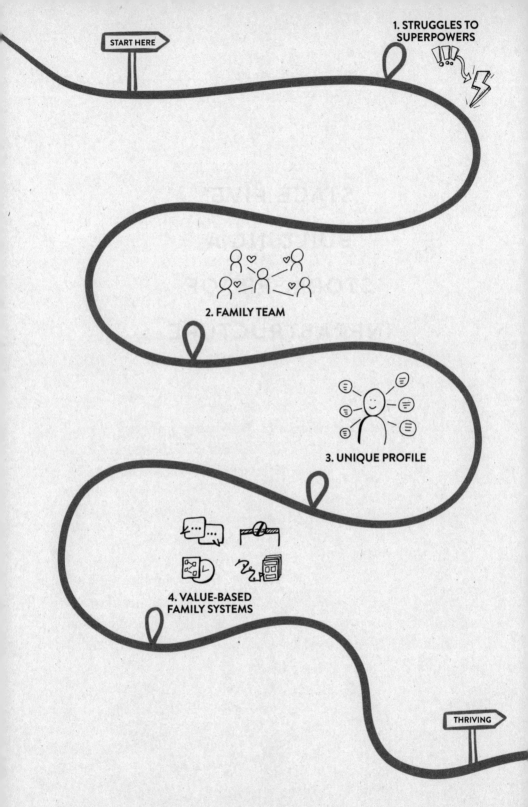

START HERE

1. STRUGGLES TO SUPERPOWERS

2. FAMILY TEAM

3. UNIQUE PROFILE

4. VALUE-BASED FAMILY SYSTEMS

THRIVING

⚑ YOUR CHALLENGE: MINIMIZE FUTURE CHAOS

"Mommy, I don't want my brother at my birthday party." The words of my five-year-old stung. After all the work I'd done over the last few years, my kids still didn't want to be around each other. Fighting back tears and frustration, I took a deep breath and simply said one word: "Why?" What came next made my jaw drop.

"Because my brother doesn't like loud noises and gets overwhelmed with a lot of people. I want him to be happy at my party too." What I assumed was a disconnect was an acute awareness of her brother's needs.

After a little back and forth, we landed on a plan that worked for everyone, including her brother. My daughter offered to have her party at 8 a.m. so we could be in the pizza place and arcade without all the lights, people, and music. We were able to celebrate without fear of it ending with tears.

I won't pretend to be perfect by any means, and thundershowers still roll in from time to time, but now my entire family works together as a team to prevent storms from taking over. We go on fun trips together. My kids enjoy each other (which I never thought possible). I have time to do things for myself (like write this book and watercolor for fun). We're all thriving as a family.

Our Family Success plan has helped us handle difficult transitions as a family, such as a cross-country move, starting new schools, getting through a global pandemic, and dealing with tough teenage topics such as death, sex, and depression. In fact, this is the same plan thousands of parents around the world have used to create the family they've always wanted.

Instead of a one-size-fits-all-approach to parenting, we need to think creatively and see each member of our family as a unique member of the team, working together to meet each person's individual needs.

This plan is not a bid for fairness in which each child:

- Gets the same amount of connection, time, and attention
- Helps around the house and pitches in the same amount
- Satisfies the same expectations and rules
- Receives no special treatment or exceptions in the name of keeping the peace
- Follows the same bedtime or electronics plan, despite different ages or interests
- Receives the exact same number of presents during holidays, so no one feels left out
- Keeps the same set routines and schedules

Gone are the days of "fair" or "equal." Over the last decade, the focus in education has evolved. Students are now expected to get their needs met through differentiated instruction, supports, and accommodations for individual learning styles, strengths, and challenges. The same shift is needed in families.

If we give everyone the same amount or the same type of support no matter what they need, we miss seeing the individual in front of us. Far more than fairness, children want to be seen, heard, and understood for their uniqueness.

If the thought of making different plans for each family member, navigating different rules per child, and getting everyone in your family on board with this individualized approach leaves you with hives, I get it! I'll show you how to make

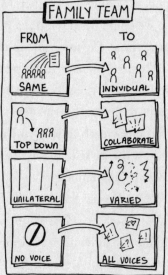

this work in your family. And know that you've already done much of the heavy lifting by creating and implementing plans for your biggest chaos causers.

Let's take a look at how this can work, even if you have a social justice warrior on your hands who is dead set on keeping track of every single rule and toy to ensure fairness.

THE PATH FORWARD: YOUR FAMILY SUCCESS PLAN

It's time to apply what you've learned in the previous stages to your entire family—to the ecosystem—instead of just one child. Creating a family that operates using this individualized approach is only possible when each member of the family works together to understand not only their own needs and wants but those of the others. This requires a deep level of connection, trust, and understanding, which is what you've been working on up to this stage.

Not only are you going to start to unravel and understand each team member but you and your family will also uncover common values, goals, and interests, while considering your family's culture and background.

This means that when a rule, routine, or boundary needs to be adjusted or revised, the focus isn't only on how this change will affect the chaos causer but on how this change could ripple into the rest of the team. Together, your family will create an environment in which each member can be successful, given their unique skills, talents, desires, needs, and challenges. Through the rest of this chapter, we'll create your family team, beginning with family huddles. Then, instead of building positive interactions with just one parent and child, you'll begin to work on a family connection plan that brings the whole family together. This way, you'll begin to learn each member's triggers, likes and dislikes, basic needs, skills, sensory preferences, and more.

In the sections ahead, I will break down this plan one piece at a time:

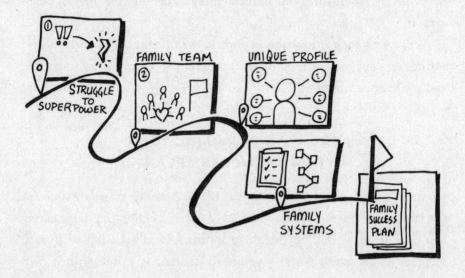

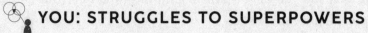

YOU: STRUGGLES TO SUPERPOWERS

You hear other adults talk about your child. They say things like:

"He's so aggressive. He needs tougher parenting."

"He's totally wild. You really need to control your kid."

"She's way too sensitive about everything. She needs to just toughen up."

You hear the slightly judgmental tone masked as helping. You've seen the looks people shoot you when your kid is bouncing off the walls, running through the store, hitting, wandering away, or crying over a disappointment.

And you can bet your kiddo sees it too. They've heard the labels, the remarks, the correcting, the reprimanding. They sink a little bit every time they hear it. But those behaviors don't define who they are. You know it, and so do they.

What if there was a way to turn your kid's biggest struggles into superpowers? What if the behaviors that get them into trouble, appear to be problems, and downright drive you batty, could be channeled to help them thrive? So that despite them, or more accurately, because of them, they're out there playing with other kids, following your directions, and able to solve problems independently?

That's what happens when you look deeper, ask questions, and get to know them. When you take the time to look beneath that surface behavior, you get to know your child and find the most amazing qualities. Nurture those qualities, and you can help them grow into who they truly are, not who they're told they should be.

What qualities can you nurture to help them go from struggling to thriving?

The first step in your Family Success plan is the powerful shift: struggles to superpowers. This is how you can take what you currently view as problems and swap them out for assets, so they become the very things that help your children succeed.

REAL-WORLD SUPERHEROES

Michael Phelps is a former swimmer who won twenty-eight Olympic medals, which is more than anyone else in history. Thing is, when Michael was a kid, he got into trouble constantly. He wouldn't stop moving, and everyone around him saw that as a problem that needed to be fixed. He would also become hyperfocused, even obsessive, about things that he loved, which, let's face it, can be awfully annoying at times.

But one person in his life thought maybe they could channel his energy and obsessive personality. Michael loved swimming, so they took him to a pool, where he could burn off his energy. Soon they discovered that swimming helped him in school, not just because he was calmer but because he learned math by doing problems related to lap times.

Michael's Olympic success was made possible because one person saw his constant movement and obsessive nature not as problems but as strengths. Where everyone else saw struggles, this person saw a superpower.

Michael Phelps isn't the only example of this.

There are thousands more.

- Billionaire Richard Branson struggled in school due to dyslexia and ADHD. But he turned his struggles into an advantage. He chose not to focus on academics and used his energy to start multiple businesses. Now he's one of the richest men on the planet.

- Hall of Fame basketball player Ray Allen is famous for having intense daily practice routines that made him one of the best shooters of all time. And he credits his borderline OCD for driving him to practice so obsessively.
- Academy Award–winning actress Emma Stone turned to theater and improv because it helped her handle her anxiety and panic attacks.

So what if instead of trying to fix or change the things about our children that make them different or challenging, we embrace those qualities and help them hone them into superpowers? In so doing, not only will you become more connected and empathetic, you will also gain unbelievable insights into your child's behavior. With insight comes the ability to meet them where they are and the trust required to get them on board with the plans you'll create together.

Flip Side of the Same Coin

Before we talk about how to swap your child's struggles for superpowers, let's first get clear on what I am referring to when I use the term "superpowers."

It's extremely important to note that a superpower is part of your child already. In fact, it's mostly likely the flip side of the very thing that frustrates and annoys you most about them.

Here are just a few traits that can be seen as a struggle, but on the opposite side are superpowers:

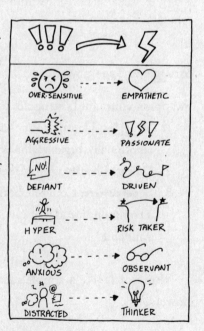

OVER-SENSITIVE → EMPATHETIC

AGGRESSIVE → PASSIONATE

DEFIANT → DRIVEN

HYPER → RISK TAKER

ANXIOUS → OBSERVANT

DISTRACTED → THINKER

Your child's superpower is the very thing that will enable them to do the things they do best. These are traits that will allow them to be successful while still being themselves, as opposed to feeling as though they need to hide bits and pieces just to fit in.

Take the Hulk in the Avengers movies. If you don't know, the Hulk is this big, green, muscular monster who emerges anytime the scientist Bruce Banner gets angry. For most of the movies, Bruce sees the Hulk as a problem, a disease, something to be gotten rid of, as opposed to a vital part of himself.

Eventually, Banner learns to accept the Hulk, then to harness him so he can grow big and strong without getting mad. He finally turns his struggle into a true superpower.

We're going to do the same thing for your child.

Instead of fighting against their struggles, you can turn them into an advantage. Those superpowers can inform the solutions to behavioral issues. Instead of feeling like no one understands them, your child will make a change in behavior because that change calls upon a strength, as opposed to a fatal flaw.

Struggle to Superpower Swap

Swapping your child's struggles to superpowers is a three-step process.

1. **Struggles:** Identify your child's biggest challenges (socially, emotionally, organizationally, etc.)
2. **Quirks:** Identify what makes your child uniquely them
3. **Superpowers:** Combine both the struggles and the quirks to find a common thread that can serve as a springboard for empowering your child

Think of it like a simple math equation: struggles + quirks = superpowers.

Note: You will do this same activity with the other members in your family one at a time. But for now, think of "that kid" who brought you to this book in the first place.

Step One: What Is Your Child's Biggest Struggle?

You'll likely find this easy because struggles cause the most pain and emotional distress in your life. You're here because your child makes inappropriate jokes, can't stand when things don't go their way, or cries easily.

The first step in swapping these struggles for superpowers is to brainstorm the behaviors that are wreaking the most havoc on your family right now. Set a timer for this step. Otherwise you might find yourself spiraling into a dark place of negativity. You've most likely done this work for one child in your family. But I'm adding this step so you know where to start when you begin to apply this to the other family members.

Some common struggles:

- Says no to absolutely everything
- Makes a ton of messes
- Gets really distracted
- Cries over the smallest things
- Extremely shy
- Extremely loud
- Climbs and jumps on anything in sight

- Kicks, hits, constantly runs into things
- Daydreamer and often distracted
- Has to have things their way
- Super picky
- Doesn't communicate with words
- Doesn't pay attention

Step Two: What Makes Your Child Unique?

Before you make the magic swap to seeing your child's struggles as superpowers, we have to spend some time getting clear on what makes your kids unique.

You might notice that this step is just a little bit harder.

I want you to think a little bit outside of the box here. It doesn't have to be things your child likes or is good at. Instead, think of anything that really helps you know your child for who they are.

Think of this list as the things that make you smile about your kid when they're sleeping and you aren't so consumed with all the things they're doing wrong.

Note: If you're still struggling to come up with something, I get it. When this happens, I encourage you to go back to the magic reset button (page 207) and take it back to connection. Without fail, doing this will reveal something awesome about your kid that you had almost forgotten about.

Step Three: Turn Your Child's Struggles into Superpowers

In this step, you will look for the places that the struggles and uniqueness intersect. You will zoom out and look for a common thread that encompasses both sides of the coin. This won't necessarily be a one-to-one correspondence, meaning there isn't always a superpower to every struggle. Instead, I encourage you to look at this more holistically.

For example:

1. Throws fits when things don't go as planned + better at organization than most adults = super planner

2. Scattered and distracted + makes inventions = visionary

3. Finds ways to break any rule + curiously asks questions = outside-the-box thinker

4. Cries easily + caring and generous = empathetic

Note: Struggles and superpowers aren't always a one-to-one correspondence. Instead, I like to look at a list of struggles and the list of quirks to see the overlap. However, for the purpose of keeping this simple, I've kept it to a one-plus-one equation here. In order to simplify the struggle to superpower process even further, I've developed a tool that is highly effective. After working with thousands of parents around the world, creating a quiz that more than a hundred thousand parents filled out, I've been able to identify five dominant behavior types that most struggles and superpowers fall into.

FIVE DOMINANT BEHAVIOR TYPES

STRUGGLES	SUPERPOWERS
Overly Sensitive • Cries over the smallest thing • Battles over socks and shoes • Doesn't like being alone • Scared of new people	**Unique** • Thrives on a plan • Cautious and pays attention to detail • Empathetic • Big heart; wants to please others
Aggressive • Yells and screams • Throws things and is destructive • Crosses arms and shuts down • Shouts "I hate you" or "Go away"	**Fierce** • Passionate about life • Takes a stand for beliefs • Big emotions • Strong and powerful
Defiant • Refuses to do what's asked • Always answers with a no • Ignores requests • Repeatedly breaks rules • Never follows directions	**Spirited** • Confident in own decisions • Likes to take the lead • Social justice warrior • Strong leadership skills • Thrives on free choice
Distracted • Struggles to complete tasks • Needs frequent breaks • Lacks motivation or desire • Extremely disorganized • Loses belongings frequently	**Creative** • Imaginative • Free thinker • Typically thinks outside of the box • Fun and playful • Tons of ideas
Hyperactive • Hyper around guests • Says inappropriate things • Makes jokes at inappropriate times • Jumps on furniture • Plays rough with others	**Adventurous** • Able to take risks • Dances to the beat of their own drum • Full of life and energy • Explores the world they live in • Inquisitive

Let me show you how to see the superpower beneath the disruptive quality you wish to tame.

Unique

Unique children are deeply sensitive. You may be dealing with a lot of crying, clinging, and resisting new people, but what lies beneath those behaviors is incredible empathy. Your child is attentive to detail and is highly attuned to other people.

Well-known fictional unique characters include Piglet and Caillou.

Fierce

Fierce children are driven by passion. You may be dealing with a lot of yelling, throwing, and aggression, but what lies beneath those behaviors is incredible strength. Your child stands up for what they believe in and prefers to take the lead in many situations.

Other well-known fierce characters include Katniss Everdeen and Kylo Ren.

Spirited

Spirited children are all about free choice. You may be dealing with a lot of nos, ignoring, and rule breaking, but what lies beneath those behaviors is focused determination. Your child is confident in their decisions and stands up for what they believe.

Well-known fictional spirited characters include the Grinch and Princess Merida from the movie *Brave*.

Creative

Creative children possess unlimited imagination. You may be dealing with a lot of disorganization and procrastination, but what lies beneath those behaviors is incredible originality. Your child is brimming with ideas and resourcefulness.

Well-known fictional creative characters include Willy Wonka and Punky Brewster.

Adventurous

Adventurous children are willing to take risks. You may be dealing with a lot of silliness and roughhousing, but what lies beneath those behaviors is incredible courage. Your child is bold and loves to explore their surroundings.

Well-known fictional adventurous characters include Peter Pan and Curious George.

HONING SUPERPOWERS

As parents, we have the power to show our kids how to harness their superpowers and use them appropriately. Through skill-building and planning huddles (page 232) you can introduce this concept of struggles to superpowers with each member of your family and start to see the entire family shift. For now, let's see what this would look like.

For my son, that means teaching him what to do if someone gets in his way so he can handle when plans don't go as expected or respond kindly when someone changes plans on him. But the key here is knowing that his superpower is that he is fierce. He trusts his decisions and ability to follow through on his plans. Some kids really struggle to make plans. Heck, I know this is *not* my superpower.

By looking at superpowers instead of just struggles, you will be able to see what your child needs when it's time to solve a problem. And remember, you can't get this wrong. Just seeing the possibility that your child's behaviors could be a superpower is a huge step forward in the right direction.

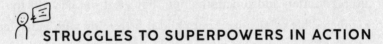 **STRUGGLES TO SUPERPOWERS IN ACTION**

Amelia: Critical and Complaining

Amelia struggled to see her son's behaviors as anything other than disrespectful. He would criticize her actions and choices, complain about anything that was given to him, and get angry if things didn't go his way. It had become the norm for her son to say hurtful and hateful things, such as "You're the worst parent ever" and "You're such a dummy." This constant criticism and complaining from her son made it hard for Amelia to want to help him or see him differently. Her feelings were hurt, and for good reason. However, one day the struggle-to-superpower swap clicked for her in a way it never had before. After her son criticized Dad for doing something wrong and screamed at him for making this mistake, Amelia realized that while this was hard to handle as the adult, her son's attunement to details and ability to notice mistakes was a superpower. Her job was to help her son turn this superpower into a helpful, not hurtful, trait. By seeing this trait as a superpower, she was able to have a conversation with her son. Together they made a plan to be on the lookout for when they noticed a mistake, how to use this to help others instead of criticize them. This new lens of "noticing mistakes" versus "critical and complaining" helped both Amelia and her son move forward in a new connected direction.

ACTION STEP

Your simple next step is to identify your child's superpowers so you can help them use these skills to solve problems, connect with others, and fall in love with themselves.

Step One: Struggles

Make a list of your child's biggest struggles that typically are seen by you or others as a negative.

Step Two: Quirks

Make a list of your child's most unique skills or interests. What makes your child uniquely them and is fun and interesting about them.

Step Three: Superpowers

Combine your child's struggles and quirks to get clear on what your child's superpowers are.

If you're struggling with this step, you can use the behavior quiz at www.calmthechaosbook.com/behaviorquiz.

CONNECT: GET OTHERS ON BOARD

The goal in this stage is to stormproof your entire family from future chaos. To prep for bad weather in the future, you need your family's buy-in and support. I know that jumping into any new approach—in this instance, the family team approach—might be met with rolled eyes and side glares, or worse, an increase in tantrums and outbursts. Yet, if you're going to have a chance to unravel and understand each team member, you're going to need to uncover common values, goals, and interests while considering your family's culture and background.

In order to ease you and your family into this transition, I've put together some simple and doable activities that will bring everyone together and get this new team mentality in place.

FAMILY TEAM-BUILDING ACTIVITIES

I've done the following exercises and activities with my own family. Grab one of these ideas and keep trying different strategies until you find something that works for your gang. Remember the ultimate goal: to change how the entire family views and talks about the family, interacts with each other, and works together to solve problems.

1. Your Family Team's Roster

One of the simplest ways to create a family team is to start by getting clear on who is part of the team. This will look different for every family in that some families might coparent, others might have grandparents who are actively involved, while others might include sitters or teachers. No family is identical, and that is to be celebrated in this activity. Now go ahead and list the team members. For extra credit, make this list visual too. Some fun ways to create a team roster include:

- Build a family photo wall
- Doodle the family with names and nicknames
- Create a scroll with family team members
- Paint or draw the family team together as a group project
- Make a collage of family photos and names

2. Establish a Team Name

Creating a team name will give your family a unique identity. There are several ways to come up with a team name. Here are a few ideas:

- Your last name or combo of last names
  (Darby + Abraham = Darbraham)
- Combo letters from each family member
  (DECA family)
- Favorite animals (Team Turtles)

3. Create a Team Flag or Crest

Make a family flag or crest and incorporate every team member's creativity, likes, and interests. This is one activity that many families are reluctant to try, but there is no wrong way to go about doing this. Some families like to collaborate ahead of time on the design, while others use a simple divide and conquer method. This is the 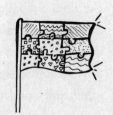 method I recommend if you know your children will still struggle to come up with one coherent plan or you have one child who dominates activities.

Each person gets a piece of paper to decorate however they wish. Then, when everyone is done, you can bring the pieces together to combine into one flag by taping the pieces together or gluing them onto another sheet of paper the same size.

When you're done with your flag, I recommend hanging it somewhere where the entire family can see it and be reminded that you are connected and unified as a team.

4. Team Connection Plan

While you're creating names and flags, introduce the idea of coming together as a family team to have fun on a regular basis. Building the bond as a family is just as important as huddles, problem-solving, and understanding each other.

Some fun team connection ideas include:

- Family game night
- Movie night
- Taco Tuesdays
- Ice cream sundae parties
- Family hikes
- Volunteer days
- Cookie baking night
- Crafting parties
- Family puzzles
- Family video game night

Start by making a list together and then choosing what you want to begin with. Set a weekly or monthly date on the calendar for the chosen event, so nothing else gets scheduled in its place. For added connection, put away the phones, computers, iPads, and video games unless they're being used in the family activity.

MAKING DECISIONS AS A FAMILY

Decision-making and problem-solving as a team are skills that need to be built, which is why we begin developing them with low-impact activities. So often, even as adults, we are used to one person being in charge of the decisions and the rest following along, whether we like it or not. To interrupt that unhealthy pattern, we practice making decisions about something with lower stakes.

If your children (or even your partner) struggle to offer an idea or choice, coach them to ensure that everyone uses their voice and is heard.

During a huddle, it's okay for your children to still get upset, not like your ideas, and you not to like their ideas. It's okay for your conversations not to always go well. In fact, expect friction, especially at the beginning. Just know that when each family member realizes the importance of every person's voice and concerns, the real change happens. Resentment falls away, frustration and the desire to assert power disappear, and connection blossoms. When each team member's needs are met, there is no reason for jealousy, resentment, power struggles, or guilt.

NOT JUST A CUTE ACTIVITY

The urge to skip this connection activity because it feels frivolous can be strong. But these activities aren't just good for building trust and a sense of belonging as a family; there are other benefits as well.

In one study done by the University of Illinois, psychologists found that working together as a team balances the strengths (superpowers) and weaknesses (struggles) within the group. Shared experiences bring members closer and build bonds that have a positive impact on emotions and relationships for life. Historically, tribe names, family crests, monarchs, and more were used to create a sense of purpose, group identity, and support.

Dipping your toe into building a family team also makes sense because you're building future life skills. Studies have repeatedly shown the positive impact on interpersonal skills when young children are given a chance to brainstorm a variety of solutions to a problem, predict outcomes of their own actions, and talk about their feelings. Who would have thought the path to world peace could start in your very own living room?

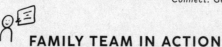

FAMILY TEAM IN ACTION

Brittney: Can't Agree on Anything

Brittney loved the idea of creating a team name and flag with her husband and four kids. However, when she went to create the flag and decide on a name with the family, everyone started fighting. She decided to table the discussion and move into creating the flag by handing each child and adult a piece of paper. Even the toddler drew with markers filling the page with "'happy lines'" that showed the family playing together. As they started to draw, Brittney had an idea. "What's something we all like to do together as a family?" Immediately, her nine-year-old chimed in, "Camping." Brittney suggested they call themselves the Happy Campers. Everyone, even the toddler, unanimously and enthusiastically nodded in agreement, and from that day forward, the family was known as the Happy Campers. Brittney taped the pictures everyone made together and framed them as the flag, and any time they needed to make decisions they remembered they were all in this together.

ACTION STEP: CREATE YOUR FAMILY TEAM

Your simple next step is to gather your family for at least one family team-building activity.

While I think it would be great if you did all the activities listed above, I want to highlight the importance of getting started versus adding to feeling overwhelmed. If you do nothing else, I encourage you to create a team name with your family to create a united identity each of you can relate to.

UNDERSTAND: INDIVIDUAL UNIQUE PROFILES

If your kids have ever wondered why big brother does *this*, or little sis does *that*, creating this next step in your Family Success plan will answer those questions and help get everyone in agreement. Because with such understanding comes a reduction in resentment, anger, and chaos.

At this stage in your journey, your parenting is less about getting everyone in the family to operate the same way, and more about embracing the members of the family for their quirks, likes, dislikes, and even their triggers. Once this happens, the family can then work to accommodate individual needs and create an environment where each member feels accepted for who they are.

That's where the unique profile comes in.

UNIQUE PROFILE

Think of the unique profile as a cheat sheet on each family member's inner workings so you can understand how they think and feel and why the heck they do the things they do, the way they do.

When you take the time to create these profiles for each family member, you will spend less time breaking up arguments, dealing with siblings constantly at each other's throats, the perpetual pushing of buttons just to get under each other's skin, and the nonstop debates over what's fair or not be-

tween family members. In fact, by involving everyone in the process of creating these profiles, you will ensure that each person in the family knows how to handle new storms when they arise. Even better, your family will be equipped to avoid storms in the first place, without having to constantly walk on eggshells.

There are many things you can include in your unique profiles, and the good news is you've already done most of this work for one child as you've gone through the previous stages.

What's included in a unique profile:

- Basic information about the individual (age, allergies, medications, etc.)
- Primary stress response (fight, flight, freeze) (page 272)
- Connection preferences or choices (page 273)
- Sensory preferences (page 274)
- Likes, dislikes, and interests (page 274)
- Unique skills (page 275)
- Warning signs (tipping points and known lead-up) (page 275)
- Calming strategies that work (page 276)
- Struggles and superpowers (page 276)

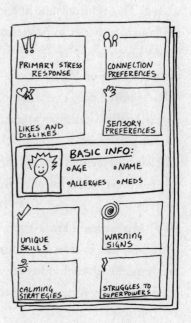

BASIC INFORMATION

This category seems self-explanatory, but focusing on this information can be extremely helpful when you're digging under the surface and assessing if basic needs have been met with the behavior funnel (Stage Three).

Age: By remembering that a child is five versus ten, it's easier to recognize that they have very different developmental skills from a sibling. This is important in choosing age-appropriate jobs to help around the house, activities to participate in, and even general expectations.

Allergies: If you have a child with, say, a nut allergy, it will be important for everyone to know what to do if this child starts to have a reaction. This category might also include food sensitivities. For example, my son's behavior drastically changes with red food dye, and he needs to take a supplement afterward, or rage is likely to follow soon after. Knowing this has prevented a lot of meltdowns after a family function.

Medication: I know there can be a lot of stigmas around medications, and this is often kept hush-hush, but the more a family can be open and honest with each other about what medications each person needs and why, the more everyone can help each other be successful.

PRIMARY STRESS RESPONSES

You might recall from Stop, Breathe, Anchor (pages 52–53) that the most common stress responses are:

- **Fight:** talking back, yelling, picking fights, kicking, and hitting
- **Flight:** walking away, hiding, leaving the room
- **Freeze:** disengaging, ignoring, shutting down
- **Fawn:** blending in, appeasing just to make it go away

Knowing each family member's go-to stress response—having it listed on the unique profile—is not only helpful when planning and tweaking your In-the-Moment and Ahead-of-the-Moment plans. It also helps family members understand why two people tend to butt heads more than others or why one person walks away in the middle of a heated discussion. Knowing an individual's primary stress response will enable each member of the family to enter arguments and difficult situations with more empathy and compassion for that other person, potentially changing the reaction to one another.

CONNECTION PREFERENCES

As you know by now, connection is key for understanding and helping children (especially our most challenging kids) feel safe, heard, and seen. You gathered this information for at least one child already when you were working on moments of safety, your 1:1:1 plan, and the magic reset button, but having it in one place can be invaluable.

Safe Person: When children feel disconnected from those around them, it can be hard for them to control their emotions and behavior. Each child needs a go-to soothing presence when they're most upset. This person can be a safe place for the child while they're in a storm. **Note:** this isn't to say that no one else can comfort a child, but knowing there is at least one comforting person is valuable information.

Ways to Connect: Every person has a preference when it comes to how they wish to be connected with. Some children may prefer tickling, roughhousing, or physical games, while others prefer to cuddle, read books together, or sit quietly in the same room. It's important to make a note of how each member of the family prefers connection so they can receive the love and warmth you're trying to give them without it overwhelming them or having the opposite effect.

SENSORY PREFERENCES

SENSORY If you recall from previous chapters, sensory preferences are how your body takes in and interprets information from the environment using any of your eight sensory systems. Understanding that each member is hardwired differently in this regard can create far more compassion.

Let's say you have two very different children. One is a thrill seeker who constantly jumps on furniture, pushes into his sibling, touches their things almost habitually, or puts everything in their mouth. The other gets easily agitated, overwhelmed, or overstimulated from sensory input. They hate getting wet; complain about socks, clothes, or tags; or get visibly upset in loud places. When as a family you make a list of the types of sensations that each member seeks out or avoids, you've got the start of a conversation. Suddenly everyone can see how sensory input, or the lack thereof, might have triggered challenging behavior such as tantrums, meltdowns, or outbursts so you can avoid feeling like the child was being vindictive or manipulative. This information, which you'll include in the unique profile, can help you create plans, provide tools and supports, and connect out of the moment.

LIKES, DISLIKES, AND INTERESTS

DESIRES & It's awfully easy to forget that each family member has a person-
AVOIDANCE alized set of likes and dislikes. When you can get clear on what each person tends to choose (what they gravitate toward or away from), planning, meals, connection, and problem-solving are that much easier.

Some categories to think about for likes and dislikes:
- Hobbies
- Foods
- Books
- Characters
- Games or activities
- Movies or TV shows

UNIQUE SKILLS

Every member has a special set of skills they bring to the team. It's easy to overlook many of these because they come so naturally for the one. However, when each family member is aware of skills they can rely on others for, and what skills other members might need help with, everyone can work together in a more empathetic and understanding way. Just as you wouldn't want a baseball team composed of all pitchers, your family needs diversity to make for a well-rounded team. List skills that each person excels at.

Note: Skills aren't fixed and can change. Now we're simply listing strong areas where this family member can be of help to someone else, and weaker areas where they could benefit from some help.

STORM WARNING SIGNS

You've identified the storm warning signs using behavior spirals (page 215). These are patterns of behaviors or triggers that lead to chaos for your challenging child. Knowing these signs will help other family members head off storms before they turn into hurricanes. But we're going to track these precursors to trouble for each family member, not just the chaos causer, because we all tend to be triggered by one thing or another.

If you aren't sure what these are for a specific family member, simply do a few behavior spirals the next time they're upset. Any contributing factor would be helpful for others to be aware of so they don't inadvertently trigger a negative reaction. When you add this information, also make note of the outside factors that can induce a spiral. This might include sensory input, like loud noises or certain smells. It can also be things like phrases or situations that tend to lead to a spiral. Also note if a family member has been set off by certain say, do, provide phrases or actions. This way, others can avoid repeating the same trigger unknowingly.

CALMING STRATEGIES THAT WORK

What works to calm one child might not work for another. So the goal here is to identify a specific calming strategy for each member that everybody can share and understand in an age-appropriate way. Even better, you can use this information to "plug and play" with the plans you've been working on all along. The more you continue to learn and add to this list, the easier it becomes to settle an upset child, navigate a challenging situation, or problem solve as a family, because instead of coming up with an entire plan from scratch, each of you has a repository of strategies to pull from that you can tweak as you go along.

STRUGGLES AND SUPERPOWERS

Last but definitely not least, sharing about each family member's struggles and superpowers can be valuable information for everyone on the team to know. Similar to the skills list we created, this can help with the balancing and understanding of each family member. Where one member excels in an area, another might need support and vice versa. When you can see that one family member is incredibly resilient rather than bossy or pushy, the others can lean on this superpower when going through hard times. Likewise, if you can identify a member who is detail-oriented rather than picky or anxious, the others can enjoy this person's superpowers to help plan a big event or make sure nothing is forgotten before a trip.

UNIQUE PROFILES IN ACTION

Cassie: Arguments and Fights with Other Family Members

When Cassie first started implementing the Calm the Chaos framework, she was focused on her daughter's explosive meltdowns and the havoc they were creating in the family. However, as she worked through the stages with her daughter, something remarkable happened. Her daughter started

to recognize not only her own triggers, struggles, superpowers, and sensory preferences but those of the other family members. For instance, when her parents got upset, she realized that loud noises, lots of movement and action, and being late caused them to get easily triggered. Knowing this information allowed all the children to head off any big outbursts when Mom and Dad weren't feeling great or were overwhelmed. Cassie's daughter's meltdowns decreased, and the outbursts from other family members started to fade as well.

ACTION STEP: CREATE A UNIQUE PROFILE

Your simple next step is to gather what you've already discovered about you or one of your children up to now and create a unique profile.

Remember, this isn't about getting it perfect or adding more to your to-do list. Instead, this is about having a system for organizing all the amazing things you already know about your family that you might not have in a place for others to easily access.

If this feels overwhelming at all, start small. Use your knowledge of yourself or the child you've been focusing on in the earlier chapters, whichever feels easiest. Then, over time, build up your family's unique profiles and add them to your Family Success plan. If even that feels overwhelming, break the task down even further and simply choose one section you will fill out for one child right now.

EMPOWER: RULES AND DISCIPLINE PLANS REIMAGINED

No turn on red. Wear a seat belt in a car. No shoes, no shirt, no service.

Rules provide structure and define expectations; they bring order to an otherwise chaotic environment and keep us safe.

We've been taught that to keep our children safe, we need to set firm and consistent rules and boundaries. How else will they avoid harm and learn to navigate the real world?

Raising challenging kids requires us to rethink and reimagine rules and discipline. Instead of viewing rules as a means of controlling behavior or gaining compliance from an early age, we must shift our focus to helping children learn autonomy, healthy boundaries, self-advocacy, and compassion for others' needs.

How do you raise resilient, independent children who are respectful and responsible members of society if you do away with rules?

You need to shift from a rigid rules and consequences system to a team-based, value-aligned system. That's exactly what the final step in your Family Success plan is: your discipline plan reimagined.

THE ULTIMATE GOAL

There are three big problems with creating rules and expectations with a top-down or rigid approach:

1. When rules and expectations don't take into account the child's unique needs, wants, and skills, we set them up for failure and a belief that they aren't good enough or something is wrong with them.
2. The focus on compliance and obedience leaves children feeling unheard and misunderstood, as though their specific needs and desires don't matter.
3. When we approach rules and limits from a rigid mindset, we are parenting out of fear of what might happen.

If our goal is to empower each member of the family, and we know that every team member is unique, why would we create rigid boundaries and expectations that don't have any room for individuality or growth?

Instead of focusing on the what-if's when our kids are grown and in the real world, what if we parents used the time we have with them to set up an environment that allows each family member to be successful? What if we shift our operating system from one of fear to one of possibility? What if we move to looking forward, leading our children, and helping them gain the necessary skills to thrive in the real world once they leave the safety of our home?

What if we could teach our children:

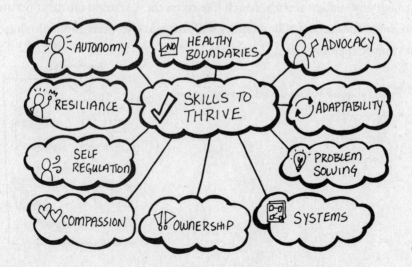

So how do we do all this without laying down the hammer or letting our kids run amok?

Contrary to what many believe, ditching strict rules and firm limits doesn't mean that you're going to let your kids walk all over you or let them go free range. Research has shown that children need structure (and warmth) to be successful. Without taking your hands completely off the wheel and letting your kids drive solo, the time has come to think creatively and explore alternative ways of providing warmth and structure that don't include rigid thinking, unilateral rules and expectations, or consequences just to teach a lesson.

More than rigid structure, firm limits, and consistent rules handed down by adults in charge, children need to be given and taught personal boundaries, values, autonomy, routines, and systems founded on their individual needs, the greater good of the family, and clear family values.

DITCHING RULES AND FIRM LIMITS

The replacement for rigid rules and firm limits is a collection of value-based family systems. These are routines and plans aligned with your family values that help your family run smoothly. Everyone knows what is expected, what happens when things go sideways, and how to work together to get through any sudden storms. Much like rules, these systems create structure and safety for every family member without being so tight and constricted that family members struggle to fit in.

Four Types of Value-Based Family Systems
- Agreements
- Boundaries
- Routines
- Plans

Creating Family Values

Values, if you remember, are those ideas that you and your family team hold near and dear to your heart. These are the beliefs that everyone in your family can agree on that will make your family culture not only function but thrive. Think of  your values as your North Star. They act as the guide for your family's actions, behaviors, choices, and systems as you move forward.

Defining family values helps each family team member remain in agreement and guides decisions and choices now, as well as into adulthood.

Note: I'm not here to tell you what values to have as a family. Every family is different, and that is not only okay, it's encouraged. This framework is designed to work with your family, not the other way around.

Here are just a few common family values to consider:

- Compassion for others
- Creativity
- Hard work
- Adventure
- Discernment

- Neurodiversity
- Acceptance
- Playfulness
- Kindness
- Spirituality

Tip: If you have young children or nonspeaking children, let them draw pictures of what is important to them. Allow all voices to be heard and valued. This is the most important part of this exercise, not coming up with the perfect value set.

Agreements

Agreements are clearly defined expectations that are created together as a family and mutually agreed upon. The key to an agreement is that they work for everyone involved, not just the adults. They consider the needs and developmental level of each member.

Agreements provide order and structure, allowing both parents and children to feel a sense of calm and safety without the rigidity of rules and expectations that are typically handed down from on high. Because agreements account for each family member's needs and current abilities and skill levels, parents aren't stuck in constant power struggles over trying to get kids to do things they aren't capable of doing yet. While your children are learning these skills, agreements will provide a gentle structure to keep them from getting lost. The result is fewer fights, arguments, and explosive behavior, therefore less chaos.

What's the difference between rules and agreements?

RULES	AGREEMENTS
• Rigid • Set by adults only • Punitive • Controlling • Based on future goals • Blames and shames • Unattainable	• Flexible • Made collaboratively • Responsive • Serve as bumpers (like at the bowling alley) • In tune with current capability or skill set • Teach and guide • Realistic

Essentially, think of agreements as common expectations that each family member abides by and lives by that are aligned with the family values.

Example Agreements from Calm the Chaos Families

- Respect each other's personal space and needs when possible
- Accept each family member's way of communicating needs
- Value each person's ideas and actions
- Accept each other's mistakes and attempts to put it right
- Consider school and homework a priority
- Always have mac and cheese dinner nights on the meal plans
- Do our best to use soft hands and gentle words
- Be honest with each other, even when it's hard

Let me be clear: I'm not opposed to the word *rules*, but the concept I want you to walk away with is the focus on collaborative overarching guidelines that the family can all agree upon versus a list of set of directives that need to be followed, or else consequences will ensue.

⚠️ **Caution:** If you're looking at your current family rules and thinking of chucking them out with the trash, hold up just a minute. Remember, you don't want to quit cold turkey or swap overnight. Instead, slowly shift from rigid, unilateral, and one-size-fits-all rules that are hard to remember, hard to meet, and even harder to follow through on to agreements for your family. Keep it simple and think of these agreements as a guideline that helps your family move forward in one direction, so everyone is on the same page.

Let me walk you through how to make that shift using the You-CUE framework we've been working with all along. Start by choosing one current rule your child is struggling to follow.

1. **You:** Assess your own beliefs and thoughts about why this rule is important. What are your own concerns if this rule isn't followed? What are the facts (not fears) about what it means if your kids don't follow this rule? Can you find proof of other successful people who don't follow this rule?

2. **Connect:** Before addressing this rule, build your positive interactions. Find proof of times your child is successful at following this expectation or it's easier for them to do so. Ask yourself, "What's in it for them?"—meaning, why would this rule be important to your child? How does this rule affect their interests and preferences?

3. **Understand:** Use the behavior funnel and behavior spiral to get a clear understanding of when and where this rule is hard to follow for your child. Remain curious and open to finding out why this is not working.

4. **Empower:** Problem solve with your child using a problem-solving huddle. Share what's working already and what isn't and why this is a concern. Ask about their concerns. Then, create an agreement using what you know about your child, their developmental level, needs, sensory preferences, and triggers.

Boundaries

Boundaries are clear guidelines on how we want to be treated based on our own needs and preferences. Boundaries are how you communicate what you're comfortable or uncomfortable with, how much time or capacity you can give, and what's important to you.

For many of us, boundaries weren't something we were taught in our family of origin. If you're an adult who grew up with no modeled boundaries, it can be easy to fall into the trap of people pleasing, allowing others to walk all over you or dismiss your feelings, or even hiding your emotions altogether.

Here's the thing about boundaries for those who are new to having them and setting them: boundaries are not about another person's actions but about your response to them. You have zero control over other people's thoughts, actions, or decisions. The only thing you can control is you. How you let others know what you like or dislike, how you interact afterward—those are your boundaries.

IN YOUR CONTROL	NOT IN YOUR CONTROL
• Your actions	• Others' feelings
• Your values	• Others' thoughts
• Your choices	• Others' actions
• Your role	• Others' responses
• How you show up	• Others' words
• How you spend your time	• Others' reactions

When making boundaries as a family, it's important that you create a few simple boundaries each person agrees to about personal space, consent, and autonomy (think everyone has the right to refuse hugs or tickles if they don't want them). Instead of focusing on parent-driven boundaries such as "I can't let you do this or that," the shift in the value-based family system puts the emphasis on modeling and teaching how to set personal boundaries, how to advocate for your own needs, and how to listen and adhere to other people's boundaries.

It's important to note that this boundary work isn't about just the parents getting their needs met like in outdated firm-boundary models, and it's not just about only the kids getting their needs met in a more child-led approach. Instead, this work is about the entire ecosystem and how every member of the team can get their needs met in a safe way. It's about how each person can choose what they will and won't accept and recognizing that our actions have repercussions. Boundaries and other family systems are created ahead of the moment, so everyone involved is on the same page.

However, you might wonder what this looks like when your kid hits you, calls you a poo butt, or refuses to eat dinner, again. Here are some examples of what this might look like in the heat of the moment.

LIMITS AND CONSEQUENCES	BOUNDARIES AND RESULTS
• You can't hit me. • Go to time out. • Don't talk to me in that tone. • Go to your room. • You didn't eat what I made for dinner, so no food for you.	• I don't want to be hit. • I will step away when you're angry. • I don't want to be yelled at. • When you call me names, I will stop talking and wait. • I'm making dinner. If you want something you like, I need your input.

⚠ **Caution:** In the heat of the moment is not when you should firmly state your boundary and try to enforce a consequence.

Instead, employ your In-the-Moment plan, get through the resistance, and then after the storm has passed, huddle with your child. Address your concerns about what happened, how the boundary was crossed, what the results would be in the future, or if this happened with someone other than you, and then teach the skills needed for both of you to get your concerns addressed.

Example Boundaries for Families

- If you don't want others to touch your toys, they belong in your room.
- I can't let you hurt me or your sibling. If you want us to stay in the same room, I need you to keep your hands to yourself.
- That hurt. I don't like it when you're so rough.
- I don't want a hug right now.
- I need a moment to cool down.
- It's too loud in here, I need to leave the room.
- We don't have to share our toys, but we do have to share the space.
- We stop roughhousing the moment someone says stop.
- We take breaks when we're upset so we don't say or do things that hurt others.

In short, boundary work is about defining what you want or need for yourself (the boundary) and what will happen if that line is crossed (the results). This is a shift from firm limits and consequences that so many of us have been encouraged to use to get control over our children and their behaviors.

When boundaries are approached from this flexible and individualized perspective, it removes the power struggles that are inevitable when firm boundaries are set and restated and the disconnect that happens when consequences and punishments are used as a way to teach.

Routines

Routines are the backbone of any family system. They relieve stress and help everyone know how things run. They provide predictability, order, and organization so you can enjoy your time doing things you want to do instead of fighting over getting out the door, nagging over picking  up toys, or wrangling kids for the bath. Even more exciting than the order they bring, routines are essential in teaching your children the habits and resilience they'll need to be independent and to feel more successful on their own.

Much like the other strategies and systems we've addressed, routines need to be made with children and personalized for their individual needs and done ahead of the moment.

Think of these as plans you make with your child to get through tricky situations throughout the day (such as coming home from school and throwing the backpack on the ground, getting dressed without becoming distracted, or cleaning the room without nagging). Whether you're dealing with what to do when your child is angry or what to do when your child comes in the door after school, both of these require an Ahead-of-the-Moment plan. The solution to both issues lies in where to put things, whether it's your fear or your child's backpack. Routines unpack and break down the steps we typically reserve in our head as parents and forget to say out loud.

Often, people consider establishing morning, bedtime, or bath routines as the first order of business and being consistent for a period of time to establish what is acceptable or not. Parents might be encouraged to set a routine that goes something like this: school, homework, playtime, dinner, bedtime.

However, this isn't a routine or system that reduces friction, this is simply a high-level schedule. Instead, look at routines as any sequence that gets you and your child through a particular time or transition from one activity to another. So, instead of simply doing mornings, you would break this down into a getting-dressed routine, getting-into-the-car routine, and possibly even a breakfast routine if your child needs things broken down into smaller steps. Start with one small time period first, one segment of a larger whole.

⚠ **Caution:** Parents often fall into the trap of assuming children should be able to do everyday tasks in five minutes without being told. However, organization, follow-through, and breaking things into small steps are skills and habits that must be built much like the Five-Minute Energy plan you created earlier in the book. By creating routines instead of simply relying on high-level expectations (everyone will keep their room clean), you reduce the need for nagging, frustration, and even a breakdown in communication over what each member of the family is capable of doing.

Here are a few tips for creating routines with your family:

- **Less is more:** Start with only one routine before putting any more in place. Think of this as your Ahead-of-the-Moment plan for a tricky part of the day.
- **Break it down:** Our minds remember thing in collections of threes, fives, and sevens. For this reason, break the day into three to seven parts when creating a routine. More than that and it's overwhelming. Less, your routine is likely going to be too broad and hard to follow.
- **Include the transition:** Don't underestimate the power of including the walk up the stairs or getting from electronics to the kitchen. You don't want any big, gaping holes in your routine.
- **Make it visual:** I'm a sucker for making any resource or tool for kids visual. The truth is, even adults need visual cues and reminders to stay on track. Turning your agreed routine into a checklist or a mov-

able to-do list can be extremely helpful for both you and your kids. Everyone knows what comes next without the nagging.

- **Practice:** I can't say this enough. Anytime you have a new skill, habit, or strategy you want to introduce to your kids, you need to practice. In fact, I recommend doing this practice when the stakes aren't as high. That means practicing a bedtime routine right after school or during the weekend when things are relaxed. Whatever you do, don't introduce a new routine in the heat of the moment when things are falling apart. These are always introduced, created, and tweaked out of the moment in huddles.

WHEN THINGS DON'T GO AS PLANNED

By now you might be wondering what to do when things don't go the way you've planned and hoped; when kids don't follow a routine, don't live up to a family value, or break an agreement.

In the past, you may have depended on punishments, rewards, and consequences. Now it's time to rely upon the value-based systems you've already created and huddles to get clear on how to move forward.

Remember, there's always a reason behind your child's behavior. The same is true when they break an agreement or push a boundary. It's time to give you and your child a structure that will keep communication lines open and expectations clear so you can keep situations from deteriorating.

Our goal here is not behavior management but mentorship. And that is done through connection, conversation, skill building, and problem-solving.

How do you now approach the situation if your kids break an agreement?

Let's say the kids can't go five minutes without hitting each other and the agreement to treat everyone kindly feels like a joke. This is a clear indicator that something needs repair.

1. **Take it back to connection:** Start with reconnection and see what's going on with the siblings' connection outside of the moment (if they're hitting this often, my guess is that there is a larger source of tension somewhere).

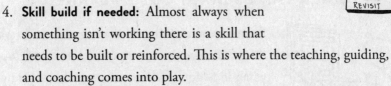

2. **Spiral it out:** Next, get clear on what's under the surface and spiral out the latest incident using the behavior spiral to see what led up to the chaos.

3. **Huddle:** Bring up the struggle in the next huddle and address the skills, challenges, and concerns you and your children are seeing.

4. **Skill build if needed:** Almost always when something isn't working there is a skill that needs to be built or reinforced. This is where the teaching, guiding, and coaching comes into play.

5. **Tweak or create a plan:** Be specific about the type of plan that's needed. In this case, I would say that a plan for what to do when we get frustrated with our siblings would be a good place to start.

6. **Revisit what will happen when:** Children need our guidance and our mentorship. Just as a coach wouldn't play a teammate who is struggling with catching the ball, you don't want to put your child in a situation that sets them up for failure. Instead, revisit what will happen if they aren't able to follow through with the plan, even if it's because of a lack of skills, dysregulation, etc. For example, they will play in a separate room for now, until you can sit with them.

I REPEAT: PUNISHMENTS, REWARDS, AND CONSEQUENCES AREN'T THE ANSWER

I will be the first to admit how frustrating it is when our kids don't follow through with what we agreed to, they hurt their siblings, or they deviate from a plan. But I want to assure you that threats, groundings, tears, and lectures aren't going to teach your children anything except how to be really good at hiding things. We want our kids to trust us with the small things, so when something big happens they can come to us with any problem they have.

We can help our children understand why a mistake has happened, make sense of where things went wrong, and help them plan for how they could navigate the situation differently next time. That is how you set them up for success. You help them love who they are, accept others for their quirks and flaws, develop a clear sense of where they can fit into the world, and create compassion for others.

For these goals, rewards and punishments aren't just useless but counterproductive.

As parents, with every single struggle that comes in our families, we have a choice. Instead of focusing on fear and control, we can choose trust and learning.

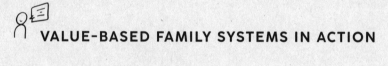

VALUE-BASED FAMILY SYSTEMS IN ACTION

Emily's Family: Consequences and Rewards

For years, professionals had convinced Emily, a working mom with two kids, that all her family problems came down to her son's ADHD and ODD (oppositional defiant disorder) and Emily's poor parenting skills. She had been told that her son needed strict discipline to control his defiance, firm rules to keep his distraction and hyperactivity in check, and clear consequences to stop his outbursts and fights with his older sister. Common consequences included no dinner, straight to bed, loss of privileges, and extra chores. However, after working together to create value-based family systems, Emily and her family decided that consequences and rewards weren't working; in fact they were making things worse. They began to huddle and problem solve when things started to go sideways. "What's going on?" became a common question Emily and her husband asked when they noticed something not working. They began to involve everyone in the plans and agreements. For example, if Luke broke something of Sydney's, they made an agreement that he would no longer be able to borrow items. Instead of expecting everyone to follow a blanket list of chores, the family worked together to create routines around bedtime, schooltime, meals, and more. These routines worked with each family member's needs and allowed room to go back to the drawing board if they weren't working. The family now works together to create plans and agreements, adjusting and revisiting when someone gets upset or doesn't follow through. The family is lighter, happier, and enjoys hanging out again. Working together as a family team, creating systems that work for everyone involved, saved the family.

ACTION STEP: CREATE ONE VALUE-BASED FAMILY SYSTEM

Your simple next step is to use your family values to create one new system that will reduce friction in your family and help your family team work together in a more cohesive way.

Step One: Choose a System

Knowing the work you've done up to this point on your number one chaos causer, choose one system that will help you create a plan for each family member, alleviate arguments, and build skills.

1. Agreement
2. Boundary
3. Routine
4. Plan

Step Two: Huddle, Huddle, Huddle

Bring the family together to have a problem-solving or planning huddle. Follow the steps in Stage Four to help you with this step. Essentially, you want to:

1. Celebrate what is working
2. Bring up the concerns and need for a new system
3. Get feedback from each family member involved
4. Identify a new solution to use moving forward

Step Three: Make It Visual

The best systems are ones that are used daily, created together, and revisited often for small tweaks. The best way to do this is to create a visual reminder of the new system. This can be a Post-it note (for agreements), a picture chart that shows an "if this, then this" scenario (for boundaries), or a visual schedule of three to five steps (for routines).

📑 PUTTING IT ALL TOGETHER: YOUR FAMILY SUCCESS PLAN

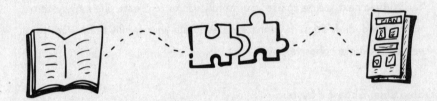

Even if you've *just* read the book up to this point without fully implementing the Calm the Chaos framework, go ahead and put on your favorite tune (mine is "Happy" by Pharrell Williams) and throw a dance party in your living room. It's okay, I'll wait for you.

Now, let's celebrate just how much you've learned in the last chapter, rock star.

By embracing the family team way of life, you've learned how to:

- Create a family that works together, enjoys spending time together, and supports each other.
- Identify each family member's likes, dislikes, triggers, sensory preferences, and more to allow everyone to feel truly seen and understood.
- Build value-based family systems that help your home and team run smoothly without constant arguments, outbursts, and tantrums.

⚠ CAUTION: PREPARE FOR PEAKS AND VALLEYS

Continue to lean into the progress that's gotten you this far and ditch the perfection mind-set. Give yourself (and your family) the permission to make small changes, continue to argue sometimes, and not be "ideal." Yes, there will be another storm; your family will hit another roadblock; and things will likely pass the point of no return more than once. But here's the cool part: with your Family Success plan, you and your family will be able to weather any storm, trudge through any valley, and conquer any challenge, as long as you're doing it together.

📑 THE PLAN

Your Family Success plan is a combination of two important parts, a living, breathing document that everyone in your family can use (even babysitters and in-laws) to know what to expect and how to solve problems together.

1. **Family team building:** You and your family will find group activities to build your experience working together and reaching agreement to achieve shared goals.
2. **The plans:** This is your family operating manual composed of individual plans that include information about each of your unique family members (such as likes and dislikes, struggles and superpowers, triggers, and more). Also contained are your family values, team name, and flag to remind each family member of your connection and commitment to the family team. This is where you will compile family agreements, routines, and plans as they're created so everyone knows exactly what to expect and when.

In this stage, I introduced you to the key elements you need to create your family team and Family Success plan.

Let's review:

1. **You: Struggles to Superpowers Swap:** Instead of only seeing the chaos causers and struggles that need work, swap your perspective to see the flip side (their superpowers). This simple shift creates a more positive and solution-focused environment and enables each member of the family to see each other's struggles as the valuable gifts they are. Instead of seeing one family member as the prob-

lem, you can now expand your focus to the whole family and how each member's struggles and superpowers counterbalance each other.

2. **Connect: Getting Others On Board:** This step is about getting everyone both excited about working toward a common goal and accustomed to advocating for and speaking up about their own needs and wants, so they can feel seen and heard. Creating a team roster, name, and flag is just the beginning of the fun. Then comes the planning of regular, enjoyable family activities that will build bonds and trust out of challenging moments. Involving your children (and partner) is a process in itself, but an important one that allows your family to solve problems together instead of being torn apart by challenges.

3. **Understand: Individual Unique Profiles:** Until now, you've likely been focusing your attention on one specific kid. Probably the one who brought you to this book. However, as you build a family team, it's important for each family member to start to understand each other on a deep level and learn what makes each person tick. This is imperative if you wish to avoid future storms and create an environment where the entire family can feel seen, heard, and accepted for who they are. With your individual profiles, you can take the mystery out of why the heck each member does what they do.

4. **Empower: Rules and Discipline Plans Reimagined:** Finally, now that you and your family are communicating and connecting on a deeper level, you have the base needed to create a strong family that works like clockwork. By ditching rigid rules, firm limits, and punishments in favor of family systems, you and your family will slowly create a family that works together, no matter the challenge. By defining your family values, they become your family's North Star, providing a guiding light. You and your family can now create new agreements, routines, boundaries, and plans that each team member knows and understands. Best of all, each of these new systems work with the individual needs of family members, instead of against them.

Creating Your Unique Family Success Plan

Your Family Success plan can be created in any form that works for you. For instance, when my husband and I recently updated ours so we could go on our first trip away together in a decade, we came at the task differently. His was typed and detailed with times and specifics, while mine was written in a little black notebook, complete with doodles on each page. Many of our Calm the Chaos families create command centers (family walls), binders, or notebooks for their Family Success plans, while others put everything in a shoebox on scraps of paper. There is no way to fail at this. Make this collection as unique as your family.

To make it super easy for you, I've included a blank Family Success plan template in the bonus package that comes with this book. You can download it at www.calmthechaosbook.com/fsp. For the sake of keeping it simple, I'll assume you already know where you're going to collect all this information if you haven't already started.

In a month, two months, or even three years down the road, you'll be adding to this amazing collection. With each challenge you face and overcome together as a family, you'll learn more about each other and be able to add more to your family operating manual. Pretty soon you'll feel even more confident.

Remember:

WHAT NOW?

THE REAL-WORLD DILEMMA

Now that you see your child for the awesome kid that they are, with all their flaws and imperfections, and you have a family that's working together to solve problems and accommodate and advocate for each other's needs, it's only natural that you see a new set of obstacles on the road ahead. In fact, here are the most common concerns of parents of challenging kids when they reach this stage in their journey:

- Other people won't care why my kid acts this way.
- There are consequences for breaking the rules in the real world.
- Who's going to care what a kid has to say?
- The real world isn't so accommodating and won't cater to my child's needs.
- What about when my kid gets a job and must show up on time, wear certain clothes, or work with others? They will have to toe the line then or be fired.
- What if my kid breaks a law and gets put in jail, or worse, hurt?
- How will my kid ever make it in college, so they can get a real job?
- Discrimination and bias are inevitable. What if I'm putting them in danger by not teaching them to comply and obey authority?

I'd be lying if I didn't admit to one (or all) of these concerns crossing my mind. In fact, as my kids get closer to eighteen, they pop up even more. I'd also be lying if I promised that the world will be kind to your kiddo, that others will accommodate them or appreciate how they advocate for themselves. In fact, in the middle of writing this book, we had a particularly hard two weeks as a family and all of these concerns and more flooded my mind.

In just two weeks, we had:

- a failure meeting at school for my oldest
- a sick kid
- a suspension
- another sick kid
- a kid with failing grades
- massive refusal to go to school
- panic attacks
- sick parents
- a broken arm
- a surgery
- more school refusal (two out of three fought wake-up time)
- and to top it all off, another suspension for a different kid

I posted this on my social media and thousands of parents resonated. To say I wanted to hide and pretend everything was perfect over here would be an understatement. But I knew I couldn't. I've included this because when I used to get to the end of a parenting book, I hated feeling like I was somehow failing, or my kid was broken. I know what I share in this book works. I know that one bad day or one rough season doesn't define our success. Despite this seemingly awful two-week period, it wasn't the end of the world for our family. In fact, we made it through more connected than when it started; we knew exactly what to do and how to handle each struggle.

We went back to the basics:

- created a Ride the Storm plan for the anxiety and school refusal
- made a Five-Minute Energy plan to get our health back
- crafted In-the-Moment plans for doctors' visits and future school refusal or schoolwork refusal
- problem solved missing assignments and roughhousing that led to school struggles

- crafted new routines and agreements that helped the house and school run smoother

All this was possible because we had a framework that works, a road map to follow, and the steps to take, so we could find our way out of the storms quickly.

Parenting is a lifelong journey with ups and downs, twists and turns, and while it's draining and frustrating at best some days, it's completely worth it. Trust the process and keep moving forward, one step at a time.

Now what about the people who criticized me for keeping my daughter home, who point to my sons' failing grades as proof that they won't be successful, or scoff at the thought that my boys both got suspensions in the same week? Oh, they still existed; only here's why their opinions didn't keep me from showing up for my kids and staying in tune with my children's needs.

1. My daughter is learning that her feelings and emotions and safety matter. She is learning how to speak up for her needs and advocate for her emotional and psychological safety.

2. My boys are developing skills and tools they need to stay on top of their schoolwork. They're learning what works, what doesn't, and

how to navigate a school system with ADHD, autism, and dyslexia. They're learning that their executive functioning skills aren't the only things that define them.

3. Instead of punishing my kids for what led to the suspensions, we were able to huddle and problem solve, and both boys were able to create plans for what to do in the future when something similar happens.

Turns out, the suspension of my oldest autistic son happened because he was trying to get his grades up. He was partnered with someone who was sleeping, and he was afraid they would get bad grades. So he tapped him on the head jokingly, and the other child punched him in the face. He grabbed his backpack, walked out, and went straight to the office. He was able to spiral out what happened, advocate for his needs, and realize that he misread the room and crossed someone's personal space. I couldn't hope for anything more than this outcome.

Because I've been able to see the Calm the Chaos framework applied to families around the world from different backgrounds, cultures, and challenges, I feel confident that our kids will not only be ready for the real world but become the change makers society so desperately needs.

Yes, they'll face opposition as they grow up, starting now and continuing until long after they've left our nests, but let's hold on to the following truths.

SEVEN TRUTHS ABOUT PREPARING CHALLENGING KIDS FOR THE REAL WORLD

1. It's Not Sink or Swim

Let's be honest: Your child won't be dropped into the real world like a player on the latest reality TV show *Challenging Kids: Will They Survive?* alone and with zero support or tools. But let's get something clear. Right now, your child is in the "real world," and they have you to help them navigate it. What you're concerned about is the "adult world," when your child is older and no longer in your home with you to be their guide.

Communication, trust, and safety are an important foundation to your parenting. By huddling, problem solving, and skill building, you help them develop the necessary tools to navigate whatever your child is up against. You're helping them make choices that keep them and others safe now and well into the future. They'll lean on this approach as they grow older and face further bumps in the road. Now is the time to rehearse responses or appropriate actions until they become automatic.

2. Your Child Is Still a Child

Your child is still just that, a child. Their brain, body, self-regulation, communication, and other skills are still being built and wired. In fact, science tells us that your child will continue to develop executive function skills and emotional regulation until the age of twenty-five. The loudness, the endless energy, the arguments with siblings, the lack of emotional control—all of it is your child being a child. As the parent, it's your role to be in tune with your child's unique needs and help them develop awareness of their own needs and those of others. You are now armed with tools to help you continue to understand your child on a deeper level, so you can help them understand themselves too. This will serve them well, even when they're sixty-five years old.

3. Focus on Skills, Not Fear

Not every grown-up is going to listen to a child who questions authority, not every boss is going to be flexible with their hours to accommodate your child's needs, and not every store owner will be forgiving if your child pockets something, like a piece of candy, because they lack self-control. That's why you must teach your children new skills throughout their childhood (and into young adulthood).

Be the safe place for your child while teaching them the skills they need to be successful in the world. Know that your child will mess up here and there, and that they might even get hurt. This isn't a sign of your bad parenting and shouldn't be something you fear or try to avoid. Many children, especially the most challenging ones who push the limits, are experiential learners. No matter how many times someone tells them not to do something, they're going to try it out themselves. This is part of the learning process and gives you a great opportunity to huddle and skill build after.

4. It Isn't Your Child's Job to Make Others Feel Better

For years, the world hasn't accepted all types of humans. The mental health crisis that so many young children are facing right now is evidence of this.

I don't want to teach our children to change themselves simply to fit in and make others more comfortable; it's not their responsibility. It's their responsibility to express themselves authentically, safely, and in a way that shows others the same respect that they deserve for themselves. I want to buttress their self-confidence and help them embrace who they are, how they're made, and their unique superpowers.

5. Calming the Chaos Can Sharpen Advocacy Skills

We have the opportunity to teach our kids how to stand up for themselves, accept themselves, and advocate for their wants and needs in a way that maintains connection for all involved. However, some people are set in their ways, and no matter how responsive your child is to their needs, habits, and beliefs, they're going to get resistance. The act of advocacy could drain their energy and deplete their capacity to show up for themselves. Perhaps, in the interim, you get a trained advocate to do the job, or you as the parent can change the environment your child is in.

6. Surround Yourself with Support

You can't do this work alone. The world can feel big and scary if you're doing it all by yourself. You won't always have the energy to take on the fight, and that's okay. That's why it's so important to find an online support group, local parenting group, or a few close friends who can be your allies and support when you have school meetings, doctors' visits, and other stressful instances requiring advocacy.

I assure you, others like you exist. If you're struggling, there are likely a handful of others struggling with the same challenges. Try the school parent list, a local outreach program, the library, or even a free social media group led by someone who's been through what you're facing. If you can't find one locally or online, create this community yourself. That's what I did almost a decade ago when I started a blog. I was just hoping there was someone else out there struggling with raising a challenging kid. Little did I know there were millions.

7. The World Is Changing

Rapid change in technology has opened up the world, and fast! People are more connected around the world through social networks, and a large segment of the population has become more aware and sensitive to the needs and uniqueness of individuals. The world you or I may have grown up in (or that of our parents) is not the same world our children or their children are going to grow into. There are changes in schools, public policy, workplace, and even in family structure. This gives me hope for a world that is more accepting and open to children who don't quite fit the mold.

As evidence of rapid change, one study recently found that only 40 percent of jobs require a four-year degree (this is down from 75 percent from just a few years ago). Leaders in corporations and businesses are having to shift their leadership style to accommodate flexible schedules, collaborative projects, and even transparency and authenticity in the workplace. Companies have adapted hybrid in-person and virtual models with more and more adults working from home instead of doing the multihour commute into the office. There's been a surge of awareness of behavior, challenges, neurodiversity, and individual needs and strengths compared to when I started working with parents just over a decade ago. I get excited when I think of the opportunities for our unique and challenging kiddos going into the world.

Trust that you're preparing your child for the world, that you are, in fact, giving your child skills that will allow them to manage their emotions, communicate effectively, and select environments that meet their needs, which will put them ahead of their counterparts who haven't been required to do the deep work.

THE OUT-OF-THE-BOX LIFE

If you had extra time in your day, what would you do with it? When I ask most parents at this stage this question, the answer is almost always the same: "I have no clue." And it makes sense why: you've spent so much time taking care of everyone else that you haven't had a moment to spend on you, your own interests or passions.

Now that you aren't spending every waking hour breaking up fights, stressing over another call from school, or fighting over bedtime, you may be experiencing a flood of mixed emotions:

- Excited that arguments are no longer part of every day, but nervous that another storm is lurking around the corner
- Grateful for the family you've built, but resentful of how much time you've spent on taking care of your family
- Happy that your family is now working together smoothly, but grieving the person you were before kids
- Proud of creating the family you've always wanted, but confused about what makes you happy beyond just being a parent

If you feel any of these emotions, or all of them, you aren't alone. Yet, creating more for yourself is easier than you might think, and you can do so on your own terms. The Calm the Chaos framework extends far beyond handling challenging kids and reducing the friction in and around your family. In fact, something magical happens each time one of our coaching students begins to apply the framework to their everyday lives.

Since March of 2020, I've helped hundreds of parents take the next step of creating a life by their design. What they've been able to do with the framework is beyond imagination.

The Life-Changing Impact of Applying the Framework to Yourself

- Consistently meet your own needs
- Make big progress on goals
- Believe in your own abilities and skills
- Have clarity on direction and priorities
- Advocate for your own space and time
- Spend time doing what you love
- Create a sustainable work-life balance
- Pursue dreams

Here's a simple rundown of what it looks like to use the four elements of the Calm the Chaos framework beyond your family. Think of it as your new action plan.

1. **You: Prioritize You**

    Building off your established Five-Minute Energy plan you cre-
    ated early in your journey, sketch out a plan that utilizes the
    extra time you have in your day to recharge and energize you. This
    means that now, instead of simply spending five minutes a day on
    each of the steps, you might stretch each out for longer periods. For
    example, you could spend twenty minutes before getting the kids up
    just shifting your inner and outer chaos with a meditation practice,
    journaling, quiet time, or planning and prioritizing your day.

2. **Connect: What Lights You Up**

    Now that you have extra time and energy on your hands, ded-
    icate a half hour here and there to rediscovering your own
    likes and interests. Explore new hobbies and activities that bring
    you joy. For many parents, this might involve sitting with a book
    (completely unrelated to parenting), taking a long walk or bike ride
    around the neighborhood, or even picking up those crafting supplies
    you've always wanted to try. Spending this time on yourself is not
    selfish or wasteful. The happier you are, the easier it will be for you
    to spread that joy.

3. **Understand: Rewrite Your Story**

    Now that your family works together and does things without
    you serving as the glue, cheerleader, and umpire all wrapped
    into one, you can explore a new story for yourself. What are your
    own struggles and superpowers, learning styles, skills you have to
    offer, passions, and dreams? Knowing how you tick, what makes you
    who you are, and how you work best will allow you to step into new
    roles you may wish to explore.

4. **Empower: Take Action**

    It's one thing to dream, and I can tell you that once you see
    your worth and brilliance in your own flaws and imperfec-
    tions, anything is possible. It's another thing to take action, and that's
    why you'll want to carve out time on your calendar each week to take
    steps toward your passions. That's how you create a life you love, one

designed by you, influenced by your own nonnegotiables. It's time to block out ten to thirty minutes each day, an hour a week. Heck, it doesn't matter, just find a regular time for you to do what you want to do. This is the stuff you've put off forever, forgotten about, or that possibly scares you. Like everything else with the framework, you can take it one step at a time and focus on progress, not perfection.

The truth is, you can do anything you want, and you deserve the life you want to live. You can't do it all at once, but if you continue to stay focused on one priority at a time, take it step by step, and celebrate progress not perfection, you can and will create a life on your own terms. Owning this next version of you will have ripple effects you wouldn't think to dream possible.

TELL ME MORE

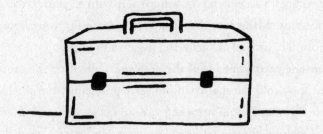

You have in your hands the tools you need to go from surviving the storm to thriving. You've begun the perspective shift that will allow you to see your challenging kid and this time you have with them as an opportunity. You now know that the very thing that makes your kiddo challenging is the exact thing that will enable them to change the world.

They just need a guide in their life—that's you—who can see them for who they are and equip them with the skills they need to succeed in today's rapidly changing world. To make the rest of this journey even easier for you—because remember, you are the most important part of this equation—I've put together some bonus resources. Included are printable plans, checklists, resource lists, and cheat sheets for specific challenges to aid you as you get started. I've added some surprise goodies, as well.

Grab your bonus resources and tools at www.calmthechaosbook.com /toolkit.

You'll likely want to get further support. This can look like one or more of the following:

1. **Community:** The old saying "It takes a village to raise a child" is popular for a reason. You aren't meant to do this parenting thing alone, especially if you're parenting a kid who pushes the limits, is usually the asterisk in other books, and breaks the mold. You need others who get what you're going through, can pick you up on hard days, and celebrate with you when you have success.

Surround yourself with other parents who are attuned to their own children's needs, can see the good in your child, and are able and willing to accept you for who you are with all your flaws and imperfections. Make sure that whatever community you choose adds to your life, instead of catalyzing negative thoughts.

2. **Someone on the outside of the problem:** One of my mentors once told me that trying to solve problems from the inside is hard to do because you're too close to the problem. You can't see the adjustment or nuance that can get you unstuck when you're inside it. You need someone from outside to help you see things from a different perspective. The key is finding someone you not only trust and have a relationship with but who is in alignment with your values and goals. This can be a trusted friend who will be open and honest, or a coach with the knowledge or expertise to help you shift how you think. This is vital when you're trying to see a cause behind a behavior, unravel a behavior spiral, let go of stressors, or swap struggles for superpowers.

3. **A guide who's been where you're going:** In addition to a community and a trusted outsider, an accountability partner who's been where you want to go can be a lifesaver. Find someone who's made it out to the other side. This person may simply be two steps ahead of you in your journey, or light-years ahead. They can point you in the right direction and get you through challenges that much faster.

Inside our Calm the Chaos community, we offer a soft place to land where you can find all of these resources. In it, you'll find an army of other parents waiting with open arms to accept you and your child for who you are. Just visit www.calmthechaosbook.com/next-step to join us.

Whether you join our community or not, I want to hear from you as you implement the plans in this book. Come back to it again and again as your children get older and you face new challenges. May you find within it a renewed sense of hope and the reminder that you're never alone on this journey.

Remember, you got this.

Dayna♡

ACKNOWLEDGMENTS

Getting this book out into the world has been an incredible journey. However, it was in no way one that was made alone. It took many people and communities to get to this point, and I am eternally grateful.

First and foremost, I have to thank my husband and my kids. Without you, Jason, I never would have made it this far. You continually push me, encourage me, and make fun of me just enough to keep me going on the hard days. And to my kiddos, Flora, Caiden, and Elijah, thank you for teaching me how to see the world differently. Thank you for being so different from one another and for being exactly who you are. In addition, thank you for giving me the space and time to put these words to paper, for working through the strategies as my guinea pigs, and for sharing your stories so other families can have the amazing bond we do.

To my mom, thank you for making me who I am. I was never an easy kid, and I pushed back against any rule you ever put in place. I know there are moments when you still say my full name from "up there" and shake your head in disbelief. However, I also know you're my biggest fan, and I've finally written the book you needed when you were raising us kids. Please know that none of the things in this book mean you didn't do a good job. You did the best you could with what you had, and I am forever grateful.

To the Dude—my dad—thank you for our weekly lunch sessions and being there for me, not just through the writing of this book but as I was growing up. I'm pretty sure I get a lot of my resiliency from you. But don't go flinging yourself from a tree to teach me a new lesson, okay?

To everyone in the Lemon Lime Adventures and Calm the Chaos communities, thank you for helping me realize I wasn't a failure, nor was I alone as a parent. I had you as the army behind me, believing in me even before I believed in myself. To my NextSteppers, Huddlers, and Calm the Chaos alumni, thank you for trusting the process, going all in on your families, and being the best damn community anyone could ask for. This book is what it is because of your vulnerability, openness to sharing your challenges, and fortitude to keep moving forward when it felt like nothing was going to work. We are creating a more accepting world one challenging kid at a time (starting in our own homes).

To my team, past and present (and future), I could not do the work I do and help the families I help without your tireless behind-the-scenes work and drive. From Jess and Kaylene, who believed in this mission before I even realized it was a thing, to Theresa, who makes sure I never miss a beat, thank you for helping me be the best version of me. To Danielle, Brian, Albert, Erin, Kayla, and the rest of the amazing growth team, thank you for helping us reach millions of parents each year and getting this work into the hands of the people who need it most. To Kylie, Galikali, Leslie, Jennifer, Kaitlin, Justeen, Beth, and Katie, thank you for supporting our amazing Calm the Chaos community in the most loving and heartfelt way, and for holding space for parents as they walk this path with us.

It's hard to imagine that ten years ago, I drove to the school office to pick up my son and listened to the principal tell me not to bring him back. In those ten years there have been countless friends who've gotten me through the roughest moments. I'm sure to miss someone, but I have to thank Angelee Brockmeyer, Sarah Esling, Ewa Torres, and Amanda Reuter for being there in some of my darkest moments in the early days and pushing me forward when I wasn't sure what the next day would bring. Thank you to Morgan, Alapaki, Sam, and GeNienne for our weekly chats when I was first building Calm the Chaos from scratch, and to Alena Wilson and Amy Small for our daily voice messages and for letting me dump on you when things felt out of control and celebrate with you when we overcame another huge hurdle.

Thank you to all my colleagues in the parenting, education, and online spaces who have taught me how to be a better human and how to grow my business to help as many families as possible, especially Seth Perler, Alissa Zorn, Rachel Macy Stafford, Amy McCready, Debbie Reber, Jason and Cecilia Hilkey, Suzanne Tucker, Debbie Steinberg Kuntz, Penny Williams, Joy Anderson, and Sarah Moore, and to Sheila McCraith for being a friend I could call on no matter what challenge we faced in business or online.

Without mentorship and guidance, my business would not be standing today, and Calm the Chaos never would have existed. Jeff Walker, Stu McLaren, Ryan Levesque, James Wedmore, Richard Cussons, Michelle Falzone, Diane Bleck, Bari Baumgardner, and Blue Melnick, thank you for believing in me before I could even see what was possible and for teaching me the skills I needed to create something this magical from websites, quizzes, and doodles. You guys all played a huge role in helping me believe in myself.

Thank you to everyone who made this book become a reality. From my amazing agent, Jan Baumer, for pushing back when this wasn't ready before the pandemic and then helping me shape it into something that was easy to follow and digest, to my phenomenal editor, Leah Miller, for shaving off the bits that weren't needed, for pushing me when I was up against a deadline, and for believing this book needed to be out in the world in a big way. To my coach Brian McCarthy, thank you for unraveling my self-doubt, fear, and procrastination so this book could become a reality, and to Ann Sheybani for being a badass book writing partner and coach who kicked me in the pants when I needed it and gave me a cushion and a warm hug when I was most vulnerable. Finally, to all the amazing people behind the scenes at Simon Element who have made sure this book is what it is today and that it's as accessible and easy to digest as possible, including Ruth Lee-Mui, Patrick Sullivan, Faren Bachelis, Benjamin Holmes, Elizabeth Breeden, Clare Maurer, Jessie McNiel, and Emma Taussig.

Finally, thank you to every single person who picks up this book, reads it (even if you don't finish the whole thing), and shares it with other parents or teachers. Without you, this book wouldn't exist. It takes strength, bravery, and vulnerability to pick up a book about calming the chaos in your life, let alone in your parenting journey, but you did it. Go you! I hope this book has given you a sense of belonging that you didn't have before, fortitude and strength to carry on through your hardest days, and hope that a better tomorrow really is possible. Don't forget: **you've got this.**

INDEX

ABOUT THE AUTHOR

DAYNA ABRAHAM, bestselling author of *The Superkids Activity Guide to Conquering Every Day* and *Sensory Processing 101*, is on a mission to create a more accepting world, one challenging kid at a time. As a National Board–certified educator, the parent of three neurodivergent children, and an ADHD adult herself, Dayna brings a unique, out-of-the-box perspective to raising kids in the modern world. She is the founder of the popular parenting website Lemon Lime Adventures, which has accumulated more than forty-one million views over the last decade. Through her compassionate Calm the Chaos framework, she has helped millions of desperate parents around the world find peace and meet their children where they are when conventional parenting tools have failed them.

With a weekly reach of more than 1.2 million people on social media and more than two hundred thousand Calm the Chaos workshop attendees, she has become a proven and trusted leader in the parenting community. Her work has been showcased in *HuffPost*, Scary Mommy, *BuzzFeed*, *ADDitude* magazine, *USA Today*, *Lifehacker*, and *Parents* magazine. She lives in Little Rock, Arkansas, with her three amazing children, her husband, Jason, and two huge Newfoundland puppies, Luna and Koda.